HC 444

Vietnamese State Industry and the Political Economy of Commercial Renaissance

CHANDOS
ASIAN STUDIES SERIES:
CONTEMPORARY ISSUES AND TRENDS

Series Editor: Professor Chris Rowley,
Cass Business School, City University, UK
(email: c.rowley@city.ac.uk)

Chandos Publishing is pleased to publish this major Series of books entitled *Asian Studies: Contemporary Issues and Trends*. The Series Editor is Professor Chris Rowley, Cass Business School, City University, UK.

Asia has clearly undergone some major transformations in recent years and books in the Series examine this transformation from a number of perspectives: economic, management, social, political and cultural. We seek authors from a broad range of areas and disciplinary interests: covering, for example, business/management, political science, social science, history, sociology, gender studies, ethnography, economics and international relations, etc.

Importantly, the Series examines both current developments and possible future trends. The Series is aimed at an international market of academics and professionals working in the area. The books have been specially commissioned from leading authors. The objective is to provide the reader with an authoritative view of current thinking.

New authors: we would be delighted to hear from you if you have an idea for a book. We are interested in both shorter, practically orientated publications (45,000+ words) and longer, theoretical monographs (75,000–100,000 words). Our books can be single, joint or multi-author volumes. If you have an idea for a book, please contact the publishers or Professor Chris Rowley, the Series Editor.

Dr Glyn Jones	Professor Chris Rowley
Chandos Publishing (Oxford) Ltd	Cass Business School, City University
Email: gjones@chandospublishing.com	Email: c.rowley@city.ac.uk
www.chandospublishing.com	www.cass.city.ac.uk/faculty/c.rowley

Chandos Publishing: is a privately owned and wholly independent publisher based in Oxford, UK. The aim of Chandos Publishing is to publish books of the highest possible standard: books that are both intellectually stimulating and innovative.

We are delighted and proud to count our authors from such well known international organisations as the Asian Institute of Technology, Tsinghua University, Kookmin University, Kobe University, Kyoto Sangyo University, London School of Economics, University of Oxford, Michigan State University, Getty Research Library, University of Texas at Austin, University of South Australia, University of Newcastle, Australia, University of Melbourne, ILO, Max-Planck Institute, Duke University and the leading law firm Clifford Chance.

A key feature of Chandos Publishing's activities is the service it offers its authors and customers. Chandos Publishing recognises that its authors are at the core of its publishing ethos, and authors are treated in a friendly, efficient and timely manner. Chandos Publishing's books are marketed on an international basis, via its range of overseas agents and representatives.

Professor Chris Rowley: Dr Rowley, BA, MA (Warwick), DPhil (Nuffield College, Oxford) is Subject Group leader and the inaugural Professor of Human Resource Management at Cass Business School, City University, London, UK. He is the founding Director of the new, multi-disciplinary and internationally networked *Centre for Research on Asian Management*, Editor of the leading journal *Asia Pacific Business Review* (www.tandf.co.uk/journals/titles/13602381.asp). He is well known and highly regarded in the area, with visiting appointments at leading Asian universities and top journal Editorial Boards in the US and UK. He has given a range of talks and lectures to universities and companies internationally with research and consultancy experience with unions, business and government and his previous employment includes varied work in both the public and private sectors. Professor Rowley researches in a range of areas, including international and comparative human resource management and Asia Pacific management and business. He has been awarded grants from the British Academy, an ESRC AIM International Study Fellowship and gained a 5-year RCUK Fellowship in Asian Business and Management. He acts as a reviewer for many funding bodies, as well as for numerous journals and publishers. Professor Rowley publishes very widely, including in leading US and UK journals, with over 100 articles, 80 book chapters and other contributions and 20 edited and sole authored books.

Bulk orders: some organisations buy a number of copies of our books. If you are interested in doing this, we would be pleased to discuss a discount. Please contact Hannah Grace-Williams on email info@chandospublishing.com or telephone number +44 (0) 1865 884447.

Textbook adoptions: inspection copies are available to lecturers considering adopting a Chandos Publishing book as a textbook. Please email Hannah Grace-Williams on email info@chandospublishing.com or telephone number +44 (0) 1865 884447.

Vietnamese State Industry and the Political Economy of Commercial Renaissance: dragon's tooth or curate's egg?

ADAM FFORDE

Chandos Publishing
Oxford · England

Chandos Publishing (Oxford) Limited
Chandos House
5 & 6 Steadys Lane
Stanton Harcourt
Oxford OX29 5RL
UK
Tel: +44 (0) 1865 884447 Fax: +44 (0) 1865 884448
Email: info@chandospublishing.com
www.chandospublishing.com

First published in Great Britain in 2007

ISBN:
978 1 84334 220 5
1 84334 220 0

© Adam Fforde, 2007

British Library Cataloguing-in-Publication Data.
A catalogue record for this book is available from the British Library.

All rights reserved. No part of this publication may be reproduced, stored in or introduced into a retrieval system, or transmitted, in any form, or by any means (electronic, mechanical, photocopying, recording or otherwise) without the prior written permission of the Publishers. This publication may not be lent, resold, hired out or otherwise disposed of by way of trade in any form of binding or cover other than that in which it is published without the prior consent of the Publishers. Any person who does any unauthorised act in relation to this publication may be liable to criminal prosecution and civil claims for damages.

The Publishers make no representation, express or implied, with regard to the accuracy of the information contained in this publication and cannot accept any legal responsibility or liability for any errors or omissions.

The material contained in this publication constitutes general guidelines only and does not represent to be advice on any particular matter. No reader or purchaser should act on the basis of material contained in this publication without first taking professional advice appropriate to their particular circumstances.

Printed in the UK and USA.

To my grandmothers, who died too young:
Cicely Fforde,
née Creswell,
and
Stella Retinger,
née Morel.

And also the late Professor
Nguyen Tri.

'Remember me, but Ah forget my fate.'

Contents

Table		*xi*
Acknowledgements		*xiii*
Preface		*xv*
About the author		*xxv*
A note to readers		*xxvii*
1	**Scene-setting and overview of the book**	**1**
	Introduction	1
	Overview	2
	Research context and literature review	4
	Vietnamese communist economy, 1954–2005	10
	Vietnamese economic development after the 1975–1976 reunification	16
	Policy and events, 1954–2005	21
	Traps and their significance	42
	Conclusions	44
	Notes	46
2	**The DRV, the development goals of unreformed Vietnamese communism and what went wrong – the limits of national liberation**	**53**
	Introduction	53
	The view from the grassroots: life in an SOE in the mid-1970s	53
	The DRV and North Vietnam prior to 1975 – the limits of statist developmentalism	54
	The north at reunification	58
	Conclusions: the importance of local perspectives	65
	Notes	65

3	**Vietnamese state industry: policy debates before 1979**	**67**
	Introduction: traditional central planning in North Vietnam and perceptions of problems	67
	The politics and political economy of state industry prior to 1979	68
	Harbingers of 'fence-breaking' – 'outside interests inside the central establishment': the local SOEs and artisanal sectors	76
	1965–1975: the effects of aid	81
	Early Vietnamese analyses: towards pro-market policy	83
	Traditional Vietnamese socialism and conservative policy: towards tedium?	93
	The trap opens: early attempts at the reform of superior levels	98
	'Reform' on the eve of reunification – plan indicators	102
	Early experience with commercialisation – policy towards the non-state sector before 1979	105
	Conclusions	111
	Notes	112
4	**Vietnamese neo-Stalinism and its feet of clay – from reunification to August 1979**	**119**
	The origins of the 1979 Sixth Plenum – what went wrong?	119
	Origins of crisis – the second FYP, 1976–1980	121
	Party organisations in small-scale industry	123
	The run-up to 1979	127
	Conclusions	129
	Notes	130
5	**The transitional model of the 1980s: a new solution?**	**131**
	The 1979 Sixth Plenum	131
	Legalising SOE commercialisation: 25-CP	135
	Conclusions	140
	Notes	141

6	**Just how important was policy? Spontaneous decentralisation, 1979–1980**	**143**
	Exogenous shocks, 1978–1979, and their immediate local effects	143
	Spontaneous decentralisation, 1979–1980 – grassroots experiences	145
	Labour relations	149
	The development of regional economies	151
	Conclusions: the impact and meanings of 25-CP	160
	Notes	161
7	**The attempted recentralisation, 1980–1985**	**163**
	Reaction and its failure	163
	Defending the DRV: SOE policy immediately after 25-CP	164
	Debate, conflict and policy development: interpretations of the new legislation – the 'new course'	169
	Grassroots response, 1981–1984: the debate, perceptions and rationalities	177
	Gathering political tensions: 156-HDBT, 306-BBT and the road to the Sixth Congress	177
	The manager's lament: chaos and its offspring	183
	Conclusions: the attempted recentralisation	190
	Notes	191
8	**From the 1986 Sixth Congress to the emergence of the SOE-focused model of the 1990s**	**193**
	Policy logic – failure hidden by success?	193
	The Sixth Congress	195
	Reforms after the Sixth Congress	197
	Towards the second trap: loss of Soviet aid, elimination of the 'two-price system' and the anti-inflationary measures of 1989	200
	The second trap and the recovery of 1990–1992	203
	The recovery of 1990–1992	205
	The start of recentralisation – SOE management councils	207

	Equitisation	208
	Renaissance? The SOE-focused model of the 1990s	209
	Notes	210
9	State industry: from the early 1990s and the 'big surprise' to the gathering problems of the late 1990s and 2000s	213
	Introduction	213
	The past and its legacies	213
	Dragon's teeth? But blue ones...	215
	Researching the 1990s: some preliminary results	216
	Notes	224
10	Conclusions – state industry and the Vietnamese experience	225
	Capitalism and the state	225
	Lessons from Vietnam?	225
Glossary		229
Acronyms		233
Bibliography		235
Index		259

Table

4.1 Capital and output in state industry 128

Acknowledgements

This study owes much to many people. It was initially financed under the Post-doctoral Research Fellowship Scheme of the Economic and Social Research Council, London (I held this fellowship from 1983 to 1987). The ESRC supplied extra funds at various times for a number of purposes: the research visit to Hanoi, hire of a research assistant during 1985 in London and purchase of a portable computer. In the nature of things research such as this cannot be pre-programmed, and I would like to express my thanks to members of the ESRC's staff for their understanding and prompt advice and assistance. Financial constraints upon the ESRC meant that a second extension of funding could not be supplied, so the closing months had to rely upon my own resources. I am extremely grateful to the Department of Economics, Birkbeck College, London, for letting me keep my room during that period.

Birkbeck provided a supportive and relaxed working environment for which I am most grateful. In particular, I would like to thank the late Hugh Davies and Nigel Foster for encouraging me to develop the portable computer facilities that I used in Hanoi and subsequently, and also for supplying the essential debugging needed to get the machinery operating effectively. The machine itself, a laptop Data General One, facilitated a revolution in work practices and database utilisation in the field and as practical research tools while writing up. I would like to record my thanks to various UK employees of the company for their help. I would also like to thank the then acting chairman of the Community of Refugees from Vietnam in Islington, Vu Khanh Thanh, who worked as my research assistant in London during the summer of 1985, for his efforts.

I would like to note my debt also to the office of the National Economics University (NEU), Hanoi, for their efforts on my behalf, and especially to Nguyen van Khanh for his assistance and encouragement. I owe a considerable debt to Nguyen Phap, then dean of the NEU, for his calming hand during moments of tension and difficulty, and for his help during my stay in 1985–1986. I need to thank Nguyen Tri, Nguyen Lang and Pham Huu Huy for their support during the same visit, and also

Hoang Kim Giao of Hanoi University's Political Economy Faculty for his help in 1978–1979. The NEU library provided valuable assistance in finding books and pamphlets, for which I am grateful. To possess and run a functioning academic library under north Vietnamese conditions at that time is an achievement that should be recognised.

I would also like to thank Nguyen Ngoc Tri, curator, Vietnamese Section, Oriental Manuscripts and Printed Books, British Library, for his help.

I would like to thank the staff, both Vietnamese and expatriate, of the Bai Bang Mill and Plantation and Soil Conservation Projects, Vinh Phu, for their ready acceptance of a consultant-turned-academic-turned-consultant in their midst. I would also like to thank various staff members of SIDA for ideas and comments over the years.

A number of colleagues at Birkbeck and elsewhere have helped me to clarify my own thinking and reduce – or so it appeared at the time – my own confusion. In particular, I would like to thank Melanie Beresford, Hugh Davies, Stefan de Vylder, Nguyen Dinh Huan, Nguyen Huu Dong, Hoang Kim Giao, Nguyen Huy, Pham Huu Huy, Nguyen Lang, Ben Lockwood, Chris Martin, Irene Norlund, Teresa Halik (née Pajor), the late Suzy Paine, Tran Huy Chuong, Anna Petrasovits, Nguyen Phap, Nguyen Tri, K.-E. Wadekin, Peter Wiles, Doug Porter, Anthony Marcus and Joerg Wischermann.

I should thank the staff of the NCDS, Australian National University, for the facilities provided during a three-month visit in 1990 which allowed me time to work on the study.

I would like to thank the Melbourne Institute of Asian Languages and Societies for giving me a room and infrastructure in 2003–2005, without which this book would certainly not have been finished.

Important parts of this work were carried out with the support of the Australian Research Council under their Large Research Grant Scheme.

I thank Suki Allen for her help and encouragement and Gilly Robson for her warm support. And also George Fforde for his ceaseless curiosity and intellectual sinuosity.

I am, of course, responsible for the many mistakes that undoubtedly remain.

Adam Fforde
Melbourne 2006

Preface:
'That forgotten world' – socialism, Stalin and the plan

War or peace?

Just what was the state sector of the Socialist Republic of Vietnam (SRV) before the market economy that emerged in 1990–1991? Was it dragon's tooth or curate's egg? Was it the basis for military strength and socialist construction, or was it something, clearly rotten, which must for various reasons be presented as 'good in parts'?

For traditional communists, those who believe in central planning, the state sector is special: manned by the proletariat, the most progressive class, and led directly by the Party through the socialist state and its planning apparatus, it is the cutting edge of progress. In the logic of Stalinism, for communists surrounded by hostile forces crash industrialisation was historically necessary, not only to show the superiority of state socialism but also to provide military strength. State industry was the place where this was meant to happen. In communist Vietnam, however, things were rather different. After national reunification in 1975, targeting the scarce resources of a very poor area upon the state sector drained the country's energies and dashed popular expectations of a happy peace 'ten times better than before', as the economy became an arena of struggle, shortages and heavy risk. Demobbed soldiers found in the late 1970s and on through the 1980s that rearing their children was full of difficulties and stress. What was promised was not delivered, either to them or to the generals who had hoped to see construction of a military-industrial complex to buttress Vietnam's new national independence. This was a curate's egg.

The contrast with the hoped-for dragon's teeth expresses the epitome of the state sector's position: so much was owed to it, yet so little came back. But how could this happen in a nation that could defeat the USA militarily, despite grinding poverty? And it was not that these hopes were a nonsensical delusion, for the USSR had shown that central planning could work, in its own terms.

In the 1920s and 1930s it was not suicidal for senior American economists, presidents of the American Economics Association, to refer to themselves as 'socialist'. Nor was it thought universally insane to think of Soviet Russia as an area where workers' rights and interests were respected. Similarly, in the early 1970s Americans of impeccable liberal credentials risked their careers to support the VCP[1] in its armed struggle against the USA. Nor, given the success of Stalin's system in creating a military-industrial complex that could first defeat Nazi Germany and then confront the West in its occupation of Central Europe, was it silly to expect that a reunited Vietnam under communist rule would rapidly create an economic and (independent) military potential that would position it well to challenge for regional influence. The 'Prussians of Asia', now granted access to the Mekong delta breadbasket, must – *surely* – have been well placed to harness the power offered by the Soviet, or rather Stalinist, programme. Soldiers, well armed, would be expected to rise from the dragon's teeth sowed in the now peaceful battlefields of Vietnam. Yet this was not to be.

While many foolish things have been written, not least about Vietnam and not just by foreigners, nobody would have dared to predict what actually happened. For within a generation of reunification the core of the Stalinist project in Vietnam, the state-owned enterprises (SOEs), were to emerge into the market economy of the 1990s. Rather than going to the wall, they often turned out well equipped, not to follow rigid plan directives and rapidly expand social production forces, but to cope with messy markets, a weak and often corrupt state bureaucracy, ideological threats and privatisation doctrines from the World Bank and other donors and, not least, severe competition from China and other SEA countries which had engaged earlier with globalisation and modernity. Through the 1990s GDP rose rather fast, the state share of the Vietnamese economy rose and many SOEs created large profits for their owners (strange coalitions of officials, managers and others).[2] Foreign investment flooded in, and by the end of the 1990s was increasingly dominant in Vietnamese industry. Through the 1990s, although many logics influenced the Vietnamese state, capitalism and profit were central concerns. This was a commercial renaissance.

Vietnamese state industry had turned out, like the curate's egg, to be 'good in parts', but, in traditional socialist terms, essentially rotten. In no sense, from whatever ideological perspective, could Vietnamese state industry in the late 1990s be said to reflect the 'planned production of use-values' that traditional socialism sought. Yet, and this is the point of the curate's egg metaphor, it was certainly better than the blind alley of militarism and muddle into which the USSR of the 1970s was heading, and where North Korea remains.

And do not forget other events of 1978–1980: the decisive shift towards the Soviet orbit by Vietnam marked by the signing of the Treaty of Friendship and Cooperation in 1978, the toppling of the Pol Pot regime in Cambodia in 1978–1979 by Vietnamese troops, China's invasion of Vietnam's northern provinces and then the start of the protracted process by which Vietnam's military presence in Cambodia terminated, opening the way to a major improvement in its international relations (Chanda, 1986). In 1978–1979, however, when Soviet troops went into Afghanistan and the Cold War was still at its height, it was reasonable to ask whether Vietnamese dragon's teeth were about to be backed by a Vietnamese military-industrial complex based upon Stalinist central planning. The world is, indeed, full of surprises.

This study

Transition

This book describes and attempts to analyse one part of the major post-reunification event in the history of Vietnam – the replacement of the traditional development programme inherited, via the Democratic Republic of Vietnam (DRV), from Stalin's Russia.

It does so from a somewhat unusual set of perspectives, with considerable weight given to the written record: the surprisingly abundant materials produced by Vietnamese analysts, politicians and officials over the years. My readings of these are influenced by my own experiences discussing and arguing related matters in Vietnamese and in Vietnam over the years. They tend to rely upon my own views as to how the country was changing, the ongoing but pervasive disequilibria in its development dynamic and an awareness that Vietnamese cultural and other predilections resulted, in this area as in others, in a range of opinions and disagreements that may appear to some readers as startling. That is, within the overall rigidities of Vietnamese neo-Stalinism there was much diversity; further, this coexisted with vast gaps between principles and practice. And, arguably even more characteristically, this led not to extreme and fraught tensions, but to philosophical stances that tolerated, willy-nilly and in different moods, 'life' (*cuoc song*) as something that, well, simply had to be put up with – and much of this during the extremes of wartime.

After the 'conquest of the South', or 'national reunification', in 1975–1976,[3] communist Vietnam maintained a large and well-equipped modern army which had proven its capacity in prolonged conflicts with such important powers as France and the USA. It was, however, almost entirely dependent upon external sources for its equipment. Vietnam's state industry, following the basic rationale of Stalin, was intended to correct that dependency. By 1995, two decades later, it was clear that this project had failed.

It is a nice comment upon the acuity of social prediction that this outcome is quite different from that expected by foreign observers and intended for the country by its leaders. In 1975, when North Vietnamese tanks took the Presidential Palace in Saigon, nobody expected that in around a decade the Vietnamese communist development strategy would have been discarded in favour of the market-oriented approach that was anathema to Vietnamese communist orthodoxy of the time, and repeatedly denounced in propaganda organs. Nobody thought that the apparatus of cooperatives and central planning of state industry adopted from the USSR would be condemned and replaced by household-based farming and SOEs competing in markets with each other and the non-state sectors.

Not only this, however: the change in Vietnam occurred, so this book argues, as a result of the breakdown from within of the chronically weak northern system – a characterisation far from that monolithic machine painted by wartime US and Vietnamese propaganda. The book argues that this breakdown started a largely spontaneous process of commercialisation.[4] This was initially resisted, but then taken up and supported by increasingly powerful elements within the communist establishment, until its support by government became unstoppable.

Yet through the 1990s the state industrial sector, I will argue, effectively saw the dynamic behind the great advances made in the 1980s undermined. As the Vietnamese Party and government saw the resources at their command recover after the loss of Soviet-bloc aid in 1989–1990, these resources were largely concentrated upon the state sector. At the same time, inward foreign direct investment (FDI) avoided light manufacturing and agriculture. Most joint ventures were with SOEs. By the second half of the decade this was resulting in a pattern of growth that created rather few jobs and was highly concentrated upon the urban areas. The rural unrest of 1997 perhaps reflected this. At least the Fourth Plenum in early 1998, and consequent pressures upon the donor community, sought a far greater level of attention to the rural areas. But the political sickness caused by the resurgence of statism in the early 1990s remained, with no real social forces outside the Party-state allowed to arise that would challenge political conservatism.

I argued in an earlier work that it was the 'state business interest' that politically drove the overall trajectory of policy through the 1980s (Fforde, 1993). This assumed that the Vietnamese political process was responsive to certain aggregated interests – certainly not to all.[5] And so it is far from surprising that the private sector, and many southern business families, remained relatively unimportant right up to the end of the 1990s. One aspect of this history is that it shows how impersonalised relationships – such as those ordered by formal bureaucratic structures – were important, for it often appears that Vietnamese politics is dominated by personalised relations. This means that the analysis has to take the formal detail very seriously. Relationships mattered, but so did the system.

In many ways post-reunification Vietnam reveals the unexpected.

There is the political continuity. The VCP maintained itself intact and in power. Why, despite the collapse and rejection of the traditional programme, was there no major political upheaval? The politburo elected at the Sixth Party Congress in 1986 was, in terms of its previous public pronouncements, deeply conservative. Yet in the next few years the Party leadership was a key active element in pushing for the conscious dismantling of the traditional neo-Stalinist system: de-Stalinisation.[6]

Again, when Vietnam was reunited in 1975 access to the rich agriculture of the south appeared to remove the single most important development constraint that Vietnamese communists had previously faced: the lack of adequate food supplies. Furthermore, they possessed the confident intensity of people who had defeated the US military effort, and, with national reunification, seen their life-long dreams fulfilled. As apparently and relatively orthodox Leninist communists, they knew that the traditional neo-Stalinist model could, under appropriate circumstances, create rapid industrialisation, permitting development and an independent military capacity that should then enable Vietnam to be truly free of the threat of foreign domination. Experience from the USSR, China and North Korea supported their expectations. Yet only five years later the economy was in ruins and the neo-Stalinist development programme fundamentally discredited. Why could it not be made to work in a unified Vietnam?

In my opinion, in the final analysis the answers are to do with a mixture of political and economic logics with how human beings cope with choice under uncertainty: learning through experience. They are not just economic questions, but also political and deeply human ones. This means – to me as a professional economist (among many personalities) – that an economic analysis has to look properly at the interaction between policy and practice, for 'reform' in Vietnam has not been a largely top-down process. This is possibly a contradiction in terms, since 'reform' is usually understood as a process consciously initiated, i.e. by policy. For that reason it is more helpful to use intransitive terms, such as commercialisation and process, which avoid the implicit assumption that it is policy that plays the determining role.

Confusion between programme and model, between intentionality and outcome, is linked to the not infrequent desire to legitimise political power by attributing to it the cause, as 'policy', of what seem to be good outcomes. Taken to an extreme, this leads to a stress upon top-down change processes, a 'policy fetishism' that focuses all upon policy and so looks for statist solutions – those that site intentionality upon the state. There are problems, however, with the common dichotomy of 'top down' and 'bottom up'. Some have interpreted my analyses to mean that change, since it came more 'from below', was coming from outside the Party-state apparatus; this is misleading, as, and I stress this a number of times below, it was to a great extent the insider status, as Party members and SOE staff, that allowed SOEs and others to participate in markets and subvert traditional central planning. This makes it easier to understand just why a normal private sector took so long to emerge (Fforde, 2005b).

While Vietnam remains a one-party state, dominated by the Party and a long way from an 'open' society, there is clearly no parallel in the political sphere between Vietnam and the new democracies of Central Europe. Basic freedoms – of expression, of organisation, of access to foreign publications etc. – are denied to the Vietnamese while enjoyed by East Germans, Poles, Czechs, Slovaks and, increasingly, others. It is perhaps only in the economic field that Vietnam was, in 1989, most strikingly advanced.

Circumstances of the research

The original research proposal was conceived in late 1982 and written up in 1983, at a time when the Vietnamese government's overall policy stance appeared to many as well as to me as reformist. The reactionary and recentralising intent behind the early 1980s' policy was not immediately obvious. Work commenced in late 1983, and finished temporarily when funding stopped in early 1987. During the winter of 1985–1986 six months were spent as a visiting researcher at the Industry Faculty of the NEU (previously the Economics and Planning University – EPU). Through 1985 a research assistant went through copies of *Nhan Dan* searching for materials describing SOE behaviour. In 1987 I started working as consultant for the Swedish International Development Agency (SIDA). This produced three reports (Fforde, 1987; Liljestrom et al., 1987; de Vylder and Fforde, 1988) and a number of visits to Vietnam in 1987 and 1988.

For the 12 months from the middle of 1988 I worked as socio-economic specialist on the forestry project attached to the Bai Bang Project in Vinh Phu, north Vietnam. And from late 1989 I was employed as socio-economic adviser to the SIDA Development Cooperation Office, Hanoi. I left for Australia in 1992. Thus from mid-1987 until 1992 I was in Vietnam almost full-time, working for the major Western bilateral aid donor and securing relatively free access to Vietnamese sources and informants. By the mid-2000s I had spent some ten years in Vietnam, starting in late 1978 when I was there to learn Vietnamese and work on my PhD (Fforde, 1982, 1987).

I spent the third quarter of 1990 on leave of absence from SIDA working as a visiting consultant at the National Centre for Development Studies (NCDS), Australian National University, Canberra. During this time I was struggling with the framework of endogenous transition[7] that can be found in de Vylder and Fforde (1996) as well as in embryo in the opening chapters of Fforde (1982, 1989). With its dominant ways of thinking thoroughly focused upon policy as the main cause of system change, the NCDS found this approach baffling and was hostile towards it. Intellectual openness was far from a characteristic of the NCDS at this time.

Research conditions thus changed very greatly during the period. In the early 1980s circumstances were less easy than they later became. Application for research permission was finally granted only in 1985, leading to the six months spent at the Industry Faculty of the NEU. And although much time was initially spent in discussion with faculty members, a relative failure to establish effective mutual understanding greatly inhibited the development of the project.[8] As at the NCDS, the idea that policy was not central and crucial was easily rejected: conservatism has many guises.

Yet during my stay in Hanoi I collected documentation and followed a programme of reading based upon both my own investigations and materials suggested by faculty members. By early 1986 progress and mutual understanding had become far better, and the university managed to begin to implement a programme of visits to SOEs.[9] By late March three had in fact been visited and some information obtained through interviews with senior management staff. The Ministry of the Interior's refusal to extend my visa then prevented further fieldwork. One reason why I give so much attention to the work edited by the late Professor Nguyen Tri (Nguyen Tri, 1972a: 78 et seq.) is that this does show clearly not only the more than somewhat chaotic nature of reality in SOEs at the time (late 1960s and very early 1970s), but that the foundation for this work was the ability to admit to, and analyse, a situation where the actual functioning of incentives was quite contrary to normative expectations.

The study benefited from the stay at the NCDS in 1990. Ideas developed for it then were an important input to the framework used in de Vylder and Fforde (1996). The work was then left, and returned to in 2004–2005 when the Melbourne Institute of Asian Languages and Societies (now the Asia Institute) offered a room and a base, and my long-standing colleague Nguyen Dinh Huan provided access to parallel histories through detailed interviews with SOE managers. More widely known for his work on rural issues, Dr Nguyen Dinh Huan worked at the Industry Department of the Hanoi Economics Institute in the late 1980s.

From 1992 to 1999 I lived in Canberra, working at the ANU and as a consultant. Production of my company's regular review of the situation in Vietnam (VECA – Vietnam: Economic Commentary and Analysis) generated access to a wide range of analyses. Publication of de Vylder and Fforde in 1996, and in translated form in 1997, had allowed us to develop our analysis of the Vietnamese transition to a market economy. This book uses that same overall framework. The ARC Large Research Grant scheme financed the Australia Vietnam Research Project through 1994–1997, which gave me various opportunities to interview participants in the transition process. Towards the end of the 1990s I received financing from the Canadian Embassy in Hanoi to examine real property rights in Vietnamese SOEs (Fforde, 2004b). In combination with work on legal changes and SOEs (Fforde, 2005d), this underpins the closing chapters.

Method

The book attempts to set out orthodox Vietnamese economic analysis and the formal policy framework. To do so it uses textbooks and the writings of Vietnamese leaders and cadres. The study places considerable weight upon official decrees and other documents. These sought from at least the early 1970s to improve the operation of the economic management system.[10] They can be found in a number of published collections as well as the official gazette (*Cong Bao*). There are also a number of specific 'guides' to new policies (e.g. BLD, 1981). From a reading of these materials it is possible to establish within reasonable doubt precisely what any policy said that it sought to do. Many of these materials, and especially the legal documents, have not been used before for such a purpose, and remain rare in the West.[11] I have given space to detailed discussion of these documents, partly to show what they were like but also to suggest that 'policy' needs to be seen not in some spuriously coherent abstract, but as highly textured and contextualised, and often contradictory (Shore and Wright, 1997). This suggests that bald statements about policy reform and suchlike need to be taken with a pinch of salt, often a rather large one.

There was much open and heated debate about economic matters, and this has also provided valuable research materials. The relative openness of the official press provided many examples of grassroots economic behaviour. This was a valuable source of information which was collected together and computerised to facilitate cross-checking. Together with a number of illuminating Vietnamese analyses, the results permit empirical study of the Vietnamese industrial economy during the period and illustration, at times vivid,[12] of the evolving pattern of events.

Notes

1. The Vietnamese Communist Party has been called by various names in its history; here I refer to it throughout as the VCP.
2. According to official data, based upon GDP measured at 1994 prices, the state share of GDP (output basis) fell from 47.6 per cent in 1985 to 39.0 per cent in 1992, after which it climbed steadily through the 1990s to average 41.0 per cent in 2000–2003. These data *exclude* foreign-invested companies, which were very often SOEs and which grew much faster than total industrial output (TCTK, 2000: tables 16, 21 and 154; TCTK, 2004: tables 27 and 109).
3. Saigon fell in 1975; the new state – the SRV – was set up in 1976.
4. By commercialisation is here meant the development of an economic system based upon voluntary interaction between consumers and independent producers who possess enough control over their productive assets to decide what to produce and where to dispose of it. This definition implies that

producers effectively control capital, and that there is therefore a recognisable 'commercial' or 'business' interest.

5. This standard political science position has been developed well by Thayer in various works (e.g. Thayer, 1983, 1995) and Vasavakul (e.g. 1993, 1997). See also Turley (1993), Riedel and Turley (1998), Porter (1990, 1993 – the 1990 version of his position is less tarnished by publishers' demands and more illuminating), Turley and Selden (1993) and, more recently, Heng (1990).

6. Normal contacts (in other words contacts that did not risk police penalties) between Vietnamese and foreigners did not start until the very early 1990s, by which time I had already spent some five years living in the country. Until then they were forbidden.

7. That is, a change process largely driven by internal forces rather than external factors, especially policy change – see p. 62.

8. I owe much to Nguyen Phap and the late Nguyen Tri, whose respect for the value of 'go and see' I greatly appreciate.

9. I used these and other site visits to develop my own understanding of micro behaviour through discussion and observation, particularly of terms used. I hardly ever refer directly to such interviews in the text, however, partly due to a long habit of desiring to protect people from the security apparatus. You never know. The grassroots panel was interviewed indirectly in 2005, when the people concerned were retired. Further, this overall stance avoids giving the reader a sense, which I think would be spurious, of 'manager speak', and also, more importantly, allows me to show just how much is available in the published texts.

10. Some Vietnamese economists date these measures to the mid-1960s, e.g. Le Trang (1990: 153), referring to attempts to overcome corruption and mismanagement in state industry 'from 1964'.

11. See, however, Vo Nhan Tri (1990) and the Vietnamese contributions to Ronnas and Sjoberg (1991), also Abrami (2002).

12. This colour, it is hoped, comes out in the quotations given in the text; see also the doggerel quoted in Chapter 8 (p. 183) on 'The Manager's Lament', which comes from an academic journal. The contrast between the wooden phrasing of much official Vietnamese and the electric timbre of real debate cannot be underestimated. See the discussion of 'stuff it' (*mac ke*) in the Glossary.

About the author

With a first degree from Oxford in engineering science and economics and a masters in economics from Birkbeck College, London, Adam Fforde studied Vietnamese at Hanoi University in 1978–1979 while preparing for his PhD (economics, Cambridge). During 1985–1986, while an ESRC post-doctoral fellow at Birkbeck, he returned as a visiting researcher to the Industry Faculty of the National Economics University. From 1987 to 1992 he lived in Vietnam, working as a consultant for SIDA. Since 1992 he has combined academic research and teaching activities with his main career focus upon consultancy, including periods with honorary positions at the Australian National University and the Stockholm School of Economics, and was a full-time senior fellow of the Southeast Asia Program of the National University of Singapore in 2000–2001. He currently resides in Melbourne and is a principal fellow of the Asia Institute, University of Melbourne, as well as chairman of Adam Fforde and Associates. He can be contacted at adam@aduki.com.au.

A note to readers

The country is conventionally divided into three 'regions' – north, centre and south. These correspond approximately to the three Vietnamese parts of the French Indochinese Union – Tonkin, Annam and Cochinchina.

The administrative hierarchy is centre, province/city, district/quarter and commune/street. Below the commune in rural areas are other levels not recognised by the state in terms of their having a People's Council – village and hamlet – though they have mass organisations and Party organisations, and some formal reporting duties.

The VCP held regular congresses; between these its Central Committee held plena. Both are numbered sequentially, with the numbering of plena reset to zero at each congress.

The Vietnamese currency is the dong.

There are many Vietnamese words that have a particular meaning or meanings which may be lost in translation. These are marked with an asterisk (*) and can be found in the Glossary.

Regarding names, apart from certain anomalies (see below), references in the text to works by Vietnamese authors give the whole name in the usual Vietnamese sequence of family name, middle name (if there is one), given name, without abbreviation. The Bibliography lists names alphabetically by family name/middle name/given name. Vietnamese who have in some circumstances, most importantly their publishing, changed to a Western convention, such as given name/middle name/family name (such as the man known as Luong van Hy in Vietnamese and Hy van Luong in English), are found in the Bibliography using the Western form and textual references are, as with Western authors, abbreviated to the family name. Any failure to follow this convention by the author is regretted and unintended. Note also that some Vietnamese authors use pen names, in which case this is assumed to operate in the same way as a normal name, i.e. the first word in the name is treated as the family name.

Scene-setting and overview of the book

Introduction

Vietnam from the early 1990s has been widely presented in the West as a developmental success story, with rapid growth and poverty reduction (Dollar et al., 1998). But in many ways by the mid-2000s this narrative masked grave concerns over its underlying stability (Fforde, 2004a, 2005a) since its politics remained dominated by a combination of a traditionally Leninist use of various facades, such as the National Assembly and the mass organisations (MOs),[1] with high levels of corruption stemming in part from weak legal frameworks combined with close relations between politicians and business, especially state business.

Through the 2000s Vietnam's state-owned enterprises (SOEs) have faced rising competition from the combination of a forcefully growing private sector and foreign-invested companies. Without Party cells or official trade unions, mediating such conflicts was a quite new problem for the regime. Through the 1990s Vietnam's rapid growth had entailed a rising state share of GDP (see Preface, note 2). It is very rare for this to happen in contemporary developing countries. Combined with macro-economic stability, this offers a 'Vietnam paradox' which can only be answered by a close examination of the nature of the state sector, and this is the main focus of this book. I argue that Vietnam's SOEs were far more private in character than has been appreciated, and that this had long historical roots and had been central to the successful transition of the 1980s, but was in part reversed in the 1990s. As one of Vietnam's leading analysts, Dao Xuan Sam, once said to me: 'In Vietnam, the public is never entirely public, and the private is never entirely private.'[2]

As in many other contexts, a society that does not perceive clear boundaries between its politics and its business faces challenges of social and political stability, typically manifest in high levels of corruption, though not necessarily in slow growth.

In this wider perspective, the book thus examines the processes involved in the transition of Vietnamese state industry from a centrally planned to a market-oriented system. These were, it is argued, predominantly 'bottom up' in character, and this means that the study has had to take special account of the interaction between policy and practice. It therefore traces four interwoven 'parallel histories':

- the economic performance of the sector;
- the history of official policy towards state industry;
- parts of the political background to changes in that policy;
- the particular experiences of a number of SOEs.

Overview

Layout of the book

In this chapter I examine relevant literature, present an outline of the changing basic parameters of the Vietnamese economy (including the changing roles of state industry within it), examine growth processes and then go over the key elements of the transition story. This introduces the argument that many of Vietnam's successes and problems have relatively long historical roots. Specifically, the potential for instability I see in the second half of the 2000s has a strong relationship with what happened in North Vietnam in the early 1960s and then during the transition of the 1980s. The two crucial turning points of 1979–1980 and 1989–1990 I see as two 'traps' which led to, first, the demise of traditional socialism and, second, the foundations of a brittle polity characterised by a blurring of boundaries between state and business that coped well with the stresses of the 1990s but faced quite new problems in the 2000s for which it was ill prepared.

The rest of the book is then divided as follows.

The study continues with a detailed discussion in Chapter 2 of the historical background to the events of the 1980s: the traditional neo-Stalinist programme adopted in the DRV and what happened to it after national reunification in 1975–1976. It also provides a short discussion of the analytical framework I use. Chapter 3 examines policy debates prior to 1979, tracing in them both evidence for conditions in the north prior to 1975 and ideas – drawn from SOE behaviour – later visible in the policies of the transition period.

The remaining chapters then examine in detail the origins and content of the transitional model[3] that arrived in 1979–1981 and operated throughout the 1980s. In Chapter 4 I look at what happened in the run-up to the crisis of 1979–1980. Chapter 5 then discusses the transitional model in detail. Chapters 6 and 7 look at SOE and local behaviour during the periods of spontaneous decentralisation (1979–1981) and attempted recentralisation (1981–c. 1985). Chapter 8 then looks at the final stage of the transition during the period 1985–1989, which ended with the emergence of a market economy after abolition of the 'two-price' system and the vestiges of central planning. Chapter 9 examines the position of SOEs during the 1990s and early 2000s, arguing strongly for the problems created by success in 1990–1991 in securing recovery from the loss of Soviet-bloc aid. Chapter 10 concludes.

In choosing this layout I have tried to take into account some of the particular problems posed for readers by the subject matter, in particular the combination of considerable institutional detail with the lack of spurious clarity that accompanies a view of change which sees it driven by 'policy' and so as a change process that can be thought of as a realisation of some intentionality. I hope that the reader will conclude with me that it would be misleading to see Vietnam's commercial renaissance, although very closely – I argue too closely – bound up with the state, as a consequence of any top-down intentionality. However, the level of institutional detail and the complexities of legal documents are burdensome. The book tends to unpack detail as it proceeds, so that the level of detail I assume the reader can cope with increases. I have also put in a somewhat unusual degree of cross-referencing that is intended to help. It is, though, evident that the 'devil is in the detail': as a wide range of site visits confirmed to me, it was very important for SOE managers to keep up with the ebb and flow of legislation;[4] this was an important part of their world. Get it wrong, and you could be denounced as anti-socialist (p. 61).[5]

A caveat

This study takes a particular view of the meaning of the transition to a market economy. It identifies this with the end of the administrative allocation of resources through a Soviet-style material balance system. Once this practice has been abolished, prices are generally free to move to reflect supply and demand, and the normal form that exchange relations take is voluntary negotiation. It is then assumed that the main economic problems have fundamentally changed: from that point on, the economy is best seen as some form of market economy. The extent to which this assumption is valid is largely beyond the scope of this book, which focuses upon the processes by which the Vietnamese economy arrived at the point at which it starts to become reasonable to make that assumption.[6] Prior to that point, the existence of central planning created an economic system whose normal operation was qualitatively different from that of a market economy (p. 9). Chapter 9 discusses the situation as it evolved in the 1990s and 2000s once central planning had vanished.

Research context and literature review

Our own research programme

The work here is part of a long-term research programme, now nearly three decades old. With three co-authors, I have developed a series of interlinked studies. Fforde and Paine (1987) examined the DRV economy and the systemic tensions within it. Fforde (1983) looked at the pre-modern rural socio-economy in order better to understand the effects of collectivisation, which was studied in greater detail in Fforde (1982, 1989). De Vylder and Fforde (1988) presented a preliminary overall analysis and critique of the transitional model which was revised and theorised in de Vylder and Fforde (1996). Beresford and Fforde (1997) looked at transition in the area of domestic trade.

These studies have seen themes and concepts evolve and have often drawn heavily upon Vietnamese ideas, as expressed in the language – the best example is the use of the word 'outside' to refer to non-plan or quasi-market activities. This term, *ngoai*, is rich in meaning (Luong, 1989), but serves here to stress important aspects of the relationships involved which are not fully brought out by terms such as 'commercial'. This is in the main because the 'inside/outside' dichotomy relates to wider issues where discussion often starts with kin relationships.[8] In addition, its use permits avoidance of the prejudice that non-plan relations are best described by the term 'market'. This and other terms will be brought into the discussion as appropriate; Vietnamese words are to be found in the Glossary. However, the reader may reflect upon the troubled meanings that accrue to Western terms when used under conditions very different from those of ordinary market economies.

One of the most intriguing conclusions of this research (one of the reasons why many mainstream economists found the approach distasteful) is that the main role played by inflation in the transition process was positive. This is because it created and then maintained a gap between official and 'outside' prices – or values – that provided a strong incentive for economic agents to shift resources towards 'outside' activities. This meant that attempts to defend the plan through subsidisation based upon inflationary finance almost always attempted to make water flow uphill, and were thus a powerful force for commercialisation of the state sector from within.

Vietnam studies and SOEs

While there are large literatures[7] relating to transition and SOEs, and for Vietnamese SOEs especially prior to 1989–1990, I am uncomfortably aware of having worked in something of a research vacuum. While Western research into the operation of the contemporary Vietnamese economy grew fast from around the mid-1990s, there has been very little work on the dynamics of transition as I define it above, which requires a close examination of the 1980s (especially the first half) and earlier. This period was indeed largely written out of history by early donor studies (World Bank, 1990a; Leipziger, 1992; Drabek, 1990; UNDP, 1990; UNIDO, 1989; but see Dodsworth et al., 1996), which seem to have been more concerned to hail the Party's apparent admission that 'market economies are best' and so thankfully attribute success to policy change. They tended therefore to concentrate upon the late 1980s, by which time the transitional model was both mature and scheduled by policy for replacement by a market-oriented economy.

Through the 1990s, however, a small number of studies emerged that treated the emergence of the market economy in Vietnam as worthy of interest, notably Abrami (2002), Vu Tuong (n/d, 2001), Digregorio (1994), Dang Phong and Beresford (1998) and Kerkvliet (2005). These tended to confirm the findings of earlier work – such as

Fforde (1982, 1989), Fforde and Paine (1987), de Vylder and Fforde (1988), Vickerman (1986) and Spoor (1985) – that previous studies which had viewed the DRV as 'strong' were wrong and widespread policy unimplementability and extensive market growth were indeed what had happened. Note work such as that by Van Dyke (1972) and Woodside (1970) which had argued for this even earlier. The Penguin book by Chaliand (1969), which went to many printings, referred to peasants during wartime actively selling their surpluses on markets. Despite this, many analyses present the DRV as a model of neo-Stalinist correctness, with extreme pressures on free markets.

Martin Gainsborough has developed a body of published work that treats policy as but one among many factors that influence change. He treats SOEs as both the objects of political struggle and at times subjects, capable of exerting influence upon historical change (for example Gainsborough, 2002).

Abrami's work, so far little published (Abrami, 2002), takes research in a similar direction, arguing that while the DRV state was certainly 'weak' in the sense that it typically failed to secure stated goals, it was nevertheless more important than other studies had argued. In particular, by comparing market regulation and support in Vietnam and China the picture emerged that for various reasons, and with the notion that certain sorts of market development appear to require focused state activities, north Vietnamese commerce appeared to be hindered in its development. This is particularly interesting and valuable as it combines comparative and highly textured analysis with an interest in the effects of what she sees with others as particular characteristics of Vietnamese state thinking – its 'managerial socialism'. I add to this, through my examination below of tensions within expert thinking, ways in which the perceived failures to implement neo-Stalinism were mediated into policy. This opens up the question of just what the limitations of local analyses were and how these may be related to the ways in which state power both was and was not used in the period 1989–1991: in other words, the second 'trap'. In other work Abrami points to the unintended effects of state actions in the 1990s as again a hindrance to commercial development (Abrami and Henaff, 2004).

An interesting attempt to theorise the position of SOEs within a wider context can be derived from Kerkvliet (2001), who takes a strongly statist 'state-society' approach. His approach is reminiscent of Mitchell (1991). Mitchell posits that the state-society boundary is usually blurred, and thus in effect unobservable and simply an 'affect' of certain techniques of rule. Thus state-society relations are to be explained by politics and how it is done. Kerkvliet (2001: 268), however, holds to the position that even if it is futile to 'distinguish between what is in the state and what is in society', it is still valid to adopt an approach that 'emphasizes arenas in which relations between state and society are problematic... focusing on two matters: how the political system works and discussions about appropriate state-society relations'.

It follows that there is great scope for examining ways in which groups whose apparent situations have 'state' or 'non-state' labels interact. This is fruitful, but my main problem with this approach is that it remains content to use terms such as state and society not as 'affects of certain techniques of rule' but as fundamental analytical categories, with terms like state power then coming back into the analysis; see Almond (1988) for an assessment and Hindess (1996) for a critique of common usages of the term power that suggest it can be treated as an ordinal variable, with agent X prevailing, or us expecting that they will prevail, over agent Y if X has more power than Y. Hindess suggests that this is very unwise, not least because 'who wins' (in Vietnamese *ai thang ai*, from the Russian *kto kogo*) depends greatly upon what actually happens, rather than the situation before the fight starts.

Parallel to the state-society approach, many analyses of Vietnamese SOEs from around the mid-1990s tend to policy fetishism – that is, excessive concern to explain things in terms of policy and what was wrong with it. A central example is the World Bank (e.g. World Bank, 1995a); others are Kokko (1998), Suiwah Leung (1996), Mallon and Van Arkadie (2003), Turley and Riedel (1998) and also perhaps Woodside (1997).

But this picture is far from universal or without nuance. For example, de Lestrange and Richet (1998: 93) stress the political factors that influence SOE behaviour, though they conclude that: 'The Vietnamese leadership will certainly have to come up with new ideas so as to launch the new stages of the economic reform.' I take this to mean that progress depends primarily upon policy change (see also Diehl, 1995).

By contrast, McMillan and Woodruff (1999) argue that informal relationships between firms – rather than formal institutions such as law – create the trust needed to maintain low transaction costs. The point is that market economy institutions can be auto-generated rather than policy-driven. This parallels McMillan's earlier work on China (McMillan, 1994).

I should also mention the path-breaking (but rarely cited) work of the neo-Trotskyite Gerard Greenfield (1993, 1994). He argues, based upon close fieldwork in north Vietnam in the very early 1990s, that SOE managers, supported by the state, were actively appropriating state assets as part of the rapid development of capitalism. This is one of the very few works that looks at real property rights rather than taking superficial legal forms as meaningful in terms of issues of ownership and control. It goes beyond simple allegations of theft and corruption to ask questions about systemic change that are lacking in other writings from a Marxist perspective, such as Beresford (1993, 1997).

SOEs and their possible roles in economic development

There is a large literature on the possible roles of SOEs in economic development. The debates and arguments are usefully seen historically, since Western orthodoxies have gone through major shifts since the Second World War.

An accessible commentary is Lindauer and Pritchett (2002). They report that an examination of the three years 1962, 1982 and 2002 reveals major shifts in economic thinking about the roles of markets and the state in development. Thus, informed by the experiences of the 1930s' Depression, most mainstream economists in 1962 were highly sceptical of the reliability and value of free markets. As a result, policies encouraged high levels of protection and economic development based initially upon import substitution. These had also been common before the war. Such market scepticism, combined with suspicion of international capital flows, encouraged SOEs through either nationalisation or direct investment. Waterbury (1999) is an accessible overview that shows the variety of ways in which SOEs were part of development efforts. UK and French post-Second World War reconstruction was heavily dependent upon large state sectors (Shonfield, 1965), and the World Bank and other important international agencies advocated these policies at the time.

However, Lindauer and Pritchett (2002) argue that by 1982 mainstream views had shifted around to scepticism about states and optimism about markets. By 1995 the World Bank was reporting studies which concluded that:

> large SOE sectors can hinder growth for a variety of reasons, in part because individual SOEs are usually less efficient than private firms and in part because the resulting aggregate SOE deficits are typically financed in ways that undermine macroeconomic stability. In addition, subsidies to SOEs often divert scarce funds from growth-enhancing public spending, such as education and health. Finally, we found that because SOE sectors tend to be larger in low-income counties, SOEs are likely to be most costly in the countries that can least afford them. (World Bank, 1995b: 25)

These ideas in political economy analyses were supported by the 'rent-seeking' literature (Krueger, 1974) which stressed that barriers to free markets offered many opportunities for gain as businesses sought to create or maintain protection for themselves, such as through tariffs on foreign trade. Business people benefited if they could secure favourable positioning relative to those barriers, which in turn (according to these arguments) weakened economic growth.

For these perspectives, of course, the apparent success of Vietnam's SOEs in the 1990s is anomaly or anathema, and not infrequently resulted in the position that development would have been still better had they been privatised. This recalls left-wing discussions of the 1960s and early 1970s as to whether there could be successful development in the periphery of the unequal global capitalist system (Warren, 1973), and does not answer the question as to why the arguments deployed by the World Bank (if we assume them to be more than self-serving) simply did not apply to Vietnam in the 1990s: for example, that macroeconomic stability would have been undermined.

Counter-arguments assert the value of SOEs. An interesting one is that mounted to defend China's SOEs by Dic Lo (1999).

Through the 1990s the apparent certainties of the early 1980s reported by Lindauer and Pritchett (2002) were eroded by the economic difficulties facing many countries that had extensively privatised SOEs, both developed and developing. Out of this by 2002 had come, they argue, a far lower degree of comfort with relatively simple generalisations. Thus by the early 2000s I could interview a bilateral-funded consultant within a multilateral agency in Hanoi working on SOEs whose remit was to protect the Vietnamese from visiting (or resident) advisers whose thinking was 'unreconstructed 1982' in Lindauer and Pritchett terms.

Vietnamese communist economy, 1954–2005

Problems of data and analysis

Data

After 1975 the quality and availability of economic data in the SRV steadily improved. Despite this, however, there remain three major difficulties with the data before the adoption of Western national income accounting (NIA) methods in the mid-1990s.

First is coverage. Orthodox communist statistical theory based itself upon neo-Stalinist assumptions about the nature of socially valuable economic activity.[9] Belief in the necessity of increasing the scale of production for economic growth (Bray, 1983), combined with the belief that this would lead, without measures to stop it, to the emergence of political forces opposed to the communist regime, led to important conclusions. Economic institutions had to be subordinate to the regime. In rural areas this meant cooperativisation, where increased scale would not require landlords since their social and economic positions would be taken by Party-dominated cooperative leaderships.[10] In industry this meant SOEs, with inputs delivered to them according to the plan.

The basis for categorising sectors was the concept of 'economic component' (*thanh phan*), based upon a class categorisation that relied upon formal ownership – in other words the property form[11] under which fixed assets were held. This stress upon *production* creates problems if one is interested in how resources are acquired and disposed of; that is, a division of economic activity according to *allocative mechanisms* – how resources are allocated and acquired. In a market economy this is mainly carried out through markets, and in a centrally planned economy (CPE) through the instructions and orders of the plan (see also note 33 on p. 115).[12]

Understanding the implications of different allocative mechanisms is fundamental to understanding the commercial renaissance in Vietnam.[13] If, as is central here, one is interested in how and to what extent SOEs are participating in markets, or, to use the technical term, the extent to which they are self-balancing (*tu can doi*), this does not show up in the official data (see the discussion of the term *tu* in Vietnamese, p. 47). Use of the official classification leads to deep difficulties. There is no official measure of the extent of unplanned activities within the state sector. Also, socialist transformation,[14] for example of petty producers into cooperative workers, could boost socialist output statistics, and vice versa. But the extent to which such practices were self-balancing was often known to policy-makers (for example see p. 173 and the data in de Vylder and Fforde, 1996: 213).

Second, wide variation in the values of crucial statistics quoted by different bodies at different times, coupled with the data's frequent internal inconsistencies, creates doubt about the reliability of any given statistic. As a senior policy adviser once said to me, referring to the IMF for whom they had considerable respect: 'They come, they ask for statistics, we give them what they ask for, and sometimes we forget to keep a copy.'

Finally, the absence of any decent Vietnamese guide to extant statistical methodology also means that it is hard to assess the relative reliability of different data.[15]

Analytical frameworks

It would be natural to assume that as a member of the communist bloc Vietnam's state industry would closely follow the Soviet prototype. Although superficially true, in reality this was not the case.

Fforde and Paine (1987) argued that under north Vietnamese conditions it would have been hard to implement traditional central planning. Indeed, the unimplementability of socio-economic policy has been a theme with which both the Vietnamese and those who attempt to study them have long had to live (Fforde, 1986). This was also central to my study of the problems arising from the collectivised rural economy in the DRV (Fforde, 1982, 1989), which drew heavily upon an earlier analysis of the traditional functions of rural institutions (Fforde, 1983).

The failed attempt to implement the orthodox central-planning model in the DRV during the first Five Year Plan (FYP) (1961–1965) was originally responsible for creating conditions of 'aggravated shortage'. By this is meant a coexistence of the classic and well-studied consequences of central planning (Ericson, 1984; Feldbrugge, 1984; Kornai, 1980), so that the same good could be at the same time in both 'abundant and short supply' (*dong thoi thua thieu), with fairly extensive development of markets.[16] Prohibition of direct relations between 'people who had it' and 'people who wanted it' meant that they could not transact to mutual advantage. The concept refers to a general characteristic of the DRV economy, macro-systemic in nature and so designed to aid understanding of system change. By 1975 the northern economy was characterised by the coexistence of a central-planning apparatus with an extensive development of autonomous[17] horizontal (*ngang) links between economic units often associated with more or less 'free' markets. The concept of 'aggravated shortage' has been found to be of great value, and to an extent the 1980s simply legalised and accepted its basic dichotomy.

By presenting economic agents with alternatives to activities carried on within the plan, such relationships aggravated (from planners' perspectives) many of the problems of systemic shortage familiar from developed CPEs (Kornai, 1980). As behaviour adapted, economic institutions revealed a strong tendency towards endogeneity, by which I mean that their content was determined in ways very different from the top-down assumptions of the textbooks. SOE autonomy, central to their sustainable participation in markets, thus emerged in the main from their practice rather than from top-down reforms. This is one reason why the terminology is so interesting and vivid.

For economists trained in the conventional and doctrinally reinforced neo-Stalinist tradition, and this was true for most north Vietnamese scholars, the unimplementability of the neo-Stalinist programme meant that the vision taught in universities lacked effective contact with reality. This had important and often dramatic implications for debates about the problems of the traditional programme (Chapter 3).

Thus the main energy for Vietnam's commercial renaissance came from *within* its SOEs. To explain this, the study concentrates on the causes and consequences of the so-called transitional model, which lasted formally from 1981 to 1989.[18] It looks at its political and macro-economic backgrounds in the experiences of the 1960s and 1970s. It also examines its immediate origins in the economic crisis of 1979–1980. It was this commercialisation which meant that the Vietnamese could, by using SOEs and their familiarity with markets, reallocate economic activities when Soviet-bloc aid was lost in 1989–1990 in ways that were consistent with the emergence of a market economy.

Transition is understood here to mean a situation where the essential characteristics of the traditional neo-Stalinist model coexisted with the market relations of what was to replace it. In the transitional model this was officially (and for most of the time legally) sanctioned. Coexistence was marked by the so-called 'two-price' system, whereby many goods were simultaneously traded voluntarily at high values[19] and subject to the state system of allocation at low accounting prices.

An important characteristic of the transition model (understood in this way) was how it provided significant access to rents[20] in the form of large subsidies to elements of the state and cooperative economies (Fforde, 2002). These appeared as the use of inputs supplied at low and fixed state prices to generate incomes through diversion into activities that were not part of the overall state plan. These low prices could result from such phenomena as the 'low' official exchange rate – compared with that on the free market – and cheap credit, as well as simple access to cheap goods. Many SOEs used these to learn about free market behaviour, build up their own capital (*von tu co),[21] construct suitable links with their external 'owners' and so on.

The North Vietnamese economy, 1954–1975

Growth, 1954–1975

Reasonably good statistics on total output (using Soviet statistical methods – p. 9) became available from the late 1950s. National income grew at an average of around 6.3 per cent yearly through the first FYP (Fforde and Paine, 1987: table 19) – a rather slow rate by central-planning standards.

In the same period state industrial output (Fforde and Paine, 1987: table 31) grew at just over 19 per cent a year. The growth rate slowed towards the end of the FYP. While the reasons for this are analysed in depth elsewhere (Fforde and Paine, 1987), it was mainly due to the region's poverty combined with the social and political context.

A very poor area ...

After 1975, as Western economists started to look at what had happened in North Vietnam after 1954, many concluded that the poverty of the area created conditions extremely unsuited to the dreams of ambitious neo-Stalinists (Fforde, 1982; Vickerman, 1986; Fforde and Paine, 1987). The French had left behind very little modern industry and, while there were a very few mines and some up-country plantations, in the main this was a region of poor peasants.

An extensive quotation from a book written in 1960 to support the political position advocating a rapid growth strategy shows this clearly:

> Industry and the artisanat also met many difficulties. Before the war [against the French] industry only amounted to 10% of the total of agricultural and industrial output. After the years of fighting, this had fallen to 1.5%. The factories and mines had almost all either been destroyed by war or taken south by the French. The tin and zinc refineries (though very small) had been bombed by the Americans and the Japanese and, left unused, were out of operation. Most large machinery and means of transport needed for the Hong-gai mines and the cement factory had been taken south so output had collapsed. Coal output in 1930 was 2.615 mn. tonnes but in 1955 had fallen to 641,544. Cement output in 1939 had been 305,800 tonnes but in 1955 was 8,450. In a number of factories, such as car repairs, locomotive repairs, boat-building, printing and spinning, the machinery had been dismantled and some of the buildings destroyed. In the Nam-dinh textile mill materials and the main parts of the turbine had been taken to the south (cloth output in the north was 55,575 m in 1939 and only 8,783 in 1955).
>
> Thus, in the newly liberated areas industry was paralysed... Nearly 100,000 industrial workers were unemployed. (Vu Quoc Tuan and Dinh Van Hoang, 1960: 15)

Official statistics (TCTK, 1978, 1985) confirm this. The starkest figure was for per capita staples output, which by 1960 was 290 kg. This figure is in paddy rice equivalent, and adds to rice other staples such as potatoes and maize. Approximately, multiply by 0.6 to get from paddy rice to milled rice, and doing so gives 175 kg a year per person, or about 15 kg a month, which was just above the minimum food ration of about 12 kg a month that people were receiving when I was a student in Hanoi in 1978–1979. With insignificant exports, North Vietnam's urban population had, under the French, largely depended upon taxes imposed on the south. By 1960 the total population of the DRV was 16.1 million, of which 9 per cent was urban and about 125,000 worked in industry (TCTK, 1985: tables 8, 12 and 78).

Fundamental to the story are the constraints to rapid economic change in North Vietnam, long an area of population saturation (Fforde and Paine, 1987). The work quoted above (Vu Quoc Tuan and Dinh Van Hoang, 1960) had to justify the attempt, and later studies had to cope with the consequences (Nguyen Duy Trinh and Nguyen Van Tran, 1966; EPU, 1970).

It is interesting to compare per capita output levels for strategic goods in 1960, after the Three Year Plan (1958–1960) had restored output levels, and 2000. Iron and steel rose from 0.5 kg to 20.4 kg; chemical fertiliser from 3.2 kg to 16 kg; electricity from 15.9 kWh to 104.5 kWh; staples in milled rice equivalent from 175 kg to 267 kg; salt from 7.4 kg to 7.6 kg; coal fell from 161 kg to 150 kg; lime rose from 12.6 kg to 14.9 kg; fish sauce fell from 2.3 litres to 2.2 litres; cigarettes rose from 4.6 packs to 36.6 packs; cement from 25 kg to 171 kg; and bicycles from 1.4 units per thousand to 2.0 units per thousand. Recall that for many items foreign trade was important.

Bearing in mind the fact that even by 2000 Vietnam's per capita GDP was recorded at only US$380 (TCTK, 2001: table 32), the deep poverty of North Vietnam in 1960 is obvious. Most people were poor farmers.

The first FYP was ambitious, with high levels of investment and rapid hoped-for output growth rates (BCH, 1963). But this was unimplementable, and so compromises had to be made, underpinned by the aid programme. The structure of aid shifted from investment goods towards consumer goods and industrial inputs, as the newly built factories could not be operated fully without such supplies, which the North Vietnamese economy was unable to provide. Thus one can understand why the slogan 'Priority to the development of heavy industry' was changed to '*Rational* priority to the development of heavy industry' (**Uu tien phat trien cong nghiep nang mot cach hop ly*). Le Duan would thus argue it both ways:

> During the construction of socialism, it is incorrect not to stress the role of material incentives in stimulating workers to work actively, but it is also incorrect not to teach them and raise their socialist consciousness, in which case no revolutionary movement will be created. Both sides of the question are factors that stimulate production and neither should be belittled. (Quoted in Doan Trong Truyen, 1965: 70)

1965–1975

A widely held opinion is that, after LBJ's phrase, US wartime efforts 'bombed them back to the Stone Age'. While the killings and destruction were immense, this is confirmed neither by the data nor by wartime US intelligence estimates; what happened, rather, was that a combination of decentralisation, Vietnamese inventiveness and massive Chinese and Soviet-bloc support not only held up industrial output levels but also permitted them to rise. By the end of the war imports were supporting greatly increased levels of both urban population and state employment. Food aid started in the late 1960s, and was feeding most of the urban population by the end of the war.

Such propaganda as Nguyen Duy Trinh (1976) therefore contained elements of truth: the north had not only won the war, but had also continued to construct socialism. The problem was, and this predated the war, that rapid growth in state industry lacked sufficient basis in the northern economy, and so it (and the urban and state-employed population that accompanied it) relied upon imports. Unlike China, domestic rates of surplus generation never reached high levels (Fforde, 1999; Naughton, 1994).[22]

Thus the DRV population rose from 16.1 million in 1960 to 18.6 million in 1965 and 24.6 in 1975 (Fforde and Paine, 1987: table 8). The urban population rose from 0.9 million in 1960 to 1.1 million in 1965 and 1.8 million in 1975. The number of state employees grew from 0.5 million to 1.7 million between 1960 and 1975 (about 300,000 of the gain was in the social sectors: education, health, etc.) (Fforde and Paine, 1987: tables 10 and 12).

SOE employment rose from 114,000 in 1960 to 220,000 in 1965 and then 356,000 in 1975. Compared with the yearly growth in the first FYP of 19 per cent, between 1965 and 1975 state industrial output grew by 6 per cent annually (Fforde and Paine, 1987: table 31). Between 1965 and 1975 output grew 82 per cent and employment by 61 per cent. The reported value of fixed assets rose by over 100 per cent. Though we know little about the extent to which war damage was accounted for, the evidence points to a situation in SOEs where assets were underemployed and staffing levels high, all floating on high levels of imports that would have to change once the war ended.

Vietnamese economic development after the 1975–1976 reunification

Overview

The fall of the south in 1975 saw the country finally reunited after decades of long and bloody struggle, so these years are quite properly viewed as being of great importance to realising hopes for rapid and independent economic development. With a population of over 65 million at the end of the 1980s, Vietnam was the third largest communist (or recently ex-communist) country in the world (TCTK, 1990: 5). World Bank estimates of per capita GDP placed Vietnam at that time among the poorest countries in the world.[23]

The period 1975–1990 covers three FYPs: the second (1976–1980), third (1981–1985) and fourth (1986–1990).[24]

Immediately after the war, after a sharp rise in total output in 1976 the two crisis years of 1979 and 1980 were marked by strongly negative growth. During the 1980s the economy settled down early in the decade to rather higher growth rates of around 6–8 per cent annually before slowing again in the second half. Inflation accelerated in the mid-1980s, then slowed in late 1987 before reaching hyperinflationary levels until the firm anti-inflation measures of 1989 took effect (TCTK, 1991: table 88; TCTK, 1990: table 96). The peak was reached in March 1988 at 28.4 per cent month-on-month (TCTK, 1991).

Then in the 1990s growth recovered rapidly from the loss of Soviet-bloc aid in 1989–1991 and settled down to around 7–8 per cent that lasted through into the 2000s. There was a slight slowdown in 1997–1998 associated with the 1997 Asian financial crisis, when FDI fell away and export markets disrupted.

After the early 1990s prices were stable and the macro-economy generally in balance. It is the combination of macro-economic stability with a large and at times rising share of the state in GDP that is so unusual: a 'Vietnam paradox' (p. 1).

The second FYP, 1976–1980

If the key problem in implementing traditional socialism in the DRV was the underlying poverty of the area, then national reunification should have solved this by granting access to the extensive development frontier of the Mekong delta: few people, much land and scope for expansion by bringing more land under cultivation. Collectivised farmers should, according to the model, have been able to provide the food needed to feed the growing cities and expanding state industrial sector. In 1975 the north and south had equivalent populations, while the Mekong delta is about twice the area of the Red River delta. Add to this scope for expansion of plantation activities (using state farms) in the central highlands, and the outlook looked good to planners (de Vylder and Fforde, 1996).[25]

But economic growth stalled from 1977: from nearly 14 per cent in 1976 it fell back to 2 per cent in 1977 and 1978, and was then actually negative in 1979. In 1980 it was back to 2 per cent, so that through the FYP (1976–1980) growth averaged 3.8 per cent and population rose 2.4 per cent yearly (TCTK, 1985: tables 7 and 25). State industry followed a similar trajectory, averaging only 2.4 per cent annual growth over the period, with falls in 1979 and 1980 (TCTK, 1985: table 27). How had this happened? Various forces came into play (de Vylder and Fforde, 1996), but central were the loss of Chinese and most Western aid and effective resistance to implementation of central planning in the south.

The targets of the second FYP were ambitious, with high levels of investment and rapid planned growth (DCSV, 1977; Le Thanh Nghi, 1977b).

Vu Tuan Anh (1985) provides a clear and (by then) uncontentious critique of what happened in 1976–1980. To summarise his main points, crucially, between 1976 and 1980 there had been an approximate doubling of the fixed asset stock in industry without any real output response, so there was even more excess capacity trying to suck in resources (Vu Tuan Anh, 1985: 37). Large-scale plant was thus often less efficient than small-scale and/or artisanal producers and there had been no reduction in the external dependence of the economy. Structural change was unsustainable, since while Group A sectors (heavy industry) had grown faster than Group B (consumer goods), agricultural output growth was far slower that industrial output growth, so the basis for industrial growth was fragile (Vu Tuan Anh, 1985: 36).

Further, Vu Tuan Anh (1985) noted that after 1981 the influence of capital investment on structural change was not great, since most capital went to projects left unfinished from the 1976–1980 period. Priority to Group A was maintained through the period 1977–1982 (Vu Tuan Anh, 1985: 39) but in practice this was unrealisable. He noted that the fall in industrial output in 1979–1980 was in light industry, whose recovery from 1981 again dominated industrial recovery (Vu Tuan Anh, 1985: 40). He strongly criticised 'priority to heavy industry' and quoted very low capital utilisation rates in 1979–1981 for various branches, including details of the proportion of output of electricity, mechanical engineering, chemicals and other branches etc. that went to agriculture, showing that the distribution of such valuable products was not helping ease the constraints imposed by the problems of labour incentives caused by weak growth (or even declines) in wage goods availability.[26]

Macro-dynamics

Conventionally, macro-economic analysis focuses upon two main questions: the determination of potential output and the determination of actual output in some given time period. In any economy the relationship between actual and potential output can vary over time, and this was equally true in the SRV. But the causes differed from those in market-oriented developing countries. The basic reason was the very high degree of static ('short-run') inefficiency generated by the SRV's planning system, coupled with the real possibility of changes to it. What was interesting about the economy at this time was the way in which increased commercialisation, and its reversal, accompanied changes in the overall efficiency of the economy in the short run due to changes in the balance between different *allocative mechanisms* – between plan and market (p. 10).

The underlying improvement in growth during the early 1980s accompanied rapid rates of inflation. If we look at the development of retail price inflation and the margin between state and free market staples prices we can see how distributional tensions rose and fell through the period. The point here is that the commercialising of the economy revealed underlying distortions. These were manifest in use of greater monetary subsidies as state monopoly control over resource allocation had increasingly to compete with the market – the gathering fiscal crisis of transition (p. 33).[27]

During the crisis of the late 1970s prices and wages were relatively stable; between 1975 and 1980 the total value of retail sales rose an average 16 per cent annually (TCTK, 1985: table 114), but from 1980 to 1985 increased an average 70 per cent annually. A similar acceleration occurred in recorded incomes. Those of state employees were broadly unchanged through the late 1970s, then rose around 6 per cent annually during 1979–1981 before racing ahead at around 70 per cent yearly in the early 1980s. The overall pattern is therefore one of relative stability in the late 1970s, followed, after a short period of transition, by rapid inflation that tended to accelerate towards the end of the third FYP. Free market prices were far above state prices (p. 63).

Data on real state employee incomes show in the early 1980s a slow fall in the percentage of family expenditure upon food – an indicator of rising living standards – but then the collapse of net savings in 1986 as inflationary expectations took hold. The surveyed share of state employee family income derived from 'other' sources rises to reflect increased 'outside' incomes – this might not include payments from 'outside' activities carried out by the factory, which by the mid-1980s had become substantial (Chapter 8). Deflated official ('plan') incomes did not rise, suggesting that workers did not benefit in real terms from increases in formal state remuneration.

Now, while the data are adequate to support formal modelling, this has not been done. But the following questions are suggestive.

- Why was it that the late 1970s saw such a stagnation in total output, and why therefore were the Vietnamese authorities unable to initiate the hoped-for rapid and stable growth? In a nutshell, what killed the neo-Stalinist project in a united Vietnam?

- What were the nature and causes of the output recovery of the early 1980s? By 1981 40 per cent of total SOE output was reported as coming from market-directed activities (p. 173).

- What was the character of the growth process during the 1980s, and what were the origins of the distinctive growth pattern – the substantial year-to-year variation in sectoral output growth and the extremely high rates of inflation?

One important aspect of policy was the way it operated upon the relationships between different allocative mechanisms (p. 10) and their relative importance. But policy could not determine the balance between pro-market and pro-plan incentives. These mechanisms had their own dynamic and were relatively autonomous, and so the outcome was highly contingent.[28]

Analysis of the available information on the pattern of industrial growth during 1979–1980 provokes a number of intriguing questions.[29]

- Why did the recorded total gross output of construction materials, earthenware, porcelain, glassware, wood, forest products, cellulose paste and paper show an *increase* of 15.6 per cent in 1980 when total gross industrial output *fell* 9.6 per cent? Employment in these categories simultaneously fell in both state and small and artisanal industry. Why, though, did the total gross output of these important sectors then *fall* 15 per cent in 1981 when total gross industrial output *rose* 4.8 per cent?

- Why did the number of so-called 'specialised labourers' in six sectors of small and artisanal industrial rise by 12 per cent in 1980 at a time

when state employment in the same sectors was falling? In all six sectors 'specialised labourers' then fell in 1981.
- Why did the number of 'specialised labourers' in food industries suddenly rise sharply in 1981 after falling steadily from 1976?
- Why did the gross value of regional industrial output rise in 1979, fall by only 5 per cent in 1980 and then reach an all-time peak in 1981 at a time when central industrial output was 35 per cent below its own 1978 peak?
- Why did the income from the so-called 'subsidiary economy' of agricultural cooperators fall by 3.7 per cent in 1980, but then jump by 40.6 per cent in 1981?
- Why did the proportion of state worker family expenditure upon food that was supplied by the state fall from 51.6 per cent in 1979 to 34.6 per cent in 1980 and 33.3 per cent in 1981?

The answer to these questions is to be found in the way in which pressure for an expansion of 'outside' activities was at certain times and in certain places irresistible. Captured clearly through the murk of the official statistical system, the figures show how resources could move sharply between sectors and components.

A final point to this discussion remains the historical relationship between economic efficiency gains associated with spontaneous commercialisation and changes in the volume of overseas resources available to the state. There is a distinct *negative* relationship: when aid increased, as in the early 1980s and 1990s, efficiency gains slowed as the balance of allocative mechanisms shifted away from markets; when aid was cut, as in the late 1970s and 1980s, commercialisation accelerated. When commercialisation accelerated, output usually performed better than expected as static efficiency gains exploited Kim Ngoc's law (see note 12).

Policy and events, 1954–2005

The DRV and its legacy

This study is not and cannot be an assessment of the origins of policy, for we lack relevant political studies (Vasavakul, 1993, 1997). I start this account, therefore, with ways in which the crisis of 1979–1980 and policy change need to be situated in the nature of the North Vietnamese economy before 1975. The reader should gain from this a sense of the endogeneity of the plan-market relationship: the perhaps surprising range of factors that influenced decisions by people linked to SOEs, and therefore the context within which statements operated. Chapter 6 gives details of just how such a 'planned economy' could and did respond to various shocks, and see p. 108 for a contemporary published analysis of considerable insight.

From 1975 to the crisis of 1979–1981, and the first 'trap': the origins of 'partial reforms'

Major changes were occurring to both the Vietnamese economy and the overall stance of policy around the time of the Sixth Plenum of the Fourth Central Committee of the VCP in August 1979. This provides a valuable historical reference point.

The meeting took place during an acute economic crisis when policy-makers had also to confront the even more important issues of national security in the aftermath of the Sino-Vietnamese border war. Yet it effectively sanctioned a variety of spontaneous and illegal processes which were destroying the central-planning system that orthodox Vietnamese communist doctrine had long asserted was the key to socialist construction in Vietnam (see Chapter 2).

In a wider perspective, the events of 1979–1981 can be seen as a trap from which traditional Vietnamese socialism was not to recover. In a series of interviews with us in the 1990s the leading Vietnamese technocrat Tran Phuong, whose political career was destroyed in 1985–1986 in consequence of his support for the 'price wages money' measures of that year (pp. 38 and 184), argued strongly that *nobody* among the advocates of the partial reforms of 1979–1981 intended to destroy traditional socialism. I am not so sure.

But from various historical perspectives, not least those of traditional communists and their sympathisers, the legalisation of SOE participation in markets, just like the legalisation of farming-family-based production in agriculture, has to be seen as creating conditions for the emergence of capitalism, which must also be seen as hostile to the socialist regime, the dictatorship of the proletariat. After all, the very basis for these institutions had, in a Marxist-Leninist analysis, to be political (Bray, 1983). Logically, therefore, the first trap, that of 1979–1981, threatened the economic aspect of the institutional basis of the Party – central planning. This would reduce its political basis to what was left – Leninist institutions, MOs[30] and the state.

The second trap, that of 1989–1991, was therefore as logically to be found in whether the Vietnamese could remove this second aspect of the Party's position, involving an abandonment of such methods in favour of a politics more suited to a market economy and globalisation (Ljunggren, 1993). Recovery of SOEs in 1990–1992 was part of the story about how this second trap was not avoided either. By the 2000s corruption and political sclerosis pointed to the same systemic instability as the attempt to combine plan and market in the transitional model of the 1980s had done (Fforde, 2004a, 2005a). The rise of the private sector and the presence of increasing numbers of foreign businesses exerted new pressures on the Party, with an open question as to whether it had the authority to address them.[31]

The initial liberal position is marked by the Sixth Plenum of August 1979 and its slogan that production should 'explode' (*bung ra) (pp. 25 and 133). The ensuing conservative reaction helped create the set of policies promulgated in early 1981 that formed the legal basis for the transitional model. Of these, 25-CP (Chapter 5) was the most important to industry and CT-100 was the key to the new 'output contract' (*khoan san pham) system in cooperative agriculture.[32] 25-CP is best seen as conservative in its thrust, given the nature of the underlying movement in the economy (see the perceptive Vietnamese analysis on p. 132). It was predated by an apparently minor decree (279-CP) encouraging SOEs to increase market activities involving non-list goods (p. 113). Further decrees on state industry (146-HDBT, p. 164; 156-HDBT, p. 177) took this reaction further. They show that policy was conservative at a time when the basis for a commercialised state industry was being created, and point to major underlying political conflicts.

A major difficulty in understanding the political economy of the SRV remains the lack of decent political analyses.[33] There are almost no documented explanations of alliance patterns within the top leadership.[34] During the Vietnam War it was common to assert the existence of factions based upon positions taken *vis-à-vis* the Sino-Soviet split, but this now seems outdated and in any case was never properly documented.[35] This would suggest that stable factions perhaps did not exist, but in the absence of better research even that conclusion is speculative.

Nevertheless, in assessing how political change bore upon SOEs, it is useful to bear in mind the underlying structural faultlines within the Vietnamese political economy. These, continually expressed in the language, were a series of dichotomies.

First was the tension between 'centre and locality' (*trung uong* and *dia phuong*). Implementation of the plan involved coordinated inputs of resources under the control of both. This led to conflicts, reflected in central legislation that attempted to assert central authority, for example between provinces that had to feed central SOEs and the SOEs' ministries in Hanoi.[36]

Second were the tensions between 'base units' (*don vi co so*) within the socialist economy and their 'superior levels' (*cap tren*). In the state sector this meant the SOEs and their planners – either central (the ministries or departments) or local (the provincial or city departments). The superior level could also be a union.[37] In the cooperative sector this tension was between the cooperative – either agricultural or industrial – and the local regulatory authority, usually the district in rural areas.

Third were the tensions between economic agents 'outside' (*ngoai*) the socialist sector and the state apparatus,[38] and those within it – 'inside' (*noi*) (see note 8). These cleavages were associated with the structural characteristics of 'aggravated shortage' (p. 11) and systemic conflicts over access to resources (Chapter 5). Once a dynamic had started, the results were the creation of the 'state business interest' and a change in the balance of political forces, encouraging a shift in overall policy towards support for a market economy.

The 1979 Sixth Plenum and *bung ra* effectively terminated the ideological hegemony of orthodox Vietnamese neo-Stalinism. However, senior leaders remained in power whose political lives had been spent advocating the neo-Stalinist programme. It was the Sixth '*doi moi*' Congress of December 1986 (see p. 189) that removed the by then elderly men who had dominated the party since the death of Ho Chi Minh: Le Duan, party general-secretary since the 1950s, had died in July 1986; Truong Chinh, who had lost his post as party first secretary after the problems of land reform (1945–1956), was chairman of the State Council until the death of Le Duan, when he took over as stopgap general-secretary until his replacement by Nguyen van Linh at the Sixth Congress;[39] Pham van Dong, long-time chairman of the Council of Ministers, lost his Politburo post at the Sixth Congress; Le Duc Tho, long-time *éminence grise* and head of the key Organisational Department of the Central Committee, also left the Politburo at the Sixth Congress; the founder of the Army, Vo Nguyen Giap, had left the Politburo earlier, at the 1982 Fifth Congress.

Early signs of difficulties in economic matters had surfaced, however, at the Second Plenum in the summer of 1977. The minister of agriculture, Vo Thuc Day, was sacked, and the more senior Vo Chi Cong, who, with To Huu, had been in charge of the collectivisation drive in the south, replaced him. These two, with Do Muoi, were, as deputy chairmen of the Council of Ministers, to spearhead the recentralisation drive after the economic crisis of 1978–1979.

During 1979–1982 policy turned to confront the breakdown of the neo-Stalinist programme with tactical concessions designed first to contain and then push back the effective dissolution of the economic management system. Events moved rapidly, and as we have seen there were sharp changes in levels of economic activity. Initially, however, the economy moved comparatively freely in 1979–1980 in response to the pattern of incentives facing local interests and individual economic agents. It was this that the ensuing reaction aimed to stop.

Collectivised agriculture in the north had experienced a spontaneous increase in the role and scope of peasant 'own-account' activity and pressure to reduce the extent of joint production within the cooperatives.[40] In the south, levels of procurement declined precipitately. In what came to be called 'fence-breaking' (*pha rao*), SOEs increasingly ignored planned allocative mechanisms and sought out suppliers and customers, threatening central control over resource allocation.[41] Attempts were made to end the state's central foreign trade monopoly by developing regional trading corporations, especially out of Ho Chi Minh City. This was well documented in the official press (Chapter 6).

Central government made concessions while moving to curb further developments along these lines and avoid a complete breakdown of the material supply system that was meant to channel resources into priority areas (the nurturing of dragon's teeth). The temporary halt to the collectivisation of southern agriculture was matched in the north by the introduction of the so-called 'output contract' system (BBT, 1981).

In early 1981 introduction of the multi-plan system through 25-CP (p. 135) for SOEs sought to make them register 'outside' activities while promising to permit them to continue. This meant, though, that for some SOEs 'outside' activities were protected while others were encouraged to start them. Policy then began to push for a higher share of SOE output, arguing that this was in return for inputs supplied to SOEs by state trading organs. The conservative direction, therefore, was to make concessions while hoping to regain control, clamp down and later withdraw them.

1979–1982: the origins of reaction

After the summer of 1979 and the Sixth Plenum the main question, for anybody who dared broach it, was the market. On the whole, decrees initially showed a radical revision of previous attitudes and a willingness to tolerate – and legislate for – an effective breakdown of the neo-Stalinist programme. This did not last more than a few months. The increased references to SOE and others' autonomy that now started to occur in the media and in policy documents drew upon far earlier formal interpretations of what had happened to the DRV economy (Chapter 3), adding to the weight of pressures upon traditional neo-Stalinist thinking. These were sometimes dramatic.

While it appears more than plausible that the 1979 Sixth Plenum saw the dominant tendency within the party leadership align itself with regional powers against the central economic organs of the state, this line of argument cannot be taken too far. There is too little information available to permit a proper analysis.

In early 1980 came the first in a series of personnel changes in top economic organs. There was a new minister of light industry. The chairman of the VCP Industry Committee, Nguyen Lam, became chairman of the State Planning Commission (SPC), replacing Le Thanh Nghi. Nguyen Lam at around that time appeared to reject neo-Stalinist doctrine, arguing for reliance upon free market relations. In the summer of 1980 he published an article in *Communist Studies*, the party's theoretical journal, which contained many striking ideas (Nguyen Lam, 1980b).[42] He asserted that the 1979 Sixth Plenum had pointed out the existence of subjective as well as objective problems: 'If the plan and economic policies are incorrect they will not be implementable... The highest standard by which to evaluate planning and economic policy is whether they raise mass living standards or not' (Nguyen Lam, 1980b: 1). And, unlike many other commentators, Nguyen Lam was willing to tackle the issue of the free market head on. He argued that the principle error in contemporary Vietnamese economic thinking was the excessive centralisation of resources and the refusal to use market relations (Nguyen Lam, 1980b: 2).

According to Nguyen Lam, in a reformed system the centre would only manage heavy industry, basic construction, transport and some important products. It would also set basic economic indicators such as investment, total output, total wages and accumulation (Nguyen Lam, 1980b: 3). As a matter of 'objective necessity', plan and markets had to coexist. The desire to 'plan everything' ignored the reality of widespread small-scale production. A rational coordination of plan and markets required three planning levels – centre, region and base; base-level planning meant that the base had to consult directly with sources of supply and outlets. This would then ensure that production would 'burst out' (*bung ra*) (Nguyen Lam, 1980b).

Furthermore, the article strongly supported the liberalising intent of the Sixth Plenum. It took a position in favour of using all economic components (*thanh phan) 'in the early part of the transitional period'. Nguyen Lam (1980b: 5) argued that nobody should be criticised simply because they worked in the private sector: 'Judged from the point of view of production, if people make a worse living once they have left the private sector to join a collective then one can say that the collective is worse than the private sector.'

By the standards of the time this is an extremely radical statement: it maintains that the interests of socialism and its construction, including the creation of a military-industrial complex necessary for the preservation of socialism, are to be placed secondary to the immediate interest of workers.

And if private or cooperative sectors could use materials more efficiently than the state, they should be supplied with them. In a discussion of the 'three interests' (state, collective and individual), Nguyen Lam stated flatly that 'for a long time' individual material interests had been ignored, so peasants had not wished to produce and export producers preferred to sell on the domestic market.[43] He stressed the use of output contracts throughout the economy, especially in industry, as a way of boosting worker incomes (Nguyen Lam, 1980b: 7).[44]

With regard to direct horizontal relations between producers, he advocated their expansion, partly to reduce the high level of idle stocks that existed throughout the country – market shortages coexisted with hoarding by SOEs. The gap between producer and customer had to be reduced. Direct contracting between SOEs and agricultural cooperatives should be encouraged. There should be reforms in the area of foreign trade; exporters and importers had to have direct relations with foreign markets. Nguyen Lam stressed the existence of an area of 'free' goods the state did not manage. He stated clearly that if the purchasing bodies did not take up their supplies within a certain period, the SOEs had the right to dispose of the goods directly (Nguyen Lam, 1980b: 8–9).

His move therefore appears to reflect the relative importance of decentralising tendencies in early 1980 before the recentralising tendency became dominant towards the end of the year. To me this suggests that Tran Phuong's position (p. 22), that the first trap was not intentionally laid, will only become clearer when we have far better analysis of the changing politics of the time. Nguyen Lam remains relatively invisible to history, and his rapid replacement at the SPC by Vo van Kiet, long-time boss of Ho Chi Minh City, arguably the key central supporter of large-scale state business in the 1990s and opponent of statist attempts to inhibit its direct and unmediated relations with global capitalism, therefore poses a series of intriguing but as yet unanswered questions (Fforde, 2004b).

Changes in the attitude of the Politburo through 1980

The Politburo's formal attitude early in 1980 is confirmed by 25 NQ/TW,[45] which said: 'With regard to the management of the grain market, it is necessary to ensure that peasants can freely use or sell the grain that they have left after they have met their obligations to the state.' (Quoted from SWB, 1980.) A similar attitude is found in a slightly earlier decree of the Council of Ministers on export incentives, which gave away to local units some of the centre's rights to control foreign currency.

This period did not last for long. By June 1980 the Politburo had changed course, and 26-NQ/TW announced the need to increase state management of domestic trade.[46] In July 1980 a conference on agricultural collectivisation in the south held in Ho Chi Minh City 'reaffirmed' the target set by the 1977 Second Plenum of a completion of collectivisation by the early 1980s.

But although the formal legislative structures of recentralisation date from around the middle of 1980, so also do the beginnings of counters to this tendency. For example, an interesting southern 'model' of SOE reform, the Thanh Cong textile SOE, reportedly started its experiments with unorthodox methods in late 1980.[47] But Politburo decree 26-NQ/TW restricting private trade was reinforced by a state decree, 312-CP, in October.[48]

Thus by the time of the December 1980 Ninth Plenum the recentralising tendency had devised a reasonably coherent policy set: concessions through legalisation to provide a basis for tightening up. This began to appear from January 1981, with 25-CP on SOE management and 100-CT on the use of output contracts in agricultural cooperatives.[49] The combination of these measures with pressure on the free market and reassertion of central authority was the essence of this tendency until 1985–1986. The recentralising intent behind 25-CP was confirmed by 64-CP.[50]

And what of the king?

The attitude of General-Secretary Le Duan to these changes remains somewhat enigmatic. He is widely seen by Vietnamese as deeply conservative and responsible for many of these difficulties (e.g. p. 188). He was from the central province of Quang tri, straddling the DMZ. As political leader at the fall of the south in 1975 he had considerable prestige, and is often blamed for the hubris apparent in the second (immediately post-war) FYP (1976–1980) with its over-optimistic growth targets. Yet the early FYPs in Stalin's USSR were also over-optimistic, and it was precisely this that was part of the heady energy that planted the 'dragon's teeth': a very specific rationality. We still lack a decent set of studies of Le Duan. Two issues in particular intrigue me.

First, it seems apparent that he had early on accepted that there were 'problems' with the economic management of Vietnamese communism. This led to conservative solutions in both agriculture and industry (e.g. p. 85 regarding agriculture, and Fforde, 1989), but it also permitted preservation of a range of publishable ideas and observations that would have been too close to the bone in many other communist countries – see for example the study edited by Nguyen Tri (1972a) discussed on p. 88, and the analyses of problems in the agricultural cooperatives by Dinh Thu Cuc (1977) and Nguyen Manh Huan (1980). In general, the overall tone of the public debate in communist Vietnam in the 1970s and early 1980s reflects a 'tolerance of the real' which possibly reflects Le Duan's acceptance that there were deep-rooted problems. This is not to say that people did not suffer for any perceived heresy, just that the parameters of tolerated debate reflected this view.

Second is the simple fact that the history of the economic crisis of the late 1970s, the partial reforms and later reaction of the early 1980s is, recalling what can happen under communist rule, remarkably lacking in violence. The logic of Stalinism required and endorsed use of enough (or more) violence to secure control over critical resources, especially food grains – thus the bloody 'liquidation of the kulaks as a class'. I cannot see (having lived in Hanoi in 1978–1979) that this would have been impossible. Understanding why it did not happen requires a better understanding of the then general-secretary than we have at present.[51]

More directly relevant to the history of SOEs is the fact that after the 1979 Sixth Plenum Le Duan published a pamphlet, *Problems of the Local Economy*. He took a broadly open-handed line, but remained conservative with regard to any real increase in the use of free markets and substantial changes in the allocative mechanisms used legally by units of the socialist economy. Furthermore, his criticisms of past failures were rather mild. These amounted to failure on the part of a number of cadres and Party members to grasp the Party's line; failure to understand the realities of the Vietnamese economy; and failure to go from a thorough understanding of the Party line to a proper stress upon the correct policies needed to stimulate economic development at the level of the branch (i.e. the centre), the region and the base. This last point was primarily to do with weaknesses in organisation and management (Le Duan, 1979: 37–8). He saw the main solution in the centre's establishing clear lines of demarcation between it and the regions, which under the circumstances of 'aggravated shortage' (p. 11 above) was an almost impossible task.

This suggests that what was to happen subsequently – a relatively mild reaction – was consistent with his position.

And the king-maker? Le Duc Tho

Le Duc Tho, Nobel Peace Prize winner and *éminence grise*, is also of considerable importance. As head of the Party's all-important Organisation Department until 1982 (*Far Eastern Economic Review*, 1984), he had his hands upon the key central organ of the Party-cadre policy. And as a man famed for his asceticism, from the impoverished north-central province of Nghe Tinh, he may have had little sympathy with the corruption that was one manifestation of 'aggravated shortage'. Granted this interpretation, he should have sought an organisational solution to the difficulties facing the Party, and stressed personal virtue.

In late 1981 he made a long speech entitled 'Realising a profound change in organisation...' that was published twice (Le Duc Tho, 1981, 1985). In it he put forward a programme based upon such measures as Party purges. This stressed the need for measures to reinforce central control over the economy by using the apparatus of the Party and state directly. It therefore relied upon organisational solutions and was antagonistic to any real opening up of either the economy or society. It was classical neo-Stalinism, threatening use of violence and the totalitarian apparatus to force behaviour that contradicted local incentives and typically offered vast and threatening power to the peak: look at Stalin himself, and countries such as East Germany, Romania[52] and Mao's China. Yet it was not really consistent either with the legacy of Ho Chi Minh's own political style or the ways in which the VCP itself, operating generally in ways consistent with its own constitution, had shared power at the peak (Duiker, 2000; Thayer, 1995; Vasavakul, 1995, 1996).

So long as the basic problems of material incentives existed, so the arguments of this book would suggest, such measures would be doomed to failure – Vietnamese cadres would be under too great a pressure from their own needs and the demands of local interests for them simply to obey directives from above. The basic premise of the Le Duc Tho programme was that the Party could be made strong enough to override these effects. Socialist construction would then create favourable conditions for further advance and everything would improve. Given different human qualities, the programme might have worked, but it did not. Why did the generals not support it?

It is therefore perhaps moving to read Le Duc Tho's speech at the Nguyen Ai Quoc Party Academy in June 1984. Much of the impetus had gone. The previous few years had destroyed the neo-Stalinist programme, which, having failed under the unfavourable conditions of North Vietnam, should have worked in the reunited country.[53] The Party and its security organs could not defend traditional socialism. By 1986 he is reduced to criticising degeneracy in the Party and calling, as before, for renovation of working attitudes and methods (Le Duc Tho, 1986a). He was still attacking 'rightists' later in 1986 (Le Duc Tho, 1986b).

And the ex-king? Truong Chinh

Truong Chinh was first secretary (then equivalent to general-secretary) from the early 1940s until the early 1950s' land reform, when he lost his position. He remained a Politburo member, though, and after a spell as deputy chairman was chairman of the Standing Committee of the National Assembly from 1960. He regained the Party secretaryship in July 1986 after Le Duan's death, but failed to get himself confirmed at the Sixth Congress. His name means 'Long March' in Sino-Vietnamese and he had a reputation as a hard-liner. Marr (1995) shows how his political position was very strong in North Vietnam during the anti-French struggle. He was born in Nam Dinh, in the Red River delta.

Histories of the so-called 'three contracts' controversy of the late 1960s show him attacking Le Duan's initially conciliatory attitude to deviations from traditional socialism (Truong Chinh, 1968/1969; Gordon, 1981).[54] And Le Duan subsequently retreated to a position that condemned these activities and saw their local protectors, Vinh Phu, Party secretary, and ex-army commissar Kim Ngoc, suffer for them. It can be argued that Truong Chinh followed a similar political tactic in 1979–1984, not shifting his own ground until it became opportune in the run-up to the 1986 Sixth Party Congress.[55] But that would be conjecture, and strongly subject to 'spin' from interested parties. It would, however, help to explain the openness of official journals to articles taking heretical positions that showed the positive results of market-oriented SOE activities: a potential stick with which to beat the leadership, as in the case of the 'three contracts' controversy?

Setting reaction in concrete? The 1982 Fifth Congress

Through 1981 VCP political contenders faced gathering pressure from the need to confront political tensions at the scheduled Fifth Party Congress. The press and media were full of debate and conflicting evidence about the effects of the new policies and the economic value of alternative ways of doing things.[56] Although the recentralising group was in some control of the central economic organs of the state, local interests, buoyed by the pattern of economic development, had growing political weight.

A plenum – the tenth – should have been held in June or July 1981, but was delayed until October-November. It is possible that this plenum, which sought to announce the imminent Fifth Congress, saw a failed attempt by reformists to prevent further advances by recentralisers.[57] Although there are reports that the USSR had been refusing to agree to meet Vietnamese aid demands (Vo Nhan Tri, 1986), there is little evidence. Indeed, its own economic interests, based upon long experience with the DRV and the powerful security arguments behind the Soviet-Vietnamese link, argued for it supporting the reformist group (Fforde, 1985), not least to reduce costs. The USSR had tolerated important deviations from orthodoxy in Poland (where agriculture was not collectivised) and, after the Sino-Vietnamese fighting, was likely to treat Vietnamese eclecticism indulgently. The situation in terms of policy direction was thus very different from the late 1950s and early 1960s.

Further debate took place at the Eleventh Plenum in December, and then again at the Twelfth Plenum of March 1982 which finally announced the calling of the Fifth Congress in late April.

At around this time, both before and after the congress, there were important personnel changes whose significance remains unclear. Nguyen Lam left the SPC and returned to head the Economics Department of the Central Committee, while losing his post as deputy chairman of the Council of Ministers (SWB, 1982). However, he retained his secretaryship and remained head of the Economics Department until the 1986 Sixth Congress. Vo van Kiet became a full member of the Politburo. From this position he appeared subsequently to have consistently supported some local Party interests against central state economic organs. Since the SPC was the central organ whose interests relied most heavily upon preservation of central planning, and was profoundly conservative and anti-market under his leadership after he replaced the apparently pro-market Nguyen Lam, Kiet's reformist reputation is something I have always found somewhat puzzling. Some argue that he had little power at the SPC, 'surrounded by northerners'; others that his main core constituency were relatively large SOE interests centred upon Ho Chi Minh City, consistent with his attempts in the 1990s to free general companies from state influence by giving them direct access to global finance and technology (Fforde, 2004b).[58]

The long-delayed 1982 Fifth Party Congress revealed the political compromises and risks inherent in recentralisation. These centred upon a fragile agreement within the Party/state apparatus that opposed abandonment of neo-Stalinism but failed to resolve either the attitude to be taken towards conflicts within the apparatus or the question of the continuing inflationary pressures and their origins in the use of state power. From around 1982 the authorities granted major increases in state employee cash incomes and prices paid for procured goods, especially staples. But inadequate revenue growth in the state sector prevented budget receipts from rising to keep pace with higher outlays, and inflation accelerated. Accompanying this were the beginnings of the 'fiscal crisis of the transition': as the economy became more marketised so the system of central planning and state-set prices that created high budgetary receipts on the back of SOEs' planned profits broke down. Revenues based upon planned activities and accruing at fixed state prices could not keep up with the state's need to compete with spiralling free market prices in areas such as cash wages and cash payments for inputs that it could not secure through the imposition of administrative targets.

The congress introduced the idea of a 'pre-stage' in the period of transition to socialism. The historical task of this was to lay down the preconditions for socialist economic construction, especially the creation of a domestic economic surplus (DCSV, 1987: 11; Thayer, 1983). There is some evidence that this was pushed by the USSR (Vo Nhan Tri, 1986).

Since it implied renewed efforts to push resources into SOE investments, this could have meant that the tensions between the different allocative mechanisms implied by plan and market again mounted. Higher free market prices and a rapid appreciation in the free market value of hard currency were creating strong disincentives to supply resources to state trading organs. But if it was to follow the pre-stage idea, state investment policy would be under pressure to change, probably in line with donor advice,[59] and put more resources into sectors supplying export and consumer goods. This probably paralleled a shift in the pattern of allocation of agricultural means of production towards the high potential surplus areas, especially the Mekong delta. But, as Vu Tuan Anh (1985) argues, the effects were muted by the momentum of planners' intentions (p. 18).

It should be remembered that these political developments took place under unusual conditions. Vietnam was adjusting to almost complete dependence upon the USSR for foreign aid (the only Western bilaterals left after the international relations shocks of the late 1970s were the Swedes and the Finns). The economy had shown rather abrupt and sharp movements in output and relative incomes. The Chinese and Western aid cuts had sharply accentuated inflationary processes which were pushing up free market prices. If the state was to retain its basic structures intact, it had to offset these trends.

1982–1984: the gathering failure of reaction and recentralisation

From the summer of 1980–1981 the authorities introduced the first substantial revision in agricultural procurement prices since the 1960s.[60] This entrenched the problems with inflation that persisted until the end of the decade.

Here the comparison with China is interesting, since the early stages of reform there – *before* market-oriented change was permitted for SOEs and collectivised farmers – also saw increases in procurement prices: the prices at which the state bought agricultural products (Bramall, 1993, 1995). The core issue is the relative failure of the DRV neo-Stalinist system to generate high levels of investible resources, typically manifest as high SOE accounting profits to create fiscal revenues to finance high levels of state investment.

The DRV economy was generating very low levels of savings, far lower as a share of total economic activity than in China – the 30–35 per cent typical of neo-Stalinist growth (Fforde, 1999). This was despite the increased levels of mobilisation by the state typical during wartime. This meant that, unlike China, resources could not easily be reallocated from sectors whose priority had been reduced (such as heavy industry) and towards newly favoured areas such as agriculture. Attempts to do so could easily run up against fiscal problems, and without monetary stringency inflation was likely – and this was what happened in Vietnam from the early 1980s.

The Fifth Congress heralded a period of around three years (1982–1985) during which the recentralising tendency maintained pre-eminence. This authority was weakened by an abrupt slowdown in industrial growth during 1983, and as inflation eroded the value of wage hikes and higher procurement prices granted in the early 1980s. By the end of 1985 this tendency had lost irretrievable ground as a result of the failure of the measures, centred upon wage-price reforms and currency revaluation, to curb inflation. This was part of the background to the 1986 '*doi moi*' Sixth Congress.

Tracking reaction – SOEs and the recentralising legislation of the early 1980s

During the period of recentralising reaction (1980–1985) the Council of Ministers issued a number of important recentralising decrees. In July 1982 113-HDBT introduced new trade regulations which greatly increased Hanoi's veto power through its demand that 'all foreign trade activities must have permits from the Ministry of Foreign Trade' (*Cong Bao*, 1982a: 266). This formed a legal basis for the effective termination of Ho Chi Minh City's own foreign trade corporations, reportedly by a taskforce sent from Hanoi by To Huu, who also signed the decree.[61]

The decree contained a list of those goods for which central authorities demanded a monopoly. In August 1982 the second of the period's three key decrees governing industrial management appeared (the others being 25-CP, 21 January 1981, p. 133, and 156-HDBT, 30 November 1984, p. 177), seeking to increase central control of those SOEs which had been developing 'unplanned' relations with suppliers and customers. Decree 146-HDBT (25 August 1982) aimed to 'systematise' the acquisition and disposal of resources by SOEs (p. 164). It sought to 'Centralise sources of goods in the hands of the state... get rid of methods of production and business that followed the unorganised market... [and] distribute profits in a way that ensures the state's supplies of funds' (*Cong Bao*, 1986: 382).

Later in 1982 160-HDBT (16 September 1982) laid out intentions for the future development of the Mekong. By this time preparations to complete the collectivisation drive must have been well advanced. This decree called for 'All provinces to concentrate their strength for a close direction of cooperativisation' (*Cong Bao*, 1982b: 362).

The Third Plenum of December 1982 stressed the difficulties caused by inflationary pressures:

> Distribution and circulation now form the most complex and hottest battleground of the 'who will win' struggle between the two roads of socialism and capitalism... The crucial problem is that the state must control most sources of goods and control money so it can stabilise prices. [Furthermore] the Socialist Transformation of agriculture in the south has been carried out in a sluggish way. (*Nhan Dan* (*The People*), 16 December 1982, quoted in SWB, 1986.)

Attacking 'anarchy in markets', the plenum called for strong administrative pressure against the free market. This supported measures already taken in November when 188-HDBT had sought to 'reinforce socialist trade and management of the free market'. The preamble to this document revealed that 'The proportion of the market that was not organised had risen from 20% in 1980 to 30% in 1981 and 40% in 1982' (*Cong Bao*, 1982d: 460). The 'organised' – socialist – market was suffering.

The recentralising tendency retained its dominant position through 1983 and most of 1984. 1983 saw an explosion in economic legislation as policy, based as it mainly was upon a logic of administrative fiat in the absence of sufficient violence, sought compliance with its goals. Pressure was brought to bear upon petty industrial producers as the authorities sought to make them register and pay higher taxes. The agricultural tax system was revised, and further moves were made to integrate it into the district structure. The Fourth Plenum of June 1983 continued this pressure, stressing the need for 'changes in work style'. In December 1983 the Fifth Plenum was apparently still dominated by the drive for recontrol (Tran Duc Hoat, 1983; Vu Quoc Tuan, 1983).

By early 1984, however, opposition to the reaction was gathering, surfacing for example in attempts to defend the family economy, especially within agricultural cooperatives. After the slowdown of 1983, 1984 saw some recovery in industrial output growth. There is evidence of attempts to entrench the dominant tendency through the establishment and development of long-term strategy and discussion of structural change: all a necessary part of an established and sustainable growth strategy. But economic conditions remained extremely tense, and there were few signs of the desired order in economic affairs.

The Sixth Plenum of July 1984 concentrated, in its public deliberations, almost entirely upon 'pressing tasks in the reform of economic management'. These were understood to be the contractual basis for relations between cooperatives and the districts – in other words maintenance of a key link in the procurement chain; the internal management of agricultural cooperatives; the collectivisation of the south; and the legal position and economic rights of SOEs. Its tone was highly conservative (*Tap chi Cong san*, 1985). The plenum probably announced the start of the final stages of the drive to collectivise the Mekong delta.

1984–1985 – towards doi moi *and the decline of the recentralising programme*

By the end of 1984 the recentralising drive was beginning to lose its impetus. The last recentralising decree on industrial SOEs, 156-HDBT (30 November 1984 – see p. 177), confirmed the intention to assert central authority, but had to include concessions, for instance permitting SOEs to return to direct horizontal relations with suppliers and customers if the state's administrative supply system did not meet supply or purchase contracts. Similar recognition of compromise can be seen in a decree, 162-HDBT (14 December 1984), on economic 'links' (**khau*). This term was an increasingly popular euphemism for unplanned relations between SOEs designed to expand their own economic activities.[62] It echoes the distinction made below between 'production-oriented' and 'distribution-oriented' approaches and policy options (p. 86).

As the failure of the recentralising tendency became more apparent, the Seventh Plenum of December 1984 reconsidered the role of the family economy in agriculture. This more or less implicitly referred to the difficulties facing farmers in some areas of the north, where the harvest had been particularly bad in 1984 and which had been starved of industrial inputs compared with the Mekong.

1985–1986: *crisis and the immediate background to* doi moi *and the 1986 Sixth Congress; the 1985 Eighth Plenum – prices, money, wages*

Economic issues were now of critical importance. First, growth had slowed and staples production per capita was starting to fall back again, suggesting that food aid would have to continue. Second, the efforts to recentralise inherent in 146-HDBT and 156-HDBT had failed to curb pressure for a return to the *de facto* liberalisation of 1979–1980 before 26-NQ/TW and 25-CP. Third, inflation was starting to get out of hand. The recentralising tendency was confronting worsening economic problems and an opposition that continued to gain material and vocal support from the state business interest. *Economic failure spoke.*

From this perspective the June 1985 Eighth Plenum appears as a last-ditch attempt to salvage the position. Industrial output growth was slowing again through 1985. The plenum concentrated on heralded wage, price and currency reforms that sought (unrealistically and based upon poor economic analysis) to do away at a stroke with the system of subsidised supply to consumers. The package did not seek to extend the area of commercialised exchange, in fact the reverse, and so was fundamentally conservative.[63]

The conservatism of the Eighth Plenum did not go unchallenged: for example, the *Nhan Dan* editorial of 24 September 1985 warned that problems were likely to be encountered switching to the new price and wage system when enterprise accounting remained unstable, and that 'failure will mean a return to the subsidy system' (*Nhan Dan*, 1985a). It also called for increases in SOE autonomy. A clear discussion of what was intended for the price system can be found in *Nhan Dan* (1985b), showing that this was to be a continuation of administratively fixed prices. Simple economic analysis would show that without major economic restructuring that got supply and demand into commercial balance this would require direct controls over resource allocation.

From mid-1985 policy reflects the renewed vigour of local and commercial interests. The trade regulations promulgated by 177-HDBT (15 June 1985) allowed more autonomy.[64] In November Ho Chi Minh City introduced various 'experimental' management methods quite independently of central authority.[65] The Eighth Plenum measures failed to curb inflation and the fiscal crisis of transition worsened as inflation turned into hyperinflation (p. 33).

In December the Ninth Plenum supported the thinking behind the Eighth Plenum, but called for dismissals as a result of the failure to implement its resolutions properly. Tran Phuong, who had been the deputy chairman of the Council of Ministers closest to To Huu and directly responsible for the measures, lost his job in early 1986. To Huu was sacked in June (*Le Monde*, 1986). Tran Phuong had come to head the Economics Institute in the 1960s after the departure of Bui Cong

Trung, who was said to have advocated a more market-oriented approach and was sacked in 1964. As such he had of course been one of Le Duan's most senior economic advisers.

In early 1986 Party policy towards SOEs went through a U-turn, with 306-BBT calling for real autonomy for SOEs. This was then *not* reflected in state policy, which remained reactionary (see p. 186). There was clear jockeying to secure support from the state business interest.

Thus, as the VCP started the final stages of the run-up to the December 1986 Sixth Congress, various arguments had already been won and lost. These can be summarised as follows.

First, the relative social value of alternative allocative mechanisms – planned as opposed to unplanned activities – had come to the fore in debate; it had been impossible to ignore this, and much evidence had been gathered to suggest that in many instances unplanned activities were superior. They were also more locally profitable.

Second, the state apparatus had once again proved itself to be weak and disorganised. Planning directives were unimplementable and the transitional model had heightened the inability of the system to resolve conflicts. It could not do what it said it set out to do: to defend the fundamental institutions of traditional socialism. There seemed to be no reliable basis here to harvest a sowing of dragon's teeth.[66]

Third, the overall macro-economic situation was appalling. Vietnam was suffering from rapid inflation and growth that was unstable and of poor quality.

Fourth, to a large extent the central economic apparatus centred upon the SPC was, compared with other political forces of which commercialising SOEs were the key, reactionary and conservative.

It is evident that, as a matter of accessible histories, the precise reasons for the failure of this recentralising reaction are not yet fully understood, in major part since we lack political studies. It would be misleading, though, to argue that the system was doomed to failure, as there were plenty of examples of central planning that, for a while and extremely unpleasantly, did create rapid growth. But these tended to rely upon a certain degree of discipline and a willingness to use force.

Rather, I believe that at root the defeat of the reaction was to do with the creation of a constituency *within* the Party (the 'state business interest' – Fforde, 1993) that favoured commercialisation and a market-oriented solution rather than the traditional central-planning programme. This constituency was a combination of local state interests with elements centred upon SOEs that had benefited from economic liberalisation. Its growth relied in part on an economic logic which said that with given resources efficiency would be higher with market-oriented rather than planned resource allocation mechanisms (p. 10).

Its presence changed the balance of power within the VCP. It was sufficient to convert Truong Chinh to a pro-market position if he wanted to regain the general-secretaryship. The essence of the transition was therefore the political-economic effects of commercialisation and their eventual reflection in national (Party) policy. This state business interest naturally found support among pro-market economic reformists. Its relationship with political reformists, keen to de-Stalinise and increasingly aware of trends in the USSR, is entirely another matter. Not to mention political opportunists.

Doi moi *and the 1986 Sixth Congress U-turn: real or fake reform?*

By the end of the third FYP in 1985, and the failure of the Eighth Plenum measures, the SRV economy was dominated by chronic dependence upon imports, rapid monetary inflation fuelled by a yawning fiscal deficit, continued tensions between the state's trading monopolies and the market and low levels of capacity utilisation in aid-financed SOEs. This was not a pretty picture, and few policy-makers could have been happy a decade after national reunification and with Soviet-bloc aid running at high levels. More than five years had passed since the 1979 crisis, the Sixth Plenum and *bung ra*. The neo-Stalinist development programme had lost its effective hegemony, but no clear alternative had yet replaced it.

During late 1986 in the run-up to the Sixth Congress the VCP struggled to shift away from compromises that underpinned the post 1978–1979 reaction.

The influence of the death of Le Duan in the summer of 1986 is, without a decent biography and associated political studies, hard to gauge. It is, however, striking that the stopgap appointment of Truong Chinh as general-secretary presented the new leader as a supporter of market-oriented reform and the abolition of what now increasingly became known as the 'bureaucratic subsidised administrative supply system' (**che do quan lieu bao cap*).

However, the results of the Sixth Congress articulated a confirmation of the policy U-turn already presaged by decision 306-BBT (p. 184) associated with the growth of commercial interests, especially the assertion of local political power. It heralded a shift towards greater liberalisation that could match the economy's increasing *de facto* decentralisation. The Sixth Congress political report stated, *inter alia*, that the neo-Stalinist system of direct administrative allocation of resources, and the bureaucratic subsidies that were its necessary accompaniment, were not consistent with the principles of democratic centralism to which all truly Leninist communist parties had to adhere (VCP, 1987). This marked clearly a dogmatic rejection of the traditional socialist programme.

1986–1989: towards the second trap – de-Stalinisation, chaos and the loss of Soviet economic support

From 1986 onwards the VCP thus returned for a while to supporting (as it had in 1979 and early 1980) rather than trying to inhibit the strong commercialising trends within the economy. A series of decrees in 1987–1988 improved the operation of internal markets, conferred greater freedoms upon SOEs and gave back much economic power to farmer families in cooperatives. Policy towards the non-state sectors was liberalised, though in practice very little changed. Foreign trade was decentralised, and since it was now SOEs that benefited real change was far more substantial. Levels of subsidies were reduced to clean up the full-scale shift to a market-oriented order. Then in 1989, as Soviet aid collapsed, anti-inflationary measures accompanied an end to the two-price system, and, as most goods and services found themselves traded on stable buyers' markets, market-based allocative relations dominated and the transitional model vanished (Chapter 9).[67]

1989 and after: macro-stabilisation, the 'great surprise' and the second trap

1989, of course, was the year of the democratic revolts in Central Europe which led to the election of governments committed to the abolition of communist economic management. It was also the year of the massacre in Beijing. Vietnamese troops withdrew from Cambodia. And in the same year, Vietnam successfully abolished central planning.

1989–1990 saw a major exercise in macro-stabilisation. Real deposit rates were raised to positive levels. SOEs were supported but required to generate revenues for the state. In this they were surprisingly successful, and effectively reconstructed as a source of support for the regime. Inflation returned in the early years of the decade, kept under control by further reduction in credit subsidies to SOEs. The resulting macro-economic stability offered an SOE-focused development programme, but now without central planning. Other sources of privileged access to resources (FDI, aid funds, land, credit allocations, etc.) remained available to marry state business and political interests.

In Vietnam central planning had now been replaced by an economy where most goods and services were allocated by voluntary exchange. Remaining subsidies were confined to cheap credits to certain SOEs, housing and some other provisions for state employees and to a limited extent in other areas (e.g. a special exchange rate for aid-financed drug imports). The general picture, however, was of an economy where almost all produced inputs and outputs were bought and sold on what appeared to be markets. The precise nature of these transactions and the implications of the lack of effective markets for land, labour and capital are not questions normally asked of a CPE. But by 1990 the change in the Vietnamese economy over the previous decade was clear: a central-planning system had been replaced by one based upon markets. However, this commercialisation had primarily involved insiders, led by Party members, and no significant private sector emerged until the very end of the 1990s.

This was commercial renaissance from the inside. In that it had had only limited macro-political effects and SOEs so far faced very limited competition from other businesses, such as foreign or private sectors, many hostages to fortune remained (Fforde, 2004a, 2005a).

Traps and their significance

The first 'trap': 1979–1980 and the transitional model – plan and market – parasitism or symbiosis?

Partly because of their importance, but also to act as useful axes to the argument, I present the idea that the renaissance of commerce in Vietnam was a central element of two 'traps'. The first opened in 1979–1980 when, facing profound crisis, the Party declared its support for anything that would increase production and then instructed its government to pass legislation that permitted *all* SOEs to engage in markets (25-CP). This opened Pandora's box and a flock of commercial devils emerged to fly around happily in the corridors of planning offices, blandishing various inducements that would support not only existing business activities oriented towards markets, but their further expansion. Getting that flock back into the box was attempted in the early 1980s but failed, and, as I argue, it gained added political strength until it helped push the Party towards *doi moi* and advocacy of a market economy at the 1986 Sixth Congress.

The trap opened; it could not safely be closed, so it sprang shut. Symbiosis between plan and market turned into a parasitism, with the ultimate death of the host, traditional socialism.

The second 'trap': 1989–1991 from the perspective of the late 2000s

The second 'trap' opened towards the end of the 1980s, when many comrades were, to change the metaphor, more or less happily hanging on to the guideropes that hung below commercialised SOE 'balloons' rising into the sky of business, profit and market-based accumulation, cruising on a combination of Soviet-bloc aid goods and resources acquired through the planning system from the domestic economy (Fforde, 2002). Their ability to hang on was strengthened by the presence of the VCP's many structures and connections with SOEs: Party cells, MOs, personal links, ideological and cultural work and so on. This enabled the regime to increase control over SOEs during the crisis years of 1990–1991, re-establish a tax base and restore financing to these structures, such as the MOs. Thereafter, with Soviet and central-planning rents now replaced by a combination of FDI happy to enter joint ventures with SOEs and donors happy to support formal structures, and after shedding some of its weaker members, the state sector could then set off on a period of rapid growth full of contradictions that I have called the SOE-focused model (Fforde, 1997; TCTK, 1995: table 54).

The trap, though, was that a globalising market-oriented economy based upon commercialised SOEs would require effective government through changed 'techniques of rule'. Centrally, what could remain of Leninism in a VCP ruling over a market economy where capital and business would inevitably demand that their operations not be penetrated and controlled by Leninist structures? Clinging tightly to the SOE balloons meant that officials would, at the end of the day, have to go where the SOEs wanted to go, no matter how close to the sun. And, perhaps inevitably, as SOEs became more capitalist they would fly higher, becoming more and more private; a private sector would emerge; and foreign investors would work out the trick and start acting like balloons themselves. Sometimes SOEs would want to get into bed with foreigners, at other times they would want to have them killed: what should the state do? The regime would then have to look for legitimacy and authority, and whether it would get this or not from the folks on the ground watching the game was by no means guaranteed. This trap opened when the regime tied itself to SOEs in the early 1990s. When and whether it will snap shut remains to be seen (Fforde, 2004a, 2005a).

Conclusions

The following chapters will discuss and analyse aspects of this story in detail. This overview should, however, have given the reader a sense of the basics. These can be summarised as follows.

First, I divide the process of commercial renaissance into three periods by reference to two rather short periods of concentrated change: what I call the first 'trap', 1979–1981, and the second, 1989–1991.

The first saw the demise of the DRV model, with its foundations in traditional neo-Stalinism and realities strongly influenced by local and specific Vietnamese conditions. This demise was probably neither widely nor openly intended; the 'trap' was that temporary adjustments, reflected in part in policies both sectorally specific and general, opened the way to the extinction of traditional socialism in Vietnam. Ideologically the DRV programme, after a period of debate and incoherence, was then replaced at the *doi moi* Sixth Congress of 1986.

The second saw the demise of the transitional model that, through the 1980s, had seen a parasitical relationship between plan and market in the Vietnamese economy. Once commercialised SOEs had shown that they could be part of a stable and growing economy, it was replaced in the 1990s by an SOE-focused policy stance, and in this commitment to the state sector, part of a politics that saw deeply conservative measures replace the far more liberal dynamic of the late 1980s, lay the trap.[68] The nature of the trap was to become clearer as corruption and dependency upon state business interests eroded the authority of the VCP. Accustomed to a formal politics that entailed penetration and control of 'society' through the institutions of the MOs and the plan, how would the VCP respond to a world with powerful commercial forces operating? And how could it, when it was so closely bound up with state capital? Failure to secure adequate political authority immediately threatened perhaps not slower economic growth or a reversal of the decline in poverty rates, but political stability.

Both of these turning points, therefore, can be viewed as both positive and negative. Positive, in that they marked rapid shifts in directions that had previously been stymied: if you like, existing disequilibria and tensions were sharply reduced. But with relatively little attention to long-term issues of social and political development, these policy successes can be seen as seriously limited: failure to shift to a market economy basis in 1980–1981 kept the economy trapped in transition for nearly a decade 'when it could have taken only four to five years' (personal communication from senior Vietnamese economist, 1991).

Failure to combine political reforms with privatisation and economic liberalisation in 1990–1991 kept the country trapped within a stifling political framework. For SOEs this all meant that the trajectory of their liberalisation moved in a surprising way: during the 1980s on the whole they become freer and more commercial, but through the 1990s interests within the state and party apparatus re-exerted their power and property rights moved back up away from the SOE. The true renaissance of commerce, the pulling of the dragon's teeth, happened in the 1980s. The recovery of the state sector as part of a resurgent state power and success – through economic growth – in building a potential economic basis for military power (though not as yet used for that) takes place through the 1990s and 2000s.

Second, this history combines two interconnected but for me conceptually distinct areas, which are expressed in the distinction between the DRV model and the DRV programme. The first is what happened, the second is what communists in Vietnam say or write *should* have happened.[69] Policy fetishism, visible in so many official and donor reports that attribute far too much to policy (both good and bad), confuses model and programme (p. xx). Much of our understanding of the former comes from trying to understand the significance of the latter. And the latter can be read to show both variations in views and to track policy, where policy is understood as statements about what should happen (rather than what actually does occur). They also show that tensions or gaps between policy and practice were not things that led people to drop dead with political angst: a reading of official public texts such as *Nhan Dan* shows clearly stories about vividly commercialising SOEs written and read despite not matching *ex cathedra* statements about the way things should be. This is especially true in the early 1980s (Chapter 6).

Third, this history is highly textured. There is no 'simple answer', though I find that some themes resonate widely and with power. In a situation where policy is often unimplementable, when there is often great intellectual puzzlement about not only what is actually happening but why, this is perhaps quite normal. One person's clear statement about ontology and epistemology, about what is and how it should be understood, becomes another's tedious generalisation. What is perhaps most startling is that one can find persuasive and intriguing analyses that amount to real critiques of events and situation written in North Vietnam well before the end of the war in 1975 and openly published. Their authors were working in wartime, subject to considerable material deprivation, but were people whose formal intellectual apparatus was that of a neo-Stalinism in a very poor South-East Asian people fighting the world's number one superpower. This, I think, is very interesting. How on earth did they do it?

Notes

1. That is, the Women's Union, the Farmers' Union, the official trade unions and other bodies that Leninism uses to manage popular pressures for association by controlling them directly by the ruling Party.
2. '*Tai Viet nam, cong khong han la cong, tu khong han la tu.*' Personal communication from Dao Xuan Sam, who was for many years a senior lecturer at the central Party school. In my opinion he, Tran Viet Phuong and somewhat differently Phan van Tiem are the most interesting economic intellects of this period.
3. By this term I mean the officially accepted combination of plan and market at the level of the SOE that arose from late 1979, was then marked by 25-CP of January 1981 and terminated when, through 1989–1990, loss of Soviet-bloc aid helped push for an end to the element of central planning in the ways in which SOEs acquired and disposed of resources. See p. 23 and Chapter 5, also Fforde (2000).
4. The reader is I am sure aware that the term is used here to refer to things very different from other countries. The DRV and SRV both lacked things like relatively independent judiciaries. The role of law in neo-Stalinist systems is often underplayed, but it remains of interest since it lays down norms and, often, policy-makers' expectations (Gillespie and Nicholson, 2005).
5. It is my impression that this is one reason why official publications such as *Cong Bao*, the official gazette, started to gain wider subscription and readership from the early 1980s. Visits to SOEs showed that they received attention, and decrees were studied quite apart from the normal introductions given to them in Party cell meetings and so on.
6. I will address these issues in a future publication.

Scene-setting and overview of the book

7. These sections focus mainly upon Western literature, following its own norms and village lives. I deal with Vietnamese literature below.
8. Thus a child's 'inside' grandparents ('*Ong/Ba noi*') are the parents of their father, and (in much of the country) if old far more likely to be living with them than the 'outside' maternal grandparents. Such terms therefore have wide semantic range linked to yin-yang ('*am-duong*') sentiments and thoughts. Thus, when I once asked an older male friend of considerable 'puissance' whether terms such as 'plan', 'order' and so on were more male ('*duong*') and others such as 'market', 'price' and 'negotiation' more female ('*am*') so that the transition from plan to market could be seen as a 'feminisation' ('*am hoa*'), he replied without hesitation, 'Of course, that is why it was successful.' My friend, a singer, told me that he was given an open radio microphone during the Christmas bombings...
9. See Fforde and Paine (1987: 43–4) for a discussion of the theoretical basis of this methodology and its relation to the overall logic of the neo-Stalinist model.
10. A significant number of English-language village-level rural studies came out in the late 1990s based upon extensive fieldwork (Dahm and Houben, 1999; Kleinen, 1999; Luong, 1992; Malarney, 1993; Nguyen van Chinh, 2000; Sikor, 1999; Nguyen Tung, 1999).
11. There were five basic property forms: state, cooperative, private, individual and family. Of these the first two were deemed 'socialist'.
12. It is a basic result of orthodox economics that, when variables like technology and growth are ignored by assuming them constant, markets allocate resources more efficiently – for given resources, output is higher. This means that if an economy becomes more commercialised and markets play a greater role, output can rise in the short term, perhaps rather sharply. I call this 'Kim Ngoc's law' (p. 31).
13. Thus central planners maintained a list of goods whose allocation was to be subject to the plan – so-called 'list goods'. See Fforde and Paine (1987: 134–5) for the list from the early 1960s.
14. This term referred to the push to bring assets and population into the institutions of neo-Stalinism (SOEs, cooperatives, groups etc.), and to control their activities through the plan, VCP and MOs.
15. For example, a statistical dictionary (TCTK, 1977) provides no definition that I can understand of the difference between rural and urban. See also World Bank (1990b).
16. It is important to realise that markets *develop*; I recall clearly meeting a representative from a southern SOE in Hanoi around 1985 who was there to buy inputs. He had at his disposal three means of exchange: dong, US dollars and cement. These resources could not only be used for direct business activities, but also for bribes and ways of opening doors. When markets are weakly developed things that we take as normal, such as the 'law of one price' or the existence of clearly defined monetary values, do not necessarily hold.
17. The Vietnamese language simply marks aspects of autonomy by use of the word '*tu*'. Freedom is '*tu do*' – literally 'self-caused'; autonomy is '*tu chu*' – literally 'self-master'. As economic practices and thinking became increasingly willing to contest the top-down ideas of central planning, so one

read and heard this word more often, in phrases such as '*tu can doi*' – 'self-balancing' – an ironic phrase as it was planners who should have 'balanced' an SOE to decide what inputs it needed to produce its planned output.
18. The sense here is essentially the legal one: many activities characteristic of the transitional model existed prior to the legislation of 1981 (see below) and self-balancing by SOEs was, I argue, accepted by the 1979 Sixth Plenum.
19. Less than pervasive marketisation (since central planning still controlled important resources, especially inputs to SOEs) and widespread shortages meant that 'value' was not necessarily expressed in price or even in money terms: barter and interlinked swaps were important, as were gold and dollars (see note 16).
20. By 'rents' here I mean, for non-economists, access to resources at costs well below those that could be expected in normally operating markets. In CPEs, where there is chronic shortage, the ability to acquire resources cheaply through the plan and then dispose of them at a high value in some way, such as on the black market, allows so-called 'shortage premia' to be captured. People can become very adept at such things (Fforde, 2002).
21. This term is central to the relationships between marketisation, accumulation of commercial capital in SOEs subject to local control and gauging the extent to which real property rights over SOEs were moving towards or away from the SOE itself. See Chapter 9 and also p. 69 discussing depreciation. Site visits and discussions in 1985–1986 and 1989–1992 showed clearly that for the mass of SOEs 'own capital' was understood to mean capital that they themselves had accumulated and which therefore should be seen as theirs. Much of this seems to have been lost, however, in the crisis years of 1989–1990 or was then appropriated by higher levels in the early 1990s. See Chapter 9.
22. I recall in 1982 how one of my thesis examiners, an expert on China, to my surprise remarked that the levels of procurement of rice from farmers (which by north Vietnamese standards were 'high') were in fact 'rather low'.
23. The World Bank (1990b: 13) reported estimates in 1988 based upon UN work with the Vietnamese GSO of so-called 'purchasing parity' per capita GDP at US$184. Vietnam was then still using the Soviet system and despite considerable efforts by the General Statistical Office there were not yet NIA based upon UN criteria.
24. The first FYP dates back to 1961–1965 and was only operational in the DRV – 'North Vietnam'. See Fforde and Paine (1987: Chapter 3).
25. The massive collection of TCTK (1982) presents nearly 900 pages of detailed information on industry during the second FYP, while TCTK (1981) gives us aggregate data showing that the rate of investment as a share of total national income was only 15.1 per cent in 1976, rose slightly in 1977 but then fell back again, averaging around 15 per cent for the period 1976–1980. Further, and more disheartening still for those looking for an independent growth process, through the period of the FYP some 23 per cent of national income relied upon external sources – the aid programme (TCTK, 1981: table 5). Aid was not only, on this basis, paying for all investment, but also for a large part of consumption.

26. The argument here is classical 'soft' traditional socialism, arguing that central planning could work so long as it paid sufficient attention to increases in wage goods' supplies and farmers' real incomes.
27. Spoor (1988) is one of the few English-language texts that looks at this issue directly.
28. See Chapter 3 for a discussion of the importance played by state administrative control over resource allocation in the neo-Stalinist development model.
29. These data are taken from various tables in TCTK (1985).
30. It was relatively widespread knowledge in 1989–1990 that MOs were threatened with loss of state funding.
31. This book draws heavily upon earlier work (de Vylder and Fforde, 1988, 1996) which presents arguments about developments in Vietnam that cover the period up to the very early 1990s. I am currently extending these on into the 1990s and 2000s, so that at the time of writing my conclusions about the 1990s and 2000s here are sketchier than for the earlier period.
32. See Fforde (1989: Chapter 12); Beresford (1989: Chapter 5).
33. Given the efforts put into the subject by various intelligence organisations during the war this is surprising.
34. An analysis of interest can be found in Darre (1985), presumably giving a view of French military sources. This refers to a 'military-technocratic alliance' opposed by 'ideologists' around Le Duan (then Party general-secretary) and Truong Chinh (one-time Party first secretary and stopgap general-secretary in 1986 after Le Duan's death six months prior to the Sixth Congress, below). That such work is possible is shown by studies such as Heng (1999).
35. The central example of this tendency was the late P.J. Honey. See also Smith (1983).
36. This was clearly marked in Vinh Phu province, where I was stationed in 1988–1989, since the provincial capital Viet Tri was a new town of the first FYP with a rather large number of central SOEs.
37. Jerneck (1995) is a good source on such unions.
38. Here the phrase 'those who work outside, eat outside' (*lam ngoai, an ngoai*) is an apt illustration of the situation.
39. During this period Truong Chinh appears to have shifted decisively away from his previous hard-line opinions to support reform.
40. See Fforde (1989); also note the thrust of such legislation as 312-HDCP (1 October 1980), which tried to impose strict control over the peasants' rural markets.
41. See the excellent article by Dam Van Nhue and Le Sy Thiep (1981).
42. It is possible that the differences between Le Duan's statement and the plenum resolution reflected the existence of thinking within the top levels of the Party that was even more radical than the plenum resolution. There is evidence to support this idea in Nguyen Lam's piece.
43. It is of interest to note that Nguyen Lam here advocates letting out idle land to agricultural cooperators – in keeping with decree 318-CP (10 September 1979) – but makes no mention at all of the 'output contract' system which featured so heavily in Party and state policy from towards the end of 1980.

44. Ngoc Van (1980), writing in November, reported that 'hundreds of SOEs were paying with unlimited output contracts and bonuses'. The 'major problem was that the system contradicted current regulations'. See also TTXVN (1981) praising large numbers of SOEs which had introduced output contracts into their plans.
45. Dated 1 April 1980, as reported in *Nhan Dan* (1982f).
46. This decree, translated in the BBC's Summary of World Broadcasts, confused many foreign observers (including the present writer) into overestimating the power of the decentralising tendency.
47. See, for example, the article by the manager in *Nhan Dan* (1982c); and that in the Ministry of Light Industry's journal *Light Industry*, revealing that the unit had at that time no quantity planning targets (Ministry of Light Industry, 1984). There is also an interesting article published in the SPC journal *Planning* by Le Mai Trinh (1984) putting a reformist argument for its 'self-balancing' methods.
48. This decree, dated 1 October 1980, can be found in *Nhan Dan* (1980m). For details of the effects of the clampdown in Hoan Kiem quarter of Hanoi see Hoang Lien (1980).
49. See Fforde (1989) for a discussion of the meaning of CT-100 in the rural cooperatives, arguing that like 25-CP it was essentially conservative and recentralising, given the pressures from farmers keen to leave cooperatives. For a detailed and depressing official history of cooperators' attempts to leave cooperatives see Dang Tho Xuong (1992).
50. Passed on 23 February 1981, this was entitled 'On the delivery [*giao nop*] of output by SOEs and the centralisation of all sources of cash incomes in the Bank'; see SWB (1981).
51. Dang Phong and Beresford (1998) present arguments as to why 'the Party would never have done it'. I find this too sanguine, especially after talking to Vietnamese about their experiences during the 1950s' land reform. See also Dang Tho Xuong (1992) for official evidence of cooperators' desire to leave cooperatives, which was not permitted.
52. See Kornai (1985) for an excellent and informative discussion of successful tightening-up in response to balance of payments difficulties in such countries.
53. See Chapter 2 and Beresford (1989).
54. Like the three-plan system of 25-CP (p. 135), this saw spontaneous efficiency-enhancing changes to traditional socialist institutions initially supported but then condemned by top leaders.
55. On 9 June 1986 he supported the U-turn back towards support for SOE autonomy in 306-BBT (p. 184). But in the early 1980s he supported 'priority to the socialist sectors' (Truong Chinh, 1981), and so on.
56. For an early and liberal examination of rural issues see The Dat (1981). Note on p. 230 the data on bloated management structures in cooperatives and pp. 202–3 on land abandonment in the north in 1978–1979 in named cooperatives.
57. See the draft political report published in *Nhan Dan* (1982e).
58. From the perspective of an aid donor, it was certainly the case that the SPC was highly conservative in the period 1987–1992 when, as an adviser to

SIDA, I had fairly close contact. It was opposed tooth-and-nail to attempts to marketise Swedish commodity support and keen to 'protect' SOEs. Its natural enemies at the time were the CIEM (Central Institute for Economic Management Research), which was moved in the early 1990s by Kiet from a position of relative independence directly under the Council of Ministers to the SPC, which it hated. This process was encouraged by the decision of the World Bank to replace the CIEM by the SPC as its main counterpart in Vietnam, largely it appeared to make it easier to start its lending programme, the absence of which (and so its low status) it found extremely annoying.

59. For the attitude of the USSR at this time see Fforde (1985); also Vo Nhan Tri (1986). See also remarks by Soviet Vietnamologists in such journals as *Far Eastern Affairs*.
60. See the piece in *Nhan Dan* (1982g) discussing 26-NQ/TW (23 June 1980).
61. This decree contained broad measures designed to systematise foreign trade activities under central control. Growth of exports out of Ho Chi Minh City fell off rapidly in 1983 (*Nhan Dan*, 1982b).
62. Others were *lien ket* and *lien doanh*.
63. It should be clear from the discussion to date as well as the definition of transition used here that a reform of administratively set prices and wages that simply sought to eliminate the gap between state and free market prices would be expected to decrease the degree of commercialisation of the economy (at least initially). What is important is not the margin between the two price – or value – levels, but the relative balance between planned ('fixed price') and unplanned ('negotiated price') transactions in the economy. This was well understood in some reformist circles; see also Kornai (1985) for similar comments upon the regressive nature of macro-stabilisation policies when such systemic issues are not faced. What was particularly inept in terms of the economic analysis behind the Eighth Plenum was that the negative effects upon 'outside' output of a sharp reduction in the money supply, while obvious to anybody who read the papers and thought about the determinants of aggregate 'outside' economic activity, seem to have been ignored.
64. Available in *Cong Bao* (1985), and also published in the Joint Publications Research Service (1985), this decree was entitled 'On policies and measures for stimulating exports and strengthening the management of foreign trade'. It assigned quotas to local authorities; above quota, output of export goods could be directly exported, with the SOE owning the resulting foreign exchange; but all local authorities active in foreign trade had to be subject to the Ministry of Foreign Trade.
65. See *Nhan Dan* (1985d). I arrived back in Vietnam for the first time in the autumn of 1985 for research at the NEU.
66. Note the argument in Darre (1985) already cited that the fundamental division in Vietnamese politics was that between the military-technocratic complex and 'ideologues' around Le Duan and Truong Chinh. The military, directly responsible for national defence, had seen in 1980–1982 the number of army divisions raised by 17 to add to the existing 26 (Darre, 1985: 107). Soldiers need guns.
67. According to some, the formal ending of the two-price system came with a decree in December 1989, but the practical decision to end it had probably

been taken some time earlier. I have not been able to find a copy, although it is sometimes referred to as decree 195.
68. My point here is about the trend – the direction in which things were moving.
69. Note that the term 'transitional model' as used here combines both senses, in that it was both legally marked and in a large sense implemented. See Fforde (1999, 2000) for a discussion of the way in which both China and Vietnam experienced transition legally marked as such, in terms of situations where SOEs legally participated in both plan and market (the start and end of the process). Such a definition is different from what happened in other countries abandoning central planning (Fforde, 2000).

2

The DRV, the development goals of unreformed Vietnamese communism and what went wrong – the limits of national liberation

Introduction

The previous chapter provided an analysis and simplified overview of the Vietnamese state sector's commercial renaissance. This chapter now looks back earlier to discuss what had gone wrong, and, more importantly, how this was seen. I start with a discussion of life at the grassroots.

The view from the grassroots: life in an SOE in the mid-1970s

The informants

So as to obtain a limited parallel history, in 2005, when many of these issues were no longer contentious, we interviewed a small number of retired SOE managers. To protect and respect confidentiality no details are given of where they were from or which SOEs they had worked in; they had worked in the north.

Grassroots comments: conditions in SOEs

Conditions in SOEs, all agreed, were very difficult in the mid-1970s. However, workers enjoyed access to state rations and other benefits, and this gave them rice, sugar, foodstuffs, fuel and other necessities such as soap and bicycle inner-tubes. This meant that they were 'better off than the peasants'.

Material conditions were very hard. A manager's salary was 95 dong a month (worth about 60–70 kg milled rice on the free market), and for workers 40–50 dong. However, they could still live, as they had access to ration goods. One informant commented: 'Spiritually, in the 1970s there was the wartime atmosphere, to liberate the south, so all workers were enthusiastic and empathised strongly with the state in its difficulties because of the south.'

War, system, or both?

The common opinion of the panel was that now, after they had retired and lived under the *doi moi* conditions, they understood that the difficulties stemmed in the main from the system being 'centralised; bureaucratised; subsidised'. But at the time they thought that the problems were because of the war.

One member of the panel said: 'Then, when we had meetings with the workers, I always stressed that we were meeting difficulties because of the war, and "tomorrow" we would be far better off, for as Uncle Ho had said, "It will be ten times better than today."'

The DRV and North Vietnam prior to 1975 – the limits of statist developmentalism

Economic logic – northern economic development after 1954

The DRV, founded in 1945, was the ruling state authority north of the seventeenth parallel until 1976, when, after national reunification in 1975, the country was reunited under the SRV.

After 1954 and French withdrawal the DRV nationalised modern industry, while the overpopulated delta areas were collectivised in 1959–1960. Aid-financed capital imports then formed the basis for the 1961–1965 first FYP's ambitious development programme. Consistent with neo-Stalinist orthodoxy, this stressed priority development of heavy industry, despite low actual and potential agricultural surpluses and almost non-existent industrial development prior to independence.

As the apparatus of the DRV nation-state developed, expansion of such socially valuable areas as mass education and medical services was accompanied by job creation elsewhere in the bureaucracy; state employment increased rapidly. Inevitably, state cash outlays swiftly rose, and as matching revenue gains were not forthcoming a buoyant fiscal deficit accompanied severe inflationary pressures. The state was unable to use its legal trade monopolies to extract the complementary inputs[1] needed to operate its new factories, partly because of the collectivised peasantry's relative effectiveness at dodging procurement (Fforde, 1989) and partly because of the inherent inefficiencies of central planning. A weak tax base therefore starved the state's material supply system of the resources needed to operate realised investment while at the same time, by pushing the fiscal (cash) position into deficit, feeding domestic inflation. The authorities found themselves unable to operate their newly installed industrial capacity. The area became relatively oversupplied with fixed (modern) industrial capital, hungry for inputs and mainly sited in SOEs.

Inability to utilise the newly established industrial capacity had disturbing implications for the validity of the development programme. What was the point of building the factories if they stood idle? But still, this very inefficiency represented a potential for increasing output.

Aid masked this deep structural problem.[2] The state's effective monopoly over foreign economic relations was crucial to these strategies. As a result, though, local adaptations of the DRV's neo-Stalinist models had become the norm by the mid-1970s. This was true for both collectivised agriculture and state industry. The resulting behaviour was frequently illegal, but responded to immediate and local economic incentives.[3]

With my late co-author I have provided elsewhere an analysis of the development programme adopted in the DRV and the problems encountered in its implementation (Fforde and Paine, 1987). This study has not gone unchallenged, mainly because of its apparent lack of attention to the effects of the war. The argument is made that the DRV's development programme was necessary in wartime to mobilise national resources for the war effort. A frequent retort to this is that success against the French did not require neo-Stalinist institutions. The DRV has been studied by other authors (Spoor, 1985; Beresford, 1989), but it cannot be said that there is yet adequate and detailed research into its economic development.

The basic conclusion of Fforde and Paine (1987) – not primarily a political analysis – was that the DRV did not succeed in attaining the tasks set for it by policy-makers. The fundamental reasons were the effects of forced industrialisation upon a poor area. As the state sector grew the newly collectivised peasantry proved able to resist extractive policies, and free market food prices rose steeply. Real wages in the state sector fell around 25 per cent during the first FYP (Fforde and Paine, 1987: tables 133 and 136). The response was the development of what came to be called the 'outside economy' – extensive exchange activities 'outside' the planned parts of the economy. These were based, *inter alia*, in the *de facto* commercialisation of the DRV programme's classical institutions in response to local interests, and SOEs came to be involved in the free market (Fforde and Paine, 1987: Chapters 5 and 6).[4] Such behaviour was typical. It implied that the norms of the orthodox development programme did not apply. The term 'aggravated shortage' describes the outcome (p. ??).

Ideological logic – the DRV programme's appeal to traditional thinking

For many years the unimplementability of the DRV programme was not interpreted by most politically influential people in North Vietnam, or its foreign sponsors, as revealing anything fundamentally wrong with it. One reason was ideology; another was its strong attractions to leaders whose goals of development were influenced by traditional issues. Neo-Stalinism was promised central bureaucratic control over a developing country whose basic units were in some sense collectives. Relations between these – mainly cooperatives and SOEs (both in a way pseudo-villages) – would not be based upon markets but upon 'the plan'. In this way the nation could remain united while the social division of labour increased, rather than being fragmented by the petty interests generated by private capital (Bray, 1983).[5]

Besides national unification and independence, the historical task of Vietnamese communism had long been interpreted as being the construction of Soviet-style socialism. This meant the neo-Stalinist development model exemplified by the USSR. It is important to stress the idealistic nature of this vision – in the most basic sense of the word a programmatic model, to be implemented as a whole. Its totalitarianism reflected its role in realising the design laid down in the textbooks being translated into Vietnamese and providing the basis for training the new cadres coming in from the Viet Minh, and then, as time went on, from the new mass educational system (EPU, 1975; see p. 68). The intellect of the North Vietnamese economic cadre was a product of the interaction between traditional literary sources, Soviet theory attached to the DRV programme and practical experience.

These ways of thinking and viewing the world appear related to Daoist and other roots, a subject about which much rubbish could be written, though from my own experience a number of points are usefully made.

First is the tendency to view evaluations made in the abstract as rather silly. Blueprints are not real and life is complicated, so taking a view of things is much better based upon something that actually exists. This supports trials followed by analysis and review. It advocates caution and scepticism. I think this has deep cultural roots. What is sometimes called Vietnamese pragmatism is not simply ignorance but draws upon philosophical roots.

Second are ideas that relate emotion to cognition and action. Within these, emotion is not seen as a source of disorder, in fact the contrary. Somehow this often translates into a tolerance of voice and diversity that underpins a relative lack of violence and a sense of process.

Third are ideas that stress understanding as process, leading to a focus upon thought as an attribute of individuals in particular contexts, thus contingent, and so a focus upon 'whether people understand yet' and, in general, the issue of cognition (*tu duy*).

It is obvious that these tend to sit uneasily with the strong idealism inherent in any 'transitive' development programme, such as neo-Stalinism, which views development as something that is done, as product rather than process (Cowen and Shenton, 1996; Arndt, 1981).

Yet, despite the problems encountered in implementing the traditional programme, Vietnamese development policy after 1975 was, if anything, more centralising and orthodox than in the early 1960s (Beresford, 1989: 201; Fforde, 1989). The visible effect of lessons learnt from the DRV experience was the drive to *strengthen* central control. Perhaps the most striking example was the repeated attempts to abolish the free rice market by decree. This policy stance reflected a number of issues.

- The internal criticisms of orthodox policy that had surfaced from the early 1960s, and the results of the debate within the establishment about the reasons for the disorderly situation within the DRV and the non-implementability of the received programme.[6]
- The political situation, and above all the strong commitment made by the top leadership – especially Le Duan, Le Duc Tho and Truong Chinh – to the DRV programme (pp. 28–32).
- The lack of effective alternative ideas within the establishment that could stand up to the traditional orthodoxy, as well as ways of coping

with the systemic problems of the DRV model. This often led to what seemed to be simply an attitude of 'if it does not succeed, try harder'.

- The lack of discipline among state cadres and their susceptibility to considerations of local interest. The ambitious intentionality of the DRV state's neo-Stalinism reduced in the end to an entrenched theatricality where the Party centre was unable to force its will upon the periphery and so lacked normal sovereignty (Kleinen, 2001; Nguyen Khac Truong, 1991).

The north at reunification

'Aggravated shortage' meant that by 1975 well-established allocative networks alongside administrative material supply 'reallocated' economic resources and loosened planners' control (p. 11). Quite contrary to official policy, market and quasi-market relations pervaded the DRV economy. Forced development and inflationary tensions, coupled with the fiscal (cash) deficit, had encouraged these extra-plan activities. Such behaviour was commonplace throughout the socialist sectors, and the behaviour of agricultural cooperatives and SOEs – the pseudo-villages – reflected this on a day-to-day basis (p. 56).

The basic dilemma for those, such as the military, concerned with the future potential for reliable supplies of military *matériel* from the Vietnamese economy rather than from China or the Soviet bloc was thus that while neo-Stalinism offered, or at least so it appeared from Soviet experience, a solution, the discipline needed to implement it was clearly lacking. How could it be secured?

Since many of the newly installed SOE assets lacked the complementary inputs required to operate them, state industry and the large state bureaucracy were dependent upon imports of both consumer goods and current means of production, and so structurally isolated from the rest of the domestic economy. At the same time these goods were supplied at costs far below their value in alternative uses. This meant not only that they tended to be used inefficiently, but also that there was pressure for their diversion into higher-value activities. The isolation of state industry from the domestic economy was an issue that deeply concerned contemporary writers (Chapter 3). This shows up in the data revealing that capital stock was not the binding constraint upon output gains (p. 128).

Systemic conflicts between allocative mechanisms were thus a fundamental feature of the DRV economy. But these interactions were neither merely an opposition between 'plan' and 'market' nor simple 'zero-sum' conflicts. Their mutual conditionality meant the exact nature of allocative choices usually varied according to local conditions.[7]

For instance, the ability of an agricultural cooperative or SOE to obtain labour effort could depend upon concessions in the form of under-the-table access to resources, the output from which could be disposed of in ways that allowed capture of higher values. Output from a cooperator of '5 per cent' land was in principle freely disposable on local markets. The crucial role of money (cash) was as a source of information, via prices and market observation, of the value of non-planned activities.[8] These might be sales on the free market, but could equally well be direct swaps for goods or services elsewhere in the non-planned economy.

Such behaviour could *support* planned activities by increasing labour effort at the level of the individual SOE or cooperative. Thus there was a close interaction between the planned and free markets (or, in the more accurate Vietnamese terminology, between the 'inside' and 'outside' economies) which could lead to positive conditionality – success in the planned sectors could rely upon granting increased access to resources for use in market-oriented activities.[9] More, rather than less; but the knock-on effects meant that local interests and negotiating rights had to be respected, which for traditional communists was a big ask.

Dependence upon imports masked these issues. Domestic political opposition had been unable to mount an effective challenge to the neo-Stalinist strategy, though much progress had been made. Policy-makers could therefore continue to act as though the main constraint upon economic development was an inadequate fixed capital stock in state industry. This assumed more or less implicitly that the complementary inputs needed to operate additional plant would be forthcoming through the state's ability to impose trade monopolies and extract resources at low cost from other producers – above all agriculture. But the DRV's experience had contradicted this argument, because by 1975 the area's precociously overdeveloped industrial sector largely depended upon aid imports for its operation. Oversupply of fixed capital in state industry daily created strong pressures for the government to set about acquiring the resources it needed. Mediated by a bulky, inefficient and ineffective administrative system, this contributed directly to the tensions between allocative mechanisms so important to the DRV economy and its potential for systemic change. Further, it encouraged a 'grab' mentality: *if* additional resources appeared, planners would seek to secure them, perhaps abandoning the agreements that had generated them. This was happening during both the unsuccessful recentralisation of the early 1980s *and*, though using different methods, the recentralisation of the 1990s.

Everyday confrontation with economic realities had led to behaviour patterns that responded to economic incentives. Work for the state or the cooperative typically had little value, paying wages that bought only small quantities on the free market. Jobs gave access to goods in short supply and distributed by ration, or offered opportunities for other strategies generating high-value goods or services 'outside' the formally planned sector. People, apart from those restrained by moral scruples or certain sorts of careerist (many of the 'conservatives' in SOEs ready to denounce 'fence-breakers' – p. 61), were attuned to seeking out strategies that could exploit local shortages and turn price and other differentials to their advantage. While such issues faced almost everybody, management cadres in particular had learnt the value of negotiating a blind eye to illegal activity, whether to implement their unit's plan or to their own direct benefit – in other words, the practical utility of conditionality. The key organs of central control, centred upon the SPC, were unable to secure adequate command over domestic resources, and, since imports plugged the gap, did not really need to: at least not yet.

Views from the grassroots: 'aggravated shortage'

The panel welcomed discussion of the creative and positive measures adopted by SOEs to deal with the shortcomings of the central-planning system. These relied upon managing the presence of different allocative mechanisms. One said: 'At this time units were not called state businesses [*Doanh nghiep Nha nuoc*] but state enterprises [*Xi nghiep Quoc doanh*]. This was because at this time there were simply no private enterprises. Besides, the latter were cooperatives, which were part of the socialist economy.'

The common opinion was as follows. To contribute to raising workers' living standards, the SOE would establish small workshops to produce products that were 'non-list' (p. 136) and would be directly exchanged with cooperatives to obtain rice or food. Enterprise XXX, apart from metal products that it produced according to the plan allocated to it, started foundries to produce agricultural implements, such as ploughshares, knives, reapers, sickles etc. An SOE producing bricks, tiles and construction materials hired transport to bring coal to the SOE, and bought firewood also. According to the plan it should have bought inputs like this only from the province, but it actively did this 'under the table' (*chui) *after the province agreed*.

The methods used here were very diverse (the panel stressed), and based upon 'turning a blind eye'. All agreed that such 'fence-breaking' (*pha rao* – p. 25) was not simple, as you could go to prison easily. In the SOEs were many 'revolutionary' people who would report to higher levels.

> If there had not been 25-CP [see p. 135] then many 'little crimes' would have been exposed. One could say that 25-CP 'muzzled' many conservative people in the SOEs and saved various managers from the sack. According to the old system such activities were quite wrong, and should have led to losing not only one's job but also membership of the Party.

Such stories were quite common and there is nothing particularly dramatic in reporting them here. 'Aggravated shortage' was part of everyday life, subject to criticism from senior leaders (for example, the attacks on it at the Tenth Plenum of 1964 reported in Fforde and Paine, 1987), yet clear from the preamble to many decrees.

State industry as a force for national self-expression – dragon's tooth or curate's egg?

Thus the economic system was far from an effective neo-Stalinist machine. 'Aggravated shortage' meant that resources did not necessarily go where planners sent them; instead they were allocated according to the complicated processes of conditionality and local adjustment in the northern economy. Imposition of this system upon the richer south, where economic rents (Fforde, 2002) were high, was unlikely to lead to a sudden expansion of the neo-Stalinist core; rather, in the absence of severely repressive measures (see the Le Duc Tho position, p. 30),[10] it was liable to exacerbate the existing strains by increasing the relative attractions of the 'outside economy'.

The nature of the northern political economy and the attitudes of the top leadership meant that the attempt to utilise the DRV's planning apparatus throughout the country after 1975 not only required its establishment in the south, but also qualitative changes in the north entailing radical increases in the effective power of central authority.

The latter would require a sharp curtailment of *de facto* freedoms. Without this, the behavioural patterns of 'aggravated shortage' would persist. Economic agents would respond to the pattern of local incentives presented to them by different allocative mechanisms, by plan and by market.

The main characteristic of the political economy after 1975–1976 thus was and remained until 1989 a systemic competition for resources between allocative mechanisms, polarised between the two ideal types of the plan's administered material supply system and the unplanned free market. This was directly inherited from the DRV. Economic agents – both workers and the institutions of the socialist economy such as SOEs and agricultural cooperatives – adapted to the pervasive presence of alternatives to participation in the planned economy. This meant the creation of a wide variety of often illegal or quasi-illegal activities that shared the common characteristic of being outside the control of central authority.

Analytical implications: commercialisation and efficiency gains

The institutional reality prior to 1989 considerably complicates macro-economic analysis. For given economic resources, 'in the short run' a planned economy will usually produce less than a market economy, due to its inefficiencies. The effects of exogenous[11] changes in aggregate resource availability (of which those resulting from climatic and international factors were the most important) were transmitted through the economy. In the short run, the plan was less efficient than the market.

Thus, far from being fixed, the economy's aggregate efficiency could alter quite sharply from year to year.[12] If this supported the plan, total output would tend to be lower. Furthermore, the balance between allocative mechanisms could and did change both exogenously, most usually in response to state policy, and endogenously.[13] The latter could occur, for example, if SOEs spontaneously set about acquiring resources through direct 'horizontal' contacts; for instance, in response to a sharp drop in deliveries from the state's material supply system. This would mean that, for a given resource availability, total output would be higher.

Political economy: commercialisation and growth

These issues had implications for growth processes. Over longer periods macro-economic analysis has to go beyond a short-run framework: the capital stock and technology change significantly. Another issue is class formation: what is happening to the nature of asset ownership? If, as is argued here, a 'state business interest' had by 1985–1986 emerged with sufficient force to be a significant element of the politics of the 1986 *doi moi* Party Congress, then what economic assets could it influence, and what did this mean in terms of the ability of individuals to accumulate commercial power? What, in essence, were the processes of 'primary accumulation' that underpinned the political economy of the transition?

There were thus two processes: first, the shift to market-based commerce; second, business-based growth. These occurred both at the level of the SOE and nationally.

Initially, effective utilisation of the human and other resources freed by the arrival of peace was the key problem. This point accentuates the analytical need to focus upon issues related to allocative mechanisms and the distribution of current resources, and therefore to examine the origins of short-run changes in the pattern of economic activity. This was the main 'real-time' game.

To repeat a point already made, the most noteworthy feature of the growth before the early 1990s was that it was weak and unstable. Only after the commercial renaissance of the 1980s could SOEs, in an economy where markets dominated allocative relations, focus on growth strategies.

The political economy of an SOE-based transition

Against this background, the political economy of commercial renaissance should have become clearer. The prior development of 'outside' activities in the DRV characteristic of 'aggravated shortage' meant that commercialisation processes already existed. While often illegal, production for the market – or at least for a valuable swap or deal – was nothing new, strange or unfamiliar. High free market prices[14] stimulated and perpetuated these processes. 'Conditionality' ensured that state and cooperative cadres were familiar with negotiating to ensure plan fulfilment for the SOE or cooperative by allowing access to resources within the plan to support expansion of 'outside' activities.

The balance between 'inside' and 'outside' activities – between plan and market – was thus to a great extent endogenously determined, and so could and did vary *independently* of policy. Commercial renaissance had a dynamic internal logic. Party leaders' attitudes set the basic frame, but within that the relative attraction of different allocative mechanisms determined outcomes. This balance depended upon such factors as the value of aid, the volumes of resource in each sector and the attitudes of the general population, economic cadres and so on.

The political economy of transition – a 'transition model' – can therefore be outlined. The commercialised behaviour already apparent in the DRV would grow from with the state and cooperative sectors. Development of commercialised market-like transactions would throw up winners and losers within the socialist economy, usually led by Party members. There would thus be political confusion as new interests would have to be contained *within* political institutions and practices – constituted by the VCP – that had not been designed to do so (Thayer, 1995; Vasavakul, 1995, 1996; Beresford, 1997). Certain of the losers might have to be compensated, others simply ignored. Within the Party establishment, certain elements would be part of the rising commercialised group and in a strong position – managers of SOEs especially, and elements within their supervisory or owning levels. The meaning of state and cooperative property would change radically. Those likely to suffer most would be cadres in cooperative agriculture, state workers in unprofitable SOEs and many middle-level cadres in supervisory levels lacking positions from which to block or support commercial activity (i.e. platforms from which to buy into emergent commercial ownership).

Great complexity would thus arise in relationships between commercialising units and their superior levels within the state apparatus. To the extent that the latter benefited – for example, through a share of profits – from commercialisation, their direct interests would lead them to support it. This is not to deny the possibility that reformers could support change not in their direct interests (AVRP transcripts and discussions with Tran Phuong). However, the overall impact in terms of economic growth and development would also influence their attitude, and thus the policies they would support. Here the greater short-run ('static') efficiency of markets would come into play in an application of Kim Ngoc's law (see note 12 on p. 47).

A private sector defined in ways that would enable it to be statistically recorded need not, and did not, play an important economic or political role. This suggests why the Sixth Congress announced (but largely failed to initiate) a positive shift in the Party's attitude to the private sector: the mass of politically relevant commerce was in SOEs, not in private business. This is discussed further later.

Conclusions: the importance of local perspectives

It seems to me that any single statement of VCP policy or views would be unwise. The range of opinions and positions was large. It is reasonable, given the weight of data supporting it (and this is developed in later chapters), that stressing policy as the origin of system change in Vietnam is seriously awry and an example of 'policy fetishism', seeking to attribute far too much meaning to what the powerful say they have done. It is not only far more complicated than that, but also very different.

The argument now examines and re-examines the central moments in the process. It mainly uses official sources, which naturally focus upon policy issues – often actually being policy, since decrees provide unique information. In terms of how the book may be read, this takes the reader through discussions that become increasingly textured.

The next chapter looks at policy debates prior to 1979.

Notes

1. By this is meant those inputs from the domestic economy needed over and above those supplied from foreign assistance to support output levels in the aid-financed investment projects – for example, labour or agricultural raw materials.
2. See Fforde and Paine (1987: 68, table 3.1) showing how imports of consumer goods rose as a percentage of total imports before 1965.
3. Fforde (1989) discusses the effects of the macro-economic imbalances upon collectivised agriculture. The distributional tensions accompanying cooperative production exacerbated the problem by further discouraging participation in cooperative work, and had the effect of encouraging peasants to supply to their private plots those resources that they were free to allocate. Given the lack of discipline of local Party cadres ('localism'), this meant that the area farmed on cooperators' own account tended to exceed by a substantial margin the statutory level of 5 per cent of the cooperative's land. Despite many complaints about this, there was little the central authorities were able to do to stop it. This is a particularly clear example of 'institutional endogeneity'.

4. For example, see the quote from Pham Hung in Fforde and Paine (1987: 62).
5. See Fforde (1989) for a discussion of the way in which the traditional view of Vietnamese society stressed the local village (or commune). See also Woodside (1976) for a discussion of the 'proletarian mandarins'.
6. Chapter 3 shows the tenor of the debates. See also such documents as Tran Phuong's (1966/1967) long article in *Nghien cuu kinh te*, reports on the situation in agriculture during the late 1960s cited in Dinh Thu Cuc (1977) and the unresolved debate over 'household contracting' in Vinh Phu province (*inter alia*, Gordon, 1981). See also the article by Le Huy Ngo (1990), Party secretary of Vinh Phu province, in the local newspaper about the output contract system as modified in 1988 by decree 10 (BCT, 1988).
7. The historical origins of conditionality include Stalin's famous 'U-turn' during collectivisation in the USSR, which led to the emergence of the so-called 'private plots' in the Stalinist institutional model for agriculture. These ended up providing a very high proportion of food supplies through the kolkhoz markets (Wadekin, 1973, 1982). The Vietnamese equivalent was the so-called '5 per cent land'.
8. It does not seem to be a necessary condition so long as there is the possibility of direct and relatively free exchange of goods. But use of cash could reduce transactions costs, like equitisation (p. 208), and so had a certain natural logic.
9. So far as I can see, understanding these mechanisms was an essential part of the mental toolkit of any competent Vietnamese economist at this time. Failure to see that steep reductions in the means of exchange available to the 'outside' economy would sharply reduce its activity, *and that this would, through conditionality, hit 'inside' activities*, was one of the main shortcomings of the analysis behind the 1985 'price-money-wages' abortive reforms (p. 184).
10. In the USSR collectivisation relied upon armed force, and the threat of it. Here it is worth recalling the reported incident of the early 1960s, when as free market prices rose farmers were permitted to come into Hanoi to sell rice illegally – the police stood by and watched (Fforde, 1989).
11. That is, forces acting from outside the economy itself, such as bad weather, policy changes, cuts or increases in aid levels and so on. Another was the 'procurement strike' that occurred during 1978–1979 in the Mekong delta.
12. Between 1979 and 1981 per capita staples output rose some 17 per cent as farmers spontaneously left their cooperatives. This is an example of the way in which output could rise rather sharply and quickly because existing resources were being used more efficiently – an example of 'Kim Ngoc's law' (p. 31).
13. By this I mean that the shift took place not in response to external – exogenous – changes, but because of the way in which interactions between various economic and other factors worked themselves out; for example, as increased market-oriented activities allowed for accumulation of resources and capital for such activities. Such resources could be and often were organisational, for example marketing departments within SOEs. These took time and effort to set up, a good example of the real resource costs required to operate markets.
14. Typically ten times those in planned transactions, according to personal observation in late 1978.

3

Vietnamese state industry: policy debates before 1979

Introduction: traditional central planning in North Vietnam and perceptions of problems

As discussed, the VCP originally took as its development programme for the DRV that created by the USSR during the 1930s. The Three Year Plan (1958–1960) and first FYP (1961–1965) thus saw creation of a collectivised peasantry, attempts to erect state monopolies over large areas of domestic trade and almost all foreign economic contacts and the establishment of central-planning organs.

Viewing underdevelopment as the absence of modern industry (Fforde and Paine, 1987), the DRV programme saw the correct development path as an accelerated programme of investment in the priority area of modern – state – industry.

The neo-Stalinist programme was the same as that widely imposed throughout Central and Eastern Europe immediately after the Second World War. It was also used by the People's Republic of China during its early development programmes. The academic literature is well developed and need not be discussed in detail.[1] I start with a 'textbook' discussion of the planning system and how the plan was meant to allocate resources. I move on to look at 'seminar' thinking, and conclude with a discussion of policy ideas.

The politics and political economy of state industry prior to 1979

Control mechanisms: planning and 'balancing' the SOE – the 'textbook' view

In principle the system of industrial ministries, subject to the Council of Ministers and backed by functional organs such as the Ministry of Finance, the SPC, the Ministry of Foreign Trade and so on, oversaw the use of administrative measures to extract economic resources and concentrate them into priority areas.[2]

Deliveries of products to their users within the planned system resulted from instructions from planners; each SOE was thus 'balanced' (*can doi) as its planned output in quantity terms was used as the starting point for norm-based calculations of the required inputs. The SOE was subject to a large number of 'legally binding plan targets' (*chi tieu phap lenh). The end result was that the SOE *formally* had no choice over the sources of its inputs or the channels used to distribute its output, for these were determined by the plan given to it. Prices existed to assist planners to control resource flows and monitor SOEs through the detailed accounting system.

Moreover, planners set prices administratively in order to generate adequate state revenues. Each SOE reported in its accounts on the costs incurred.[3] The distinction was made between the 'SOE wholesale price' (*gia ban buon xi nghiep) and the 'industry wholesale price' (*gia ban buon cong nghiep). The former could vary from unit to unit, while the latter was equalised for each product by varying the margin (called the 'state income' – *thu quoc doanh) so as to ensure that the price paid by the wholesaler was the same notwithstanding the source of the product. By setting prices suitably planners could ensure that SOEs generated high profits to finance state investment.[4]

Incentives to reduce costs at SOE level existed, in that cost-cutting which reduced the actual 'cost price' (*gia thanh) below planned costs would increase profits earned by the unit. These were simply set in the plan as a fixed proportion of planned costs. 'Economising' (*tiet kiem) therefore increased this margin. By the 1970s such retained profits were paid according to fixed proportions into the so-called 'three funds' (*ba quy).[5] There was therefore some incentive to economise, but with 'outside' values so much higher than state prices and with planners' natural tendency to 'grab' at additional resources and so ratchet up plan and cost-cutting targets, the effects were not great.

A further confusing aspect was so-called 'depreciation' (*khau hao co ban*). This is best seen as a capital charge imposed by the state. It was certainly not subject to the SOE's formal control. In SOE accounts a cost was entered proportional to the value of the unit's assets. This varied from branch to branch. However, like all other costs and revenues, this was entered *automatically* in the SOE's account at the state bank. The use of administratively set prices based upon initial costs (themselves often founded upon valuations of aid goods using Council for Mutual Economic Assistance internal exchange rates) for valuing capital assets meant there was no clear relationship between these costs and any trade-offs involved in resource allocation decisions. Since most capital assets – especially in industry – were imported, the irrationalities early became clear to some officials.[6] Valuable assets had to be entered into accounts at prices so low that the surplus they generated under the form of so-called depreciation was quite inadequate. One reason for this was the 'overvalued' exchange rate.[7]

The SOE had almost no control over credit and debit entries in its bank accounts. These were not carried out in response to its orders; rather, they were part of the integrated system of accounting and control within the state sector. They were indeed historically a *control* mechanism.[8] But cash was used, though primarily for payment of wages, and, since cash was usually controlled by whoever had it, provided an opportunity for the development of direct 'outside' relations; the SOE's superiors therefore monitored it tightly.[9]

Recruitment and dismissal of personnel (especially the managers) were the prerogatives of the SOE's superiors and the Party. The specialised staff offices of the unit (finance, planning etc.) had direct links to the corresponding supervisory organs. SOE independence was thus very limited. Indeed, internal reorganisation to prevent these offices being used to monitor and control management was a key indicator of SOE commercialisation.

Three aspects are worth stressing.

First is the lack of technological dynamism and incentives for demand-oriented innovation at the level of the SOE.[10] Linguistic references to the 'passivity' of SOEs under the old system and the radical shift towards a more active attitude as behaviour became more commercial reflect this directly.

Second is the 'input-constrained' nature of production. Rather than seeking to secure static efficiency by choosing an appropriate input mix, SOEs felt no real cost pressure and indeed were neither profit maximisers nor cost minimisers in the ordinary sense. Rather, they tended to try to maximise their input stocks to insure against non-delivery of binding inputs at crucial moments – most especially when meeting output targets was threatened (Kornai, 1980). Thus the output actually produced was largely determined by the availability of the particular binding input in short supply. This was not usually fixed capital, but effective labour inputs and/or other current produced inputs (often imported). Capital stock was not a binding constraint upon output gains: increases in its supply were like 'salt in the sea'.

Third, it offered myriad opportunities for higher levels to interfere.

Views from the grassroots: Party and state control mechanisms?

The common opinion of the panel was as follows.

Before 25-CP in 1981, control by superior levels was very strict and followed the plan. The superior level managed the plan in terms of supply of materials and fuels (inputs) and outputs. The Party managed in accordance with the Party line, and relied upon reports from the SOE and other Party cells sent upwards.

However, they could still do things 'under the table' (*chui*) because they reported their non-plan activities directly and orally to their superiors. The superior level would give them the 'green light', for example by treating their behaviour as an experiment. Of course the superior level also benefited (through presents and envelopes[11]).

Small SOEs (typically 'local' or even artisanal – p. 77) found it easier to 'fence-break' as they were less closely controlled, and their workers less educated so they would be less likely to report their manager to higher levels, while 'extra' products were easier to sell to peasants and cooperatives.

Conservative non-political views from the late 1970s – the operation of the traditional economic programme and the rationale for continued priority to the state sector

There is little real difference between these recollections expressed in the mid-2000s and many of those held at the time. This can be seen from the following, which[12] predates 25-CP of January 1981 as well as 279-CP of August 1979 (pp. 135 and 171).

In the second half of the 1970s the operation of the traditional economic model in Vietnam was 'far from trouble-free'. However, mainstream doctrine clung to the absolute superiority of the socialist – state and cooperative – sectors. Although private production was reportedly an area of policy stimulation, the expectation was that the sector would be phased out within five to ten years because state and cooperative production units would by then be better equipped and therefore produce higher quality and cheaper goods.

The employment limit in the private sector was 'one to two people'; 'non-list'[13] goods were seen as more or less freely tradable, even by people who had not themselves produced them. Taxes on petty producers were low, but they had to register with the relevant authorities. Incomes were extremely high – higher at least than those of an economics professor – but they did not have (free) access to certain goods and services in short supply: an example here was the hospital, where they had to pay. The buoyancy of the sector led to problems for the state – materials were damaged so that they could be classified as waste materials and therefore sold on the free market. Perhaps 10 per cent of materials used 'outside' were pilfered from the state.

Problems of corruption, low work effort and poor quality of workmanship extended from top to bottom within the state sector, from managers to workers. It was thought possible to combat this and enforce state property rights in two ways: economic methods, or so-called 'administrative' methods, such as expulsion from the Party or Youth Movement, imprisonment or sackings (recall the Le Duc Tho programme, p. 30).

People's economic interests led them to steal, either because they were poor or because they were bad people, or simply because it was more profitable to sell on the free market where prices were far higher. This implied that getting rid of the wide gap between state and free market prices was essential. State prices were not, it was argued, too low, because the state made a profit on sales. On the other hand, free market prices were high because there were relatively few goods in circulation and, since cash holdings were large, monetary demand was high.

The difficulties created by the free market were not simply the result of the price problem, for there was considerable inefficiency in the state and cooperative sectors – many materials were simply unused. This implied, it was argued, that a freeing of the activities would increase the volume of resources available without increasing prices.

Policy conclusions: an 'organisational' focus of reform and its rationales

The 'correct' conclusions drawn from such considerations, though, were for the 'organisational' focus to change. I argue later that this was characteristic of conservative positions (p. 86).

SOEs had been encouraged to use 'by-products' (pp. 77 and 107) for some two to three years,[14] but without much success, since the state still kept low the prices they could earn, and the retained profit percentage was also too low, at 60 per cent.

Within the state sector were considerable difficulties with labour motivation. Wages were too low, and the salary structure had not been changed since 1960. There was no effective system of penalties, and in any case these could not be severe in a socialist country – SOE managers were 'not allowed to scold or beat workers'. The difficulties with labour motivation had grown sharply after 1972 (*not* 1975). Similar difficulties arose in trying to obtain non-labour resources. Higher cash payments would raise inputs, and therefore output, but would also push up prices. An interesting example was a northern soap-producing factory that was unable to secure coconut oil from the south.[15] Raw materials contracts signed between SOEs as part of the administrative supply system were not reliable; in any case, how could one penalise a supplier which simply did not have the products that it was contracted to deliver?

Party-state relations

In discussion of the system of industrial management, a number of issues came to the fore.

Party-state relations were far from being rigidly systematised. Under some circumstances a Ministry's Party Unit (*Ban can su*, previously the Party Workers' Committee) would calculate the raw materials needed to attain output targets. The Party, formally a political rather than an economic organisation, could get too deeply involved in management; it was expected to 'lead' rather than 'manage'. This confusion was not too serious, partly because people 'knew each other well'. An SOE manager could override the Party organisation within his unit, although that would only happen very rarely.

The key guiding principle of relations within organisations was that of democratic centralism – in VCP style. This meant, put simply, that superior levels had to listen to lower levels,[16] but that when a decision had been reached, 'all had to obey'. An intriguing analogy was here made with the split between the different activities of an SOE. It managed some of its products and raw materials on its own, to meet the state plan,[17] and was subject to the state in the implementation of the state's plan. The split between areas of authority was seen as an example of democratic centralism. Another field was workers' participation in decision-making, although the situation here 'was not yet good'. Another instance of democratic centralism could be found in the field of relations between SOEs and cooperatives. If an SOE should, according to the state supply plan, have obtained resources from one cooperative but favoured another, it had the freedom to ignore its previous contract so long as the ministry agreed.

The freedoms implied by this understanding of democratic centralism had already started to be felt. SOEs could search out raw materials and sell the output broadly as they wished. An example given was the Ha Dong agricultural implements factory, making children's tricycles using rubber bought from a rubber factory that it sold for a substantial profit, either to the state or privately. The SOE was also starting to make bicycle spares.

Conflicts within the bureaucracy: confusion

A striking area of confusion was the division of functions among the topmost economic organs of the Party and state, primarily the latter. Here the key technical terms were the 'owning' (*chu quan*) ministries or localities, the 'branch' (*nganh*) ministries and 'functional' (*chuc nang*) organs. The Party's organisation was far simpler. Below the Central Committee were a number of specialised economic departments, such as agriculture and industry. In principle, all Party committees were 'functional', and so there was no equivalent to the owning ministry. They corresponded to functional ministries, but often had to oversee more than one. The Industry Committee, in particular, had to oversee more than one functional ministry.

The basic difference between owning and branch ministries was as follows.

A branch was a group of SOEs with similar conditions of production, for instance the use of similar raw materials, the same types of machines or workers of equivalent skills. An SOE thus belonged to both a branch and a ministry. In general, a branch was the responsibility of a ministry – the branch ministry. Such a ministry was essentially involved with technology and planning. Such ministries had existed for many years, but had only recently started to exert themselves. Originally, they had not existed. Their ministers were in principle of the same rank as any other, but they had various ways of getting their own way, such as working through the SPC.

An owning ministry was the residual power-holder with regard to an SOE. Here its rights to control and supervise the SOE's employees and its finances were most important. When a branch ministry issued the state plan to an SOE, it had to go via the owning ministry. In assessing plan implementation, though, it had the right of direct access. It could not remove a poor management team, however, for that right remained the prerogative of the owning ministry. This made it easier to understand the distinction between 'local' (*dia Phuong*) and 'central' (*trung uong*) management (p. 24), for a locally managed SOE was essentially one where the owning functions were carried out not by a ministry, but by a province or possibly a district.[18]

The locality, however, had additional powers. A central SOE planned for a province could not simply be imposed upon it. The province had some choice over where it would be built. Since it would have to supply food and other resources such as housing and medicine for the workforce, its position was strong. Furthermore, its supervisory powers were in some ways greater than those of an owning ministry. The province dealt with Party members within the SOE, and 'led with respect to the Party'. It also organised the trade union and other MO activities – formally, everything political was dealt with at local level. Since it was responsible for security within it, and for food supplies, it had to confront 'leakages' and violation of state property rights. It was responsible for, and in a position to influence if it wished, the quasi-legal behaviour characteristic of 'aggravated shortage' and its conditionality games. The province's main weakness in its relations with a centrally managed SOE was thus usually its inability to control management.

These 'seminar' opinions contrast with the 'textbook' exposition. They are more consistent with what we can see going in on the wider arena. They confirm the reality of 'aggravated shortage' and the texture of planning, with the wide gap between textbook principles and practice. They are also suggestive as to just why the 'local' should have been more 'female' (p. 24 and note 8 on p. 47).

Reform stance in the early 1970s: organisational solutions

Within industrial ministries, an important organisational reform in 1970 had introduced two systems where there had previously only been one.

The old system divided the ministry into 'sections' (*Vu*) and 'departments' (*Cuc*). The sections took responsibility for functional areas, such as planning, labour and pay, cadre organisation, finance and raw materials. The departments directly managed production. For example, in the Ministry of Engineering and Metallurgy there had been two departments responsible for the engineering and the metallurgical SOEs respectively. This system had caused problems.

First, if there were very many SOEs, the departments simply had not coped with the administrative load placed upon them. There were often too many departments, and this imposed unnecessary staff costs.

Second, the departments were not economic organisations, and merely had planning and technical functions: they had neither money nor raw materials nor capital. They therefore tended to become rather unimportant – 'formal' – and powerless. The department was not superior to the section.

Reform had aimed to combine the functions of the sections and departments in one organisation. This was the 'union', which essentially 'replaced the department'. In the late 1970s efforts were made to set up a union to replace the Engineering Department of the Ministry of Engineering and Metallurgy. Unlike the departments, the unions had money, raw materials and capital, and the right to allocate these among their SOEs. The crucial changes were, first, that the union, unlike the department, was not dependent upon the sections; and, second, that the union had powers in the allocation of capital and raw materials between its SOEs in addition to the department's rights to issue plans and technical standards and allocate production. Although unions were based upon branches, it was not yet clear whether they should also be locally organised.

Perspectives

Orthodox opinion regarding industry and industrial organisation in the late 1970s is reasonably summarised by the above. This accepted the problems presented by the unfavourable incentives offered by the plan. Simply raising prices might improve things, but only in so far as output rose, costs fell, economic efficiency got better and the fiscal position improved. There had been little change from the earlier work done before 1975 (p. 86 et seq.). There is clear awareness of the existence of problems and a pervasive 'outside' economy.

Peripheral autonomy, of both producers and lower levels within the Party-state apparatus, was anathema but a fact of life. Attempts to coerce – either individually or collectively – did not guarantee compliance. In fact, reality rather suggested the contrary. The role and legitimacy of interests other than those of the state were thus *de facto* accepted. In a rather strange way, this was seen as a proper part of democratic centralism, in that it permitted different levels to express their interests politically. Thus the fact that the economic management system clearly did not operate cleanly and effectively matched the existence of conflicts of interest; these were not only to be expected, but were not necessarily illegitimate. It was the task of the state, as manager of the national economy, to find ways of reconciling them. However, solutions remained almost entirely organisational.

Pointers to the option of increased SOE autonomy were there, but not formally accepted. But SOEs were producing 'non-list' goods from waste materials (pp. 77 and 107) and 'list' goods where the SOE self-balanced. Marketisation processes were therefore finely referenced as sited *within* the formal planning system. This relates in its turn to the extent to which certain industrial producers remained *visibly* outside the plan, and so necessarily largely self-balancing. The language reveals much about what should have been, what was and what could be, suggesting relatively balanced relationships between the 'textbook' and the 'seminar'.

Harbingers of 'fence-breaking' – 'outside interests inside the central establishment': the local SOEs and artisanal sectors

As we have seen, our panel referred to the value of extra-plan activities and their tendency to be housed in 'workshops' (p. 60), justified in terms of their ability to generate supplements to workers' incomes. This tactic drew upon elements of classical neo-Stalinism that I now examine in greater detail.[19]

It is useful to recall the poverty of the area. With per capita GDP around the US$100–150 level, technologies that used very little fixed capital were capable, so long as inputs and valuable disposal channels were available, of being highly attractive to both producer and purchaser. Trades such as the tinker remained highly profitable, as cooking pans wore through. Many earlier studies during the French period pointed to the extensive presence of artisans with well-organised trading networks.[20] The sector was fairly large (pp. 79–80). Access to SOEs' so-called 'waste products' (**phe lieu*) offered considerable commercial potential. These could be used not only to 'push' list products into the plan (if that suited local interests) but also to support products that utilised them – the so-called 'by-products' (*phe pham*). In this way an SOE could produce 'non-list' goods outside the plan. Alternately it could form commercial relations with other units and swap or deal in such materials.

Local SOEs and the artisanat were often close to such activities, with technologies that were less 'modern', and also typically located close to farmers, who not only needed such goods but also had things to swap or sell for them.

Thus debate often circled around organisational solutions that involved better planning of SOEs and/or bringing artisanal activities either *directly* into cooperatives or somehow *within* agricultural cooperatives (Fforde, 1989). So-called socialist industry thus in fact contained two areas not directly controlled by central planners. As parts of the approved socialist economy these could not be banned, and their presence had to be tolerated. They were therefore important to the development of autonomous economic activity *outside* the formal plan. They were elements of local state industry (owned by the local authorities – primarily provinces and cities) and cooperative industry, consisting mainly of collectivised artisanal workers. There was a tendency for the technical definition of this sector to become confused with a property definition – i.e. that small-scale artisanal industry was often identified with cooperative or private production.[21] But they were of considerable interest to observers, who frequently had strong personal links to the villages where they were often sited.

Artisanal industry

For reasons at root to do with the poverty of the area, there are good grounds for supposing that small and artisanal industry (**tieu thu cong nghiep*) would play an important role in explaining the structural development of the Vietnamese economy, especially in the north. According to received dogma, this was a sector from which private property and 'capitalism' threatened to rise. The attitude taken was therefore revealing.

The sector was often associated in discussions with issues to do with 'local' industry (**cong nghiep dia Phuong*). This was the locally owned state sector, of second priority to central industry but often competing with both petty producers and the state for inputs and markets at the local level, though such boundaries could blur as deals were made. As markets grew, of course, the 'local' would start to transcend its formal definition, for example as local SOEs started to deal across the Red River delta. This process, as elsewhere, had eventually to be pushed through by the central government in the very late 1980s, thus using state power to enforce national markets (as elsewhere – Polanyi, 1975).

The situation prior to 1965

The VCP's position regarding petty industrial production for many years compromised between the desire to concentrate resources in 'priority' areas and the importance of small-scale production. Within the regional economies, low incomes and productivity meant that there was ample scope for the use of simple technologies that used relatively little capital and provided products much in demand. As the overall policy stance moved away from a strict neo-Stalinist position, non-state industry thus came to hold a rather stronger position, at least in principle.[22]

A difficulty with its expansion, however, was the distributional effects. Since its products were often easily marketable, and since input suppliers frequently possessed high-value alternative uses, the sector could command relatively high returns. This proximity to and involvement in the 'outside' economy meant that an expansion of small and artisanal industry would probably accompany and facilitate expansion of the free market, with, it was expected, adverse as well as positive effects upon the real incomes of important sectors of the population and the socio-economic basis of the DRV state.

The classical method for overcoming this dilemma was 'socialist transformation' of petty producers to bring them under better control and also, by exploiting 'conditionality' (p. 59), manage development of the free market. Thus the Fourteenth Plenum in November 1958 on the 1958–1960 Three Year Plan advocated 'development of state industry, reform [*cai tao] and development of artisanal industry and reform of capitalist industry' (NXBST, 1980: 5 et seq.).

In practice, however, these policies tended to worsen tensions as petty producers sought better terms of exchange and pushed to increase their 'outside' activities. Imposition of targets for sale at low prices to the state trading organisations was hard to enforce; materials supplied at low state prices were often diverted on to the free market. Thus the relationship between the sector and the state became the issue; reform of this so that the sector became easier to control was thus for the moment the central policy goal.

Control organs

For such units outside the state sector planners confronted a choice between directive planning and full-scale balancing. The latter would imply that adequate resources be allocated so that quantity targets could meaningfully be set. The former would entail setting looser targets. Neither was an easy option.

The central agency responsible for industrial cooperatives was the Central Cooperative Association.[23] In practice, however, the inability to coordinate input supplies centrally meant in most cases that the province or district took on supervisory responsibilities.

Development of local state industry, although of low priority, was never discouraged: in March 1960 the VCP secretariat issued order 191-CT/TW on the subject, which asserted that 'Local industry plays an increasingly important role, and needs to be reinforced and developed widely' (order 191-CT/TW: 33). Furthermore:

> We have a great potential that can be used to develop local industry – the artisanal cooperatives, private artisans, cooperating SOEs and JSP[24] enterprises. In some places there are the Army's state farms and ordinary state farms... which all make up a very good basis for the development of local industry. (Order 191-CT/TW: 37–8)

At this stage, local industry was seen as an appropriate supplier of agricultural means of production, including fertiliser, food processors etc.; consumer goods such as cloth, silk, pottery, crockery, tea-things, sugar etc.; construction materials; industrial inputs, including steel and cast iron, bauxite, coal etc., for supply to both central and local industry; and exports, for example oils, fruit, processed meat, handicrafts and art objects (order 191-CT/TW: 41).

By 1959–1960 there had apparently not yet been much progress in the socialist transformation of the large numbers of people active in petty industry. There were thought to be some 500,000 in the sector, of whom around 300,000 were either in urban areas or concentrated in specialised artisanal areas in the countryside. The remainder were closely involved in agriculture. Yet artisanal industry was producing just over 45 per cent of total gross industrial output, and had been successful in supplying inputs for the restoration of agriculture since the end of the war against the French in 1954 (NXBST, 1980: 46).[25]

This weakened arguments for its socialist transformation, and these, given in the Politburo resolution of April 1960 that called for it, are worth quoting at length:[26]

> Artisanal industry allows many peasants, petty traders and other workers to have an additional way of making a living; it helps agricultural cooperatives to develop their economic activities in many ways, reinforces the relationships between industry and agriculture, and contributes to the strength of the worker-peasant alliance...[27]
>
> But, in general artisanal industry is a backward mode of production; many of the goods produced are of poor quality and costly, and inappropriate to the rising needs of society. In addition, individual production is itself hard to stabilise, and *has a strong tendency towards the spontaneous development of capitalism*, more or less leading to differentiation in artisanal industry – precisely what happened towards the end of 1956 and the beginning of 1957. That is the shortcoming of artisanal industry. (NXBST, 1980: 46; emphasis added.)

Socialist transformation remained policy. Until the formal termination of the campaign, increasing pressure was applied to members of the artisanat, so that the sector was considered 'transformed' by the middle of 1961 (Fforde and Paine, 1987). But the Party admitted serious problems with the early stages of the movement, primarily to do with the adverse effects of collectivisation and registration upon output levels. In some areas output fell, leading to shortages of consumer goods and unemployment among the workforce (NXBST, 1980: 81, quoting 21-NQ/TW, 5 July 1961).[28] But by this stage the sector's share of total industrial output was still high, at around 40 per cent (NXBST, 1980: 82).

A key problem was the basis of the new production forms in traditional socialism's hostility to petty production. Since this attitude remained dominant, advance had naturally to be based upon improvement in the existing cooperatives and their strengthening. The call was for larger cooperatives and higher-level as opposed to lower-level forms; the existing widespread use of putting-out contracts, it was hoped, would be replaced by more formal contracting work (NXBST, 1980: 85).

The first FYP: commercialisation, 'aggravated shortage' and the response of the non-state sector – a view in hindsight

Tran Trong Huy (1967) provides useful and revealing confirmation of issues we can also access through other sources.

Although the author maintained that industrial cooperatives produced around two-thirds of local industrial output, and furthermore that the push for local self-sufficiency after 1965 had also encouraged support for the sector, it is clear from his data that the sector came under considerable pressure during the first FYP. Some provinces, he asserted, tended to view small and artisanal industry as unimportant and 'needing guidance'. He did not say which ones they were, but noted buoyant small-scale production of metal, rubber and plastic consumer goods in Hanoi, Haiphong and Thanh Hoa province. By 1965 small and artisanal industry was producing 58.6 per cent of local consumer goods output, which equalled 30.6 per cent of total industrial consumer goods output (Tran Trong Huy, 1967: 49). Small and artisanal industry supplied agriculture with 57.1 per cent of all local industry's supplies of means of production – nearly all simple tools were produced and supplied by the sector.

Tran Trong Huy (1967) concluded that small and artisanal industry, simply because of its substantial contribution, was important and so should be supported. Furthermore, dynamic effects upon growth processes occurred via technological change and the agricultural division of labour. This suggested that increased input supplies to the sector, especially of equipment, were needed – and these had to come from the state. Like many others, he criticised the putting-out (*gia cong*) system (Tran Trong Huy, 1967: 58).[29]

1965–1975: the effects of aid

During US bombing the small and artisanal sector continued to reveal its basic vitality. The data show that whereas state industry averaged between 1965 and 1974 an annual increase in gross output of nearly 6 per cent, the small and artisanal sector managed just over 4 per cent.

By 1968, when falling staples production in the north was beginning to push official indicators of gross per capita subsistence availability to below starvation levels (Fforde, 1989: 20–1), the government took measures to control inflation and the allocation of materials and output. In February 21-TTg/TN of the Premier's Office sought to reinforce control of trade and prices regarding local industry, and especially small and artisanal industry.[30] This decree traced problems back to 1961. Local industry, understood to include small and artisanal industry, had reportedly proved itself unable to move away from the 'putting-out' (*gia cong*) system to the system of managed production and material supply practised in central SOEs – 63-TTg and 3-TTg had been widely ignored (NXBST, 1978: 73).

As a sector that was still politically weak, artisanal cooperatives had been severely leaned on by local interests:

> Many places overstress the passivity of the cooperatives, and do not realise that it is their own passivity that is the root of the problem, leading at times to confrontations [between them and the cooperatives]... contracts are implemented at convenience... in a number of cooperatives there are many examples of 'passivity', such as deceptions, slipshod work, paring of raw materials, padding of costs and diversion of materials delivered for putting-out work on to the free market. (NXBST, 1978: 74)

This decree sought compliance with the basic principles of the unreformed neo-Stalinist programme, of which a deep hostility towards the free market remained a fundamental part. 100-CP, on the principles governing the financial management of small and artisanal cooperatives, supported it in the summer.

Yet through the turn of the decade this sector retained its importance. Given the levels of great poverty in the region, a tonne of cloth diverted from Chinese aid to an SOE into an industrial cooperative or artisanal group, and then, after the deals and swaps were all over, manifest in a situation where the SOE manager had a dozen shirts to give away was no small thing.

A 'proto civil society'?

Many policy-makers and their advisers were concerned about Vietnamese industry prior to 1979.[31] The classical management models were seen as weak and difficult to implement. Furthermore, systemic tensions were rooted in conflicts over resources. Macro-economic pressures exacerbated these problems. However, while this pointed to concern with the nature of allocative mechanisms, acceptable solutions remained organisational in form. These sought to smother or weaken the effects of incentives favourable to participation in 'outside' activity. But debate could not and did not escape from an economic reality within which choice was far greater than it should have been and incentives mattered.

The focus, however, was upon helping the existing planning system, via the state sector, to utilise the existing capital stock better. It was therefore inherently conservative. There was not much attention given to what an independent private sector could do in terms of economic efficiency and dynamism. This was, after all, a very poor area whose modern industrial capacity was almost entirely obtained from aid imports and sited in SOEs whose management and MO leaders were organically part of the Party-state.

The problems that were to be solved were thus 'close' to the deep interests and concerns of people who had fought to secure national independence and unity and now occupied positions in the Party-state apparatus. What, then, were their 'solutions' to these problems?

Vietnamese solutions and problems: grassroots views

The common opinion of the panel about the situation before 1979 was that the system was deeply irrational, but they thought that it resulted from war. Also, they had studied Marxist-Leninist political economy and understood that to advance to socialism they had to do it. Difficulties today, but tomorrow they would be like the USSR, rich and strong. Now they saw that this was infantile, but when they were young it was like that.

Early Vietnamese analyses: towards pro-market policy

Discussion so far confirms the gap between the apparently clear textbook ideas of traditional socialism and the practical realities of economic life. While this was fertile ground for *ad hoc* local solutions, what would be needed for new ideas to come into formal policy debates?

The Vietnamese followed no model in their change process.³² In any case, Chinese SOE reforms (rather than experiments) did not really start until well after the Vietnamese, and were initially far less thorough and wide-ranging than 25-CP (Fforde, 1999). Soviet reformers of the mid-1980s appear unaware of what had been happening in Vietnam since early 1981 (Prostiakov, 1998; Ellman and Kontorovich, 1998; Conyngham, 1982).

I turn now to look further back in time, to attempt analysis of ideas relevant to policy change in the 1980s. Two central issues can be found in these very early discussions of possible ways forward. These were the notion of 'separation' – the isolation of modern industry from the domestic economy; and a contrast between two tendencies that I call *productionist* and *distributionist* (p. ??).³³

The issue of separation is of course closely related to the consequences of an aid programme that had imported factories into a neo-Stalinist project at very low levels of GDP facing strong limits to the extent to which rice could or would be extracted from farmers. In consequence, it was hard to feed the workers and hard to find inputs from the local economy that they could use. As we have seen, in response to this the aid programme shifted towards consumer goods and industrial inputs before the end of the first FYP (1961–1965), a pattern than continued through the war.

Put this way, solutions that sought to use organisational methods, once there was sufficient tolerance of markets and 'aggravated shortage', do not look feasible. One reason was the symbiotic side to the relationship between plan and market: negotiations would take place, and out of that the planners would get something and so would many others at the table.

The problem of 'separation' – isolation of modern industry from the domestic economy

The need to attain an integration of the national economy was deeply felt. Traditional perceptions of the state had (p. 86) set attainment of a certain degree of harmony and order as an important goal. Beyond a given limit confusion and tension were signs that something was fundamentally awry, risking the view that the state was not ruling in accordance with 'natural law' (*quy luat*). In addition, there is a plausible link between national reunification and the idea of a national plan that expresses a unified national will.

However, daily life revealed tensions along a number of axes: between the plan and the market ('inside'/'outside' – *noi/ngoai*); between central and local authority (*truong uong/dia Phuong*); and between production (or base) units and their superiors (*don vi co so/cap tren*) – p. 24. Within the drive for national economic development and the war effort, the desire to reconcile these tensions was an important concern. Further, they formed the obvious building blocks of 'reformist' narratives.

However, so long as direct and autonomous horizontal relations between units of the socialist economy were literal anathema, proposals for reform of the industrial management system had to take the form of administrative changes. But so long as the macro-economic imbalances persisted, and one basic reason for this was the forced development of sectors that would not be supported by voluntary exchange with domestic suppliers, organisational means had to be found to override unfavourable incentives and somehow drive resources into the input-constrained state economy. The profound shifts in relative incomes and politico-economic power implied by a shift to a more incentive-based system were not (yet) acceptable.

Prior to 1979 reform and debate thus concentrated upon three broad areas:

- the internal organisation of production units;
- the administrative relationships of production units, both with higher levels and with other production units, both horizontally (*ngang*) and vertically (*doc*);
- the conditions under which production units acquired and disposed of economic resources – supply (*cung cap*) and disposal (*tieu thu*).

Early policy debates

By the 1970s[34] many policy-makers viewed the state of the North Vietnamese industrial management system as deeply unsatisfactory. The important speech by Le Duan in 1970 was a call for reform, and in agriculture this resulted in the highly centralising policy package known as the 'new management system' for cooperatives (Fforde, 1982, 1989) adopted after 1974. From the start of the 1970s there is evidence of efforts to devise proposals for reform throughout the DRV economy well before the end of the war.

Le Duan stressed the slogan of the advance from 'small-scale production to large-scale socialist production'. This was asserted to be based upon a correct and scientific analysis of the Vietnamese situation. It had great dogmatic weight. Coming after the agrarian 'three-contracts controversy' of the late 1960s (p. 31), and in the light of the spontaneous erosion of the planning system described here with the term 'aggravated shortage', Le Duan's position in favour of organisational solutions is not hard to appreciate.

This bore policy fruit in state industrial organisation with measures culminating in the 1977 statute for state industrial enterprises (Le Thanh Nghi, 1977a). A clear marker was 19-CP of 29 January 1976 on 'Reorganising the organisation of production, bring order in one step into economic management, create the conditions for – and demand that – each SOE and each worker implements well the 1976 state plan'.

'Productionism' and 'distributionism'

In the early 1970s debates about the causes and nature of the problems facing industry were already surfacing.

The study edited by Nguyen Tri (1972a) highlighted a number of points.[35] The deep split between *productionists* and *distributionists* was to recur through the coming years. This broad classification in a confusing debate can be seen as a sharp difference in the emphasis and value placed upon direct central control, and so also upon the level of autonomy at the 'base' (*don vi co so*), meaning the SOE as well as the industrial and agricultural cooperatives.

In a classical neo-Stalinist manner, productionism asserted that the basic problem facing industry (and indeed the economy) was organisational, and in particular the organisation of production. Integration of different production units, and the efficient and effective coordination of their activities, were therefore to be resolved by the correct choice of organisation rather than by an examination of the relative value of different allocative mechanisms.

Decentralisation therefore meant giving lower levels greater responsibility for interpreting and implementing the plan. *Productionists* assumed that the informational and other costs involved in such centralised coordination of activities were low, and that the costs of issuing the wrong instructions were also not very high. If people would only go along with the central idea, things would work out and the nation could act as one, with strength concentrated rather than dissipated. One particularly clear example was the attempt to solve difficulties arising from the coordination of producers by establishing organisations to integrate them directly (e.g. the unions, p. 75). This encouraged support for mechanisms to link industrial cooperatives directly to the SOE they supplied.[36]

Such a view is opposed to those termed here *distributionalist*, which assert the importance of incentive structures and therefore the role played by different allocative mechanisms, of which the plan-market dichotomy was central. Downplaying the implementability and rationality of any central idea that 'sought to manage everything', distributionalists had to take a sceptical approach to their ability to understand precisely what was occurring in the economy. Long experience with the unimplementability of economic policy had taught them much about the limited validity of received neo-Stalinist theory.

Since one did not know precisely what went on in any given SOE, it followed that the industrial economy was operating with considerable *de facto* peripheral autonomy on a day-to-day basis.

In trying to establish what did happen, the pattern of local incentives – and therefore the role of unplanned activities – was of primary importance. For distributionalists, therefore, advocacy of centralisation or decentralisation depended upon the view taken of the likely results in terms of immediate economic goals rather, and here they differ sharply from the productionists, than subordination of the economic system to a central idea. They were therefore pragmatic, interested in 'life' (**cuoc song*) and often enthusiastic about both variation and signs of local autonomy and creativity. For such people, 'confusion' (**lon xon*) and 'spontaneity' (**tu phat*) were often positives rather than negatives.

The distinction between these two tendencies was far from being the sole important difference. The basically idealistic nature of the productionists' position often gave them considerable polemical power, for the more realist position adopted by their opponents, coupled with the complexity and confusion of DRV industry itself, meant that distributionalists had to work hard so long as they had no clear alternative model to offer,[37] which I think they had managed to do by the mid-1980s. This was no mean feat.

The political hegemony of the neo-Stalinist position gave support to the productionists, whose influence could only begin to wane when that ended. One of the most important aspects of the Sixth Plenum of August 1979 was that it greatly energised that process. It should be noted here, however, that the distributionist position was somewhat narrow and economic, focused on advance from the 'here and now', which while giving it strength in certain contexts weakened it in others. What political developments could or should be set in train to match the economic changes? What would a 'Party without the plan' look like? What could or should then be the role of the state, the base upon which the VCP rested? But in the 1960s and 1970s this was far in the future.

The 1972 Economics and Planning University study: awareness of problems without politically valid options

In his introduction to the 1972 EPU[38] collection, Nguyen Tri (1972b) provides an exposition of problems facing industrial organisation and their possible solutions. According to him, the two basic 'laws' of socio-economic change in socialist Vietnam were the law of the centralisation of production and the law of the advance from small-scale to large-scale production.[39] Granted this statement of doctrine, what could follow?

These laws were (Nguyen Tri maintained) superficially similar to those of capitalist development, but, since they were occurring under socialist conditions, were in essence quite different. In North Vietnam centralisation processes were both complicated and extremely difficult. This appears to me as a strong attack upon the viable extent of central planning.

Thus advance in the social division of labour to accompany economic development would happen 'low down' – at the base. As there already existed a substantial artisanat of family-based and scattered producers in addition to the modern factories, the key problem was to raise employment and reduce the proportion of social labour needed to support the population as a whole ('necessary labour'). *Such a strategy would have to rely upon low-level technology.*

There were two key issues: first, building a close alliance between family artisanal work and SOEs; second, organising industrial production inside agricultural cooperatives (Nguyen Tri, 1972b: 7). Both problems meant exploiting the potential for higher productivity by increasing the division of labour in the economy. The latter, however, was still contentious, although said to be official policy (Nguyen Tri, 1972b: 8). *Many people apparently still believed that industrial accumulation and growth should only occur outside agriculture.*

This shows very clearly the direction of industrial reform in the very early 1970s, and its superficially orthodox nature. The author is both puzzled and concerned, and not too chary of pointing to important issues that threaten various shibboleths. The hostility felt towards small-scale production, and its corollary, support for large-scale organisation, narrowed for the moment the rhetorical space to changes in organisation. As a necessary evil, small-scale petty production had to be tolerated, since there was no real alternative. Control had to be found by integrating it into the state sector vertical structures – in other words, giving such producers over to their customers for more direct control under the form of putting-out relations, or perhaps a union. Similarly, the solution to the problems of state industry was to be found in the reallocation of SOEs to branch ministries.

Thus allocative mechanisms were to be altered only in two limited senses: first, by changes within the centrally planned system itself; and second, by extending the boundaries of that system. There was no discussion of the possibility for expansion of the existing but illegal autonomous horizontal links between SOEs, and between them and units outside the plan, characteristic of 'aggravated shortage'.

Although it was party policy, many were still hostile to any development of industry within agricultural cooperatives, and therefore to investment by them in industry of resources that, it was obviously thought, would otherwise be free for the state's use.[40] The tensions are obvious.

Local industry in economic policy

Nguyen Tri's (1972a) contributions place him in an intermediate position. Nguyen Lang (also at the EPU) in a number of pieces, the earliest of which dates from 1969 – although he was still actively publishing in 1985 – took a different position, thoroughly productionist. Both were on the staff of the Industry Department. Nguyen Lang's contribution to the 1972 study is discussed below, but here mention should be made of an earlier piece on the structure of local industry (Nguyen Lang, 1969). This, from a conservative, reveals much of the sector's underlying dynamism.

He points out that local industry had continued to grow despite US bombing (a near 6 per cent annual growth in gross industrial output – Nguyen Lang, 1969: 73), with faster growth in mechanical engineering, fertilisers and chemicals and food processing. Particular provinces, such as Ha Tinh, Thanh Hoa and Nam Ha, had seen buoyant growth.

In some provinces local state industry had started from scratch, as in Hoa Binh (later part of Ha Son Buon), Yen Bai and Lao Cai. Local industry had received supplies of capital, equipment, cadres and workers from the Party and state, but had been unable to use these efficiently.

Economic results were poor, and many products were unusable and 'could not be disposed of' (*khong *tieu thu duoc*). There had been overinvestment, in that many new factories could not operate because of materials' shortages, while important artisanal products were not being produced – for example, the conical hats worn by women (Nguyen Lang, 1969).

The above comments are of great interest, and the analysis of the origins of the difficulties is revealing. The author focuses almost entirely upon the 'irrational' way in which the structure of local industry had been fixed in many places; a rational structure, as he seems to understand it, would enable the branch to play its leading role in the local economy. For Nguyen Lang, rationality derives from a harmony in certain relationships. Thus the basis for fixing a rational structure was as follows (Nguyen Lang, 1969: 75 et seq.).

First, it had to be aimed at meeting local needs (especially mass consumption) as well as those of the country as a whole and exports. This would ease the existing imbalance between light and heavy industry.

Second, there had to be an effective relationship between the centrally run industrial branches and the locality's principle industrial and non-industrial branches.

Third, there had to be an effective division of labour between regions, based upon primary resource availability, production traditions or other characteristics. Nguyen Lang stressed that there was no contradiction between local specialisation and the division of responsibilities between the localities and the centre.

While the above may superficially appear as unrealistic and infeasible, it is nevertheless a good example of a productionist approach that seeks to establish a central idea, in this case of a rational local industrial structure, around which may be constructed both a political compromise and an improvement in industrial organisation. But the focus remained upon essentially organisational solutions.

Reintegration of artisanal industry – two views

Nguyen Lang's two contributions to Nguyen Tri (1972a) followed a similar vein. One argued strongly for the positive value of petty production when combined properly with state industry (Nguyen Lang and Nghiem Phu Ninh, 1972a). The piece identified two ways of doing this. The first, and here the example given was clothing, was essentially a form of putting-out work (**gia cong*) superficially similar to that under the capitalist conditions described by Marx, but arguably quite different. The arguments are interesting (Nguyen Lang and Nghiem Phu Ninh, 1972a: 100–3).

While capitalism used putting-out to increase exploitation (in the Marxist sense), in the DRV such arrangements would use people who would not otherwise be employed in production; pay sufficient to the workers to raise their incomes;[41] and permit the SOE to concentrate upon those links (*khau*) of the production process where it was most effective, thereby again raising incomes. Again, while under capitalist conditions putting-out was a strategy to bring women and children into the labour force, under socialism the aim was not to exploit them, although putting-out methods were a valuable way of absorbing labour and such elements as street hooligans (Nguyen Lang and Nghiem Phu Ninh, 1972a: 103). Finally, the creation of dependency inherent in capitalist putting-out was simply absent under socialist conditions.

The authors therefore simultaneously argue for the positive value of petty production and the possibility of exploiting it under socialist organisational forms by the creation and encouragement of cooperation between such producers and SOEs that would be based upon putting-out mechanisms. Apart from the example of clothing already cited, the authors mention textiles, bookbinding and syringes as products where such methods were in use.

The second form of combination was also based upon putting-out contracts, but used the services of a trading company as an intermediary. Examples here were sleeping mats and knitting. This method, though, posed doctrinal-theoretical problems since there was no organisational basis in production. The authors maintained that the rationale for such contracts was essentially to do with SOE interests, as they could result in savings in the value of capital invested by the SOE while they did not increase the SOE's cost price (*gia thanh*) (Nguyen Lang and Nghiem Phu Ninh, 1972a: 106–7).

This paper makes other interesting observations. Artisanal activities had 'grown strongly' in both rural and urban areas during recent years (Nguyen Lang and Nghiem Phu Ninh, 1972a: 105). The tone tends to confirm a rather buoyant autonomous development which the authors have, in some sense, to reinterpret in doctrinal terms. Thus they state that 'in recent years' a number of SOEs had started to use putting-out methods in response to a demand for children's clothes (Nguyen Lang and Nghiem Phu Ninh, 1972a: 113), allowing families to make the sleeves, collars, buttonholes and buttons. Family output reportedly rose rapidly as a result. But while there was great potential, some of which arose from the inability of SOEs to operate efficiently, with by-products otherwise wasted (here a glaring example was sawmills), many people were deeply distrustful of anything that encouraged putting-out work.

Such opinions encountered conservative arguments that putting-out activities should be treated like private sector activity, and therefore there should be no cash payments, close registration of the people involved and high taxation (Nguyen Lang and Nghiem Phu Ninh, 1972a: 115). The authors disagreed with this.[42]

The second area where artisanal activity could legitimately be encouraged (in doctrinal terms) was within the agricultural cooperatives, the subject of Nguyen Lang and Nghiem Phu Ninh (1972b). Debate about this seems to have been intense, and stimulated by the Nineteenth Plenum of February 1971. Many cooperatives had established such activities; by the late 1970s it was orthodoxy (Fforde, 1989).

Early debates and their meaning

There was deep concern over development policy, openly expressed. VCP opinion was greatly divided.

The discussion shows that the fundamental question of incentives had become the 'King Charles' head' of the debate. Organisational solutions were presented as ways of overcoming plan unimplementability. The distributionist position, which at root asserted that incentives had to be respected, was there on the table, waiting for conditions to be right for it to be able to be developed into viable policy. In this way we can see (to look ahead) why the frequent slogan of reform policy in the early 1980s was to 'free up the base' – to allow SOEs to do what they wanted, trusting that this would benefit the economy.

Grassroots views: the situation before 1975

The common opinion of the panel was that before 1979 the main factors influencing policy were as follows.

Central was the old model of socialism in the USSR. This was continually praised in the press, which asserted the richness and strength of the USSR and its victory in the Second World War. As a result, people believed in it. Everybody thought that the difficulties were temporary, and with efforts the future would make Vietnam like the USSR.

Also, in 1975 when the south was liberated the Party became doubly proud of the superiority of the Soviet model. This made the cadres as well as the people believe even more in the line and policies of the Party at that time. Aid from the USSR was large, and restored the Vietnamese economy after the war.

Contradictions between Vietnam and China, the border war with Cambodia and in the early 1970s the border war in the north took Vietnam again into conflict. People easily accepted the difficulties and believed that the Party's line – central planning – was suitable.

The subsidy system on the one hand constrained development, but on the other contributed to the peace of mind of workers and staff, strengthening the system of centralised bureaucracy. Workers were proud that the state paid attention to them, that they could buy rice, pork, cooking fuel and fuel at low prices (with ration coupons). They mistakenly thought this was the superiority of socialism and that the system of centralised bureaucratic management was a necessary part of the advance to socialism. This made policy-makers more careful when discussing proposals to abolish the two-price system, for if this was to be done then the working class and the cadres – the pillars of society – would suffer most.

These views suggest strongly that the main political forces within the system were the perceptions and interests of 'insiders' – SOE workers and cadres. It follows that, as the incentives they experienced shifted, so would politicians.

Conclusions

These arguments suggest that what was really needed for greater policy tolerance of market forces within the state sector included ideas to improve SOE marketisation *without* attacking socialist taboos, especially planning; change to macro-incentives that would push 'fence-breaking' (*pha rao) and shift the parameters of 'aggravated shortage' so as to increase the numbers of SOEs engaged in market activity, whose patrons would then, all other things being equal, support them against orders to stop (as they had been doing already); and peak political conditions that would protect even these conservative steps against high-level condemnation (unlike the late 1960s' three-contracts controversy – p. 31).

Traditional Vietnamese socialism and conservative policy: towards tedium?

In Chapter 1 I commented on the influence of traditional thinking upon Vietnamese socialism (p. 56). Themes of harmony, quasi-totalitarian national unification through the plan and hostility towards markets ran through the debate prior to 1979.

The discussion has shown the limited acceptability of small-scale production to policy-makers, in favour of the creation of a 'working class' based upon SOEs. It has also pointed to the strong tendency of petty production to grow up spontaneously within and outside the socialist sectors. It is worth noting that this is not condemned greatly in mainstream texts produced and published by official institutions such as the EPU/NEU. The extent of the market was in part set by the limits upon the use of the police and security apparatus to enforce neo-Stalinist dominance of distribution and exchange. This was one reason why it was so extensive compared to neo-Stalinist norms. Policy sought to support state industry and, through organisational reforms designed to combine petty production directly with socialist institutions, to bring it under control. It was therefore consistent with the basic tenets of Vietnamese communism at the time.

The productionist position asserted that the solution to the difficulties facing industry was to be found in managed top-down organisational and institutional change. It was dominant. Small-scale industry, with its latent and often actual potential for expansion under Vietnamese conditions, was thus only to be encouraged in so far as it was closely integrated into the two key neo-Stalinist forms: the SOEs and cooperatives. There was hostility to the notion that petty producers could be progressive in the absence of such control. Cunning exposition was therefore required if a critique was to be mounted.

A basic tenet of official doctrine was the historically necessary nature of the advance from small-scale to large-scale production. One aspect of this was the so-called 'law of centralisation of production' (p. 88) which formed the basis of Vu Ngoc Hoanh (1972). Arguing that the organisation of production had to be appropriate to the 'stage of development', he referred to Le Duan's (1968) study as calling for effective planning of post-war economic development.

In fact, this author had a sceptical attitude to the value of centralisation as a universal means for raising output, and implicitly questioned its value as a 'law'. Furthermore, he asserted that it was only really of use once the level of specialisation had reached a sufficiently high level (Vu Ngoc Hoanh, 1972: 27), and that prematurely increasing centralisation led to higher costs, most importantly in the areas of transport and administration.

His stress upon specialisation then allowed him to support the development of artisanal activities on the grounds that they could, if integrated into some sort of organisational framework involving cooperatives or SOEs, represent a consolidation of an improved division of labour in the economy.

Ngo Dinh Giao (1972) discussed the internal organisation of SOEs in the high-priority engineering sector. Again, he blamed poor performance upon weak organisation (Ngo Dinh Giao, 1972: 49).

Examination of investment during the first FYP revealed how the main determinant of asset allocation had been bureaucratic and political rather than economic. For instance, the Ministry of Engineering and Metallurgy only managed some 14 per cent of all engineering factories; the Chemical Department managed 32 per cent of chemical plants; the Forestry Department had only 54 per cent of factories exploiting wood; and the Ministry of Construction managed around 60 per cent of factories producing construction materials. There were some 1,000 SOEs (Le Huy Phan and Ho Phuong, 1972: 160 et seq.).

In fact, centrally owned SOEs were scattered around functional and non-functional ministries and departments. Local SOEs were either owned by the provincial or city industry offices or, even worse, by transport, communication or trading organs. Interestingly, though, this scattering allowed a comparison of the economic results obtained with the same resources by different 'owners', and these varied enormously.

The administrative supply system had created a widespread psychosis of 'dependency' (*y lai) upon the state and had not stimulated plan fulfilment. But the sheer ineffectiveness of the central-planning apparatus meant that SOEs could not rely upon the central authorities even to know clearly what resources they would need to fulfil the production plan (Le Huy Phan and Ho Phuong, 1972: 165). The Party had to tolerate SOEs' *de facto* autonomy.

Despite this understanding of the situation, the solution offered followed the line and remained organisational and bureaucratic. Use of the ubiquitous unions (pp. 75 and 86), coupled with orderly organisation of the ministries themselves, was seen as the way to increase output and efficiency. A crucial aspect was the formal centralisation of the right to issue instructions in one place within the ministry, plus a strengthening of the notion that the plan was binding upon the ministry as well as the SOE. Thus:

> From now on, only the Minister has the right to issue plan indicators and to change them... these are legally binding upon both the SOE and the Departments of the Ministry; for example, the Finance Department has to ensure that the SOE is supplied with

enough capital, and the Materials Department that it has adequate inputs. (Le Huy Phan and Ho Phuong, 1972: 177)

Existing legislation, however, already stipulated that 'The responsible organs must ensure that there is an appropriate materials supply plan when they issue a production duty' (*nhiem vu)[43] (120-HDCP, 3 August 1967, quoted in To Duy, 1969: 46). *It is reasonable to conclude that this was inoperative.*

Dragon's teeth?

Such optimism regarding the efficacy of organisational integration contrasts with the actual experiences of the engineering branch documented by Ngo Dinh Giao (1972).[44] This was a branch where a great variety of techniques had to be used to produce a wide range of products. The production process appeared to lend itself to a rational analysis in terms of production links (*khau). It was therefore disappointing to observe that labour, which was subject to a complicated system of skill categorisation, was often not used rationally – highly skilled people often did low-skilled jobs, and vice versa (Ngo Dinh Giao, 1972: 53). SOEs often did not bother to work out their need for skilled labour properly. Poor planning was blamed for the existence of storming cycles, time-wasting and poor output quality observed in some factories (Ngo Dinh Giao, 1972: 63). A dire picture was painted.

Formal policy change – early legislation on state industrial management

Reform prior to 1979–1980 can be divided into two stages by reference to the 1977 statute on state industrial enterprises, which marked a statement of the desired path forward comparable to the legislation of 1976 on policy towards the agricultural producer cooperatives. After the 1976 Fourth Party Congress the VCP appeared, to a limited extent, to have re-established some sort of order and direction into industrial policy.

Reform before 1977 can be dated back at least to the Nineteenth Plenum of February 1971.[45] According to Ho Phuong (1977), the Nineteenth Plenum could only call for order in large-scale engineering factories as a solution for the acute problems there. Prior to this plenum there had been experiments in a number of areas, for instance to do with the establishment of the 'three funds' system on an experimental basis, which apparently derived from a secretariat resolution of November 1969. This was then legally supported by 236-CP of 10 December 1970 (EPU, 1975: 325). EPU (1979) dated the reform of SOE management to 1969, as did Le Huy Phan and Ho Phuong (1972: 163).

Some sources trace formal policies on decentralisation from a Party decree in January 1968 (EPU, 1979) and there was certainly some legislation on this topic even earlier (e.g. 119-CP of 1 August 1967). Problems with the relations between levels within the hierarchical state structure were to dog reform, and were reportedly dealt with in some length in the Council of Ministers' report to the National Assembly in 1970.[46] Legislation supporting the creation of product groups dates from 1970, in the form of 274-TTg of 26 December 1970 (Le Thanh Binh, 1972).

The Twentieth Plenum of April 1972 and the Twenty-second Plenum of April 1974 also marked activity in the field. The former's role in inspiring early steps is confirmed by such sources as Nguyen Nien (1974a),[47] who asserted that the Nineteenth, Twentieth and Twenty-second Plena all sought to attack the administrative supply system. According to Nguyen Nien, the 1972 Twentieth Plenum sought a reinforcement of Party control over the economy from top to bottom, and better administrative effectiveness. Its resolution sought to:

> Overthrow the administered supply system of management; abolish an artisanal [*thu cong] and scattered way of organising management that is in the style of small-scale production; construct the way of organising management of large-scale production that aims to stimulate the transition of the national economy from small-scale production to large-scale socialist production. (Quoted in 525-HDCP, 23 June 1975.)

As policy formulations developed, the Twenty-second Plenum inspired such theoretical studies as Ta Nhu Khue (1974) and Hoang Quoc Viet (1974). Nguyen van Tran (1974: 5) stated bluntly that 'Socialist industrialisation, the key link of the process of socialist construction and transformation [*cai tao], had not been firmly grasped and implemented fully and actively in accordance with the line and direction of the Party.' Vu Khien and Vu Quoc Tuan (1974) wrote that the plenum stressed the legally obligatory nature of the plan. According to Hoang Quoc Viet (1974) the plenum was strongly opposed to small-scale production, advocating a 'unification of the principal of management by branch and by territory'. And so on...

In hindsight, much of this legislation and policy-making activity is most interesting in its analysis of the attempt to implement the neo-Stalinist programme in North Vietnam. Its rhetoric of a strong line, within which there was yet considerable autonomy for local initiative, reflected the need to come to terms with the *de facto* decentralisation of the planning system that had occurred during the first FYP. This was reflected in the literature and pointed towards radical policy ideas (and valid interpretations of reality even if policy was awry). The basic neo-Stalinist programme was, however, unchanged.

But the policy explosion that followed the economic crisis of 1979–1980 drew upon ideas visible in these early measures. They come conveniently under three main headings, dealing with:

- aspects of organisational relations between levels of the state planning system;
- the internal organisation of SOEs;
- the small and artisanal production units usually brought together in the industrial cooperatives.

I now deal with these issues.

The trap opens: early attempts at the reform of superior levels

It is natural to blame poor planning on poor planners, and natural for poor planners to blame other parts of the bureaucracy. Organisational definitions of the problem lead to organisational definitions of solutions. From the early 1970s until 1979 these themes dominated policy, and it has to be said that they are very dull.

Internal reform of the state planning system: 1973 and the attempted assertion of state authority through 172-CP

172-CP (1 November 1973) issued a statute on the organisation of the Council of Ministers and regulations 'On the duties, rights and responsibilities of ministries in the area of economic management'. This was later supplemented by 24-CP (2 February 1976) that issued regulations 'On the duties, rights and responsibilities of the provincial level of state government in the area of economic management'. Both of these were published in the lengthy collection of *Economic Management Law – Basic State Regulations* (NXBST, 1976) which responded to 19-CP (29 January 1976) on the wide-ranging economic reform mentioned above (p. 86).

In a formally highly centralised system, such documents aimed to provide a foundation for orderly relations between some of the most important constituent elements of the state: ministries, provinces and the Council of Ministers. As such, the natural expectation is for them to provide clear and relatively unambiguous guidance to the resolution of conflicts of interest and other problems. The existence of a considerable degree of *de facto* autonomy within the formally highly centralised system made this all the more important. Thus:

> Being the executive organ of the highest responsible organs of the state and its highest administrative organ, the Council of Ministers[48] manages every aspect of social life correctly in accordance with the line and policy of the Party and the law of the state; it organises implementation of every resolution of the Central Executive Committee of the Party and of the National Assembly. (NXBST, 1976: 40)

But things were, as we have seen, far from orderly. There was, for example, no clear resolution of the tension between local and central authority:

> In the organisation and management of the national economy, it is necessary to harmonise the principle of [management by] the branch [*nganh*] with that of [management by] the locality [*dia phuong*]. This is realised in the harmonisation of Ministerial management of technico-economic branches throughout the country with management by administrative Committees at appropriate levels in each administrative region. Management by branch must always be in harmony with management at the appropriate [local] level. (NXBST, 1976: 41–2)

The document explicitly states that departments and companies in the localities were simultaneously responsible to the 'head' ministry (*Bo Chu quan*) and the provincial People's Committees 'In accordance with the principle of dual leadership' (NXBST, 1976: 55). The minister nevertheless had certain important rights and responsibilities with regard to activities belonging to the branch but carried out in SOEs that were directly managed by the province (NXBST, 1976: 55 et seq.).

These measures in principle placed the branch ministry in a powerful position. This is confirmed by the rights and duties of the provincial People's Committees (NXBST, 1976: 56 et seq.). These rights were not great, and were limited essentially to a committee giving its opinion on the plan of each economic unit situated within it that had an impact upon the general plan of the locality, as well as other aspects of the branch such as the establishment, dissolution and siting of central SOEs. Its duties, however, were many, and reduced in effect to making every effort to enable the centrally managed SOE to fulfil its plan. As we have seen, however, evidence suggests that local authorities had their own sources of power. Policy was thus inconsistent.

The meaning of state industrial reform prior to 1979

It is not a great oversimplification to view such legislation, and indeed the overall tenor of reform prior to 1979, as simply an attempt at recentralisation – to assert the subordination of the local authorities to those of the centre – carefully defined as the branch (*nganh*) ministries rather than head ministries (*Bo Chu quan*), which were in effect comparable to the provinces in the desired power structure. From this perspective it is not surprising that the legislators also liked to point out that organs of the state had to use legal methods (NXBST, 1976: 42). This could be funny: ministers who could not attend the monthly meetings of the full council had to 'report to the Premier' (NXBST, 1976: 46).

A main aim of state management was to 'reinforce the all-round, centralised and united management function throughout the entire country of the Council of Ministers, as well as its managerial power over the entire national economy and every social activity' (NXBST, 1976: 43). Also included was the intention to strengthen the rights and responsibilities of economic units – SOEs, cooperatives, enterprise associations, unions, companies etc. (NXBST, 1976: 44); *this, however, was subordinate to the drive to assert central authority.*

A key organ of central economic authority was the SPC, which was given responsibility for preparing the most important general balances for approval by the Council of Ministers. It had the right to approve, in the name of the council, material balances set up by ministries and localities. The latter were to approve balances for items outside the centrally managed 'list' (see note 13 on p. 113). The SPC also had the right to give its opinion on major plan balances that were the direct responsibility of functional ministries and other departments (NXBST, 1976: 77–8). 'When necessary', the SPC could regulate directly the plans of branches or localities to ensure that they were in accordance with the quarterly and monthly state plan (NXBST, 1976: 79).

There was some attempt to balance the interests of ministries and localities. The branch plan, once approved by the Premier, was divided into tasks to be carried out by the branch ministry and those that were the responsibility of the province (NXBST, 1976: 79). The ministry was responsible for constructing and implementing the branch's plan, including material balances and concrete indicators. It allocated plan targets to centrally managed economic units within the branch, including SOEs; it was also meant to guide and direct the departments and companies of the localities in implementing the local part of the branch's plan (NXBST, 1976: 80). While the provinces and cities appeared to have a strong residual position, in that they set up their own general development plans, their legal position was not strong, and they were enjoined to 'Fulfil their duties to supply to the centre (labour, materials, staples, food and other goods), while simultaneously meeting as well as possible the consumption and cultural needs of their populations' (NXBST, 1976: 82).

This framework is one within which the desire for strong central control has clearly to coexist with a respect for peripheral autonomy and wishes. Apart from the localities, the other important peripheral institution was naturally the production unit itself, whether state or cooperative. These were primarily seen as simply the recipients of plan instructions.

The issue of the 'branch'

A crucial element of this organisational reform was the rationalisation of industrial asset ownership and use through the strengthening of branch (*nganh*) ministries. This, it was hoped, would coordinate more effectively the activities of SOEs allocated to them on the basis of their similar or related technologies. This posed the immediate problem of the precise basis upon which this was to be done, and there was debate about this. Many felt the lack of an unambiguous 'scientific' framework for taking such decisions. Similar arcane questions arose in pondering the technical foundation for other forms of organisational integration, such as the unions.

'Reform' on the eve of reunification – plan indicators

A further attempt to clarify and systematise these relationships occurred in 1975 with the issue of 135-CP, 'Promulgation of a system of legally binding plan indicators for the 1976 state plan' (*Cong Bao*, 1975). Formally, these orders were issued either by the Premier or the SPC – mostly the former. Examination of the list reveals the depth and scope of the economic power sought by central authority.

These two authorities could formally issue plan instructions to two types of institution.

The first type of institution was ministries or departments.[49] This section was again divided into two categories. First there were the orders to 'head' ministries; by this was meant those central organs that retained production installations from a variety of different branches. For such organs, the plan orders covered nine main headings (*Cong Bao*, 1975: 199–201).

- Production, construction, distribution and transport. These include values, mainly of output, but also including new capital installation; materials, both produced and sold; goods received and delivered, including transactions between ministries; and transport activity.
- Exports in value and volume.
- Technology and primary exploration.
- Basic investment, including changes in the capacity of the existing stock.
- Materials.
- Labour and wages. This covered the total number of workers, the wage funds and the planned growth in labour productivity.
- Training and allocation of cadres and workers.
- Cost prices and distribution expenses.
- Accumulation. This included profits.

The second category was for organs classified as planning by branch (*Cong Bao*, 1975: 201–4). Here were included certain functional organs such as the Ministry of Domestic Trade. In total there were 18 such organs.

The second type of institution was People's Committees of provinces or cities. The system of plan orders applicable to provinces and cities was divided into two, making a distinction between the economy directly managed by the locality and the territorial economy (*Cong Bao*, 1975: 204–7). The former were similar to the plan instructions issued to non-branch ministries and departments. They included agricultural and forestry output as well as the value and volume of goods to be procured. For local industry, two plan targets were handed down from the centre: the value of local industrial output and the physical output of various goods. Detailed orders covered local trade, investment, materials supply, labour and wages. It is interesting to note that these covered the training of workers and cadres.[50]

The position of local authorities vis-à-vis *central government: 24-CP*

Policy was ambitious in its attempts to bring local authorities under control. 172-CP (1 November 1973) was supported by another decree that dealt solely with the provinces' role in economic management – 24-CP (2 February 1976). This confirmed, with other legislation, the unchanging direction of policy in 1975–1976. One of the intentions of this legislation was to ensure that there would be effective material balances at both central and local levels – an indication that the authority sought by 172-CP had not been forthcoming.

24-CP asserted the 'objective necessity' of combining management by branch with management by locality (NXBST, 1976: 119–20), and the locality's responsibility for securing consumption goods supplies to those people working within its geographical area. The locality's rights to organise and manage its own staff and cadres were made explicit (NXBST, 1976: 127) – thus, power over the local nomenklatura (*sic*) (Dang Phong and Beresford, 1998).

This legislation therefore sought to strengthen the position of the centre *vis-à-vis* the localities while encouraging the latter to formalise their *de facto* independence with a more sophisticated and detailed examination of their own resources and medium-term potential. By encouraging such trends while strengthening the rights of the centre it would be possible to create the local resource flows needed to supply the 'complementary inputs' required by central industry. Of these, wage goods took high priority.

The overall planning framework remained neo-Stalinist in the low attention paid to material incentives. The stress upon organisational change implicitly assumed that conflicts over resource allocation would be resolved within the administrative structures of the Party and state. Policy remained inconsistent and clearly infeasible.

The direction of state industrial planning reform in the early 1970s – the trap

From this legislation and discussion three main conclusions can be reached.

First, the system is formally based upon a philosophy of command; superior levels issue orders to inferiors that carry moral and coercive force. This is assumed to energise the system and lead to progress; without top-down direction production will not develop. The model appears militaristic and obedience is required by discipline. In practice strong elements of negotiation enter, but these are *outside* the formal system.

Second, the legislation is precocious. It does not provide a realistic guide to managing the planning system in general and the industrial sector in particular. There is a striking absence of prerequisites for an effectively functioning system. For example, there are few clear guidelines as to how grey areas are to be resolved. Much of the language is exhortational.

Finally, the documents tend to confirm the basic conservatism, combined with a degree of acceptance of local and peripheral authority. Thus the widely ignored plan instructions were seen, on a day-to-day basis, as part of bargaining between and within various levels of the socialist economy. It was therefore quite consistent for the academic commentators cited earlier to view problems and solutions in terms of changes in this formal structure, centred around organisational solutions and without clear analysis of the balance of incentives. There is almost no discussion of any macro-economic or efficiency-based reasons for the isolation of state industry from rational and reasonably voluntary relations with the rest of the domestic economy. There is also very little acceptance in the legislation of the systematic non-observance of legal instructions that was characteristic. Like state industry, formal principles of economic management were deeply isolated from day-to-day realities. More realistic thinking, however, arose in policy towards the non-state sector.

Early experience with commercialisation – policy towards the non-state sector before 1979

The political significance of local party and state organs and the role of the non-state sector during the first FYP, 1961–1965

As the ambitious and unrealistic development programme of the first FYP progressed, mounting pressure on input suppliers tended to reinforce the dominant view that the non-state sector should remain firmly subordinate to SOEs. This is confirmed by the Seventh Plenum of June 1962, where the political strength behind the priority attached to key central 'heavy' industries is clearly evident. The Eighth Plenum of April 1963 held even more strongly to this line, stressing that 'It is essential to concentrate even more upon investment in industry, and above all in the principle heavy industrial branches' (NXBST, 1976: 141).

But towards the end of the first FYP policy increasingly allowed the relative advantages possessed by small and artisanal producers. In 1964 Politburo resolution 105-NQ/TW was critical of previous policies that had underplayed the value of local and small-scale industry (NXBST, 1976: 161). It called for a balance between the various sectors, with, in essence, each having to rely upon its own resources. With food supplies becoming increasingly strained, this implied that central industry situated in poorer provinces would, unless of very high priority, probably face great difficulties. Concrete policies adopted at this time reveal the beginnings of a compromise position with regard to the artisanal cooperatives; these are worth stating in some detail (NXBST, 1976: 178 et seq.). First, it was necessary to preserve if not strengthen socialist transformation of individual artisanal producers. Second, there should be an improvement in the putting-out system, to establish 'fair' relations between the cooperative and its supplier. Third, cooperatives' disposal and acquisition of economic resources had to be centralised under the control of state trading organisations and the purchase and sale cooperatives. A list of those goods to be supplied by the state was to be established, and cooperatives 'were not allowed to buy, sell or exchange such goods' (NXBST, 1976: 180). Output disposal had to follow order 3-TTg of the Premier's Office dated 8 January 1962, and:

> All goods subject to the state's management must be sold by cooperatives to the state, and not sold 'outside' or used to exchange for raw materials; other goods should still be sent to the state's stores, or to purchase and sale cooperatives, although in some circumstances cooperatives are allowed to sell them in their own shops, subject to the supervision of the local trading organisation. (NXBST, 1976)

Fourth, the tax and credit systems had to be reformed. Cooperatives had to stop making loans to each other and bank supervision had to improve (NXBST, 1976: 181). Fifth, there had to be changes in the prices paid for putting-out work and for the cooperatives' ordinary products.

While policy in the mid-1960s appears hard-line and so, granted what was happening, unimplementable, it had to tolerate much.

But by 1970, well before the Paris Agreements and around the same time as the early attempts at policy change discussed above, 143-CP (3 August 1970) aimed at stimulating small and artisanal industrial output. This reaffirmed the Party's commitment to the sector, albeit somewhat disingenuously:

> Since 1955, the Party has pointed clearly to the necessity of stressing small and artisanal industry, because it is the source of commodities for millions of people and provides a livelihood for hundreds of thousands. The Party has also pointed petty producers towards the road of cooperativisation to advance to socialism. (NXBST, 1976: 97)

As was well known, small and artisanal industry was an integral part of local industry, playing a crucial role in the production of consumer goods – as the decree pointed out, small and artisanal industry produced around 30 per cent of total gross industrial output and around 50 per cent of local gross industrial output (NXBST, 1976: 98). Tensions were clearest in the sector's relations with the state; there was a strong tendency for individual production to grow, especially in the cities, with adverse effects upon the cooperatives – some people had left to work on their own.[51] The substantial urban family labour supply, which was the major source of workers for petty production, remained 'unorganised' (NXBST, 1976: 99). In a clear statement of the need for an *organisational* solution to the problem, blame for this state of affairs was placed squarely upon inadequate policy implementation.

Policy towards small and artisanal industry therefore sought to 'Stimulate output, strengthen and reinforce socialist transformation, and disseminate technical improvements and new equipment to all branches of the sector' (NXBST, 1976: 100 et seq.).

To meet these goals, the decree advocated more and better planning, with a possible extension of 'product groups' (*nhom san pham*) to overcome difficulties in establishing stable relations between state industry and the cooperative sector (NXBST, 1976: 113).

Again, policy remained hard-line. But there were chinks in the wall. The 1970 decree took the position that the acquisition and disposal of resources had to permit the state to exercise its trading monopolies, *but that in certain cases producers were allowed direct relations with suppliers and customers*. Specifically, 'own-procured materials' (*vat tu do co so san xuat tu dam nhiem lay cung cap*)[52] were of the following types (NXBST, 1976: 118–19).

- Agricultural products used as raw materials that the state did not purchase (the formal list had not yet been concretely fixed).
- Forestry products such as wood, bamboo, etc. The provincial or city Cooperative Association could represent cooperatives in the contractual purchase of materials from the local forestry management organ. On this basis individual cooperatives could then buy direct from state forests.
- Waste materials and by-products from both central and local state industrial enterprises, apart from certain materials subject to state control such as lead, copper, aluminium, gold and silver. Again, SOEs could, so long as the city or provincial Cooperative Association 'introduced them and managed affairs', sell directly to small and artisanal industry. Furthermore, in order for such materials to be used properly, they could also be provided with supplies of other 'list' inputs.

Industrial cooperatives were also encouraged to purchase second-hand materials from the general population (e.g. rubber, metal, paper, etc.). The waste material and by-product companies were to cease 'occupying themselves' (*kinh doanh*)[53] with these goods and supply them to small and artisanal producers.

Output disposal followed a similar path. A clear attempt was made to distinguish between those products disposed of by delivery to the state and those where the producer had some right to 'own disposal' (*tu tieu thu*).

Also, where the producer had had to obtain inputs directly, the producer had the right to demand from the state trading organ a negotiated sale contract at a 'rational' price; products that utilised raw materials either grown or bought in directly by the producer could either be bought in part by the state trading organs or they could 'guide the producer in own disposal'.[54]

Products where the producer had a strong right to direct disposal (a concept and practice associated with the private plots – the '5 per cent land') were identified as follows.

- Products resulting from inputs supplied from retail sales from state economic organs that had not gone through the state trade network.
- Products that the state trading organs either did not buy or had left some unbought.
- Simple miscellaneous products such as embroidery, knitted trifles, drawings and pictures could all be given to workers for them to produce and dispose of themselves (NXBST, 1978: 120–1).

These 1970 measures show 'conditionality' (p. 59) used openly *and now formally* to justify policy that approved development of autonomous horizontal relations outside the system of state planning control.

Policy towards the non-state sector just prior to 1979

After 1975–1976 the authorities moved, in the small and artisanal sector as elsewhere, to reassert the economic rights of the centre. This took the form of a further development of administrative power and organisational solutions to economic problems.

1976 saw the appearance of legislation. The preamble to 134-CP (3 August 1976) stated clearly the authorities' perceptions regarding the nature of these difficulties. In 1975 the sector reportedly produced in the north around 27 per cent of total recorded industrial gross output (*Cong Bao*, 1976). It employed around 800,000 people (*Cong Bao*, 1976).[55]

The main problems derived from the lack of respect for policies on the part of many cadres and workers:

> Cooperatives themselves and artisans still suffer from the influence of the ways of thinking and working of small-scale producers.

> In places there are serious incidents of various problems such as poor workmanship, slipshod work, 'hooking' [*moc ngoac] and embezzlement of state and cooperative property. (*Cong Bao*, 1976: 38–9)

Policy maintained that the sector had an important and long-term role to play in the national economy. Small industry was to be planned and subject to thorough reorganisation. The basis for this was to be the branch-managing ministries. Possible lines for this reorganisation were the establishment of Cooperative Associations, when the cooperatives were in the same branch, and associated cooperatives, if the cooperatives were involved in co-production. The decree overtly sought to reinforce and improve state management of small and artisanal industry 'at one step', and saw three ways of doing so.

The first requirement was reform of the planning system. This had a number of different aspects. Planning had to be extended so as to cover the entire state system, with the stress placed firmly upon the local administrative level – the province and district. The industrial cooperatives had to be 'balanced'. Supplies of inputs to them were to be based upon contracts that they themselves signed. Cooperatives were encouraged to have 'supplementary plans' (*ke hoach bo sung) to meet their members' consumption needs (NXBST, 1976).

Such behaviour, effectively permitting a wide variety of activities conditional in principle upon respect for the state's interests, was also visible in the attitude to cooperatives' inputs. Here, while the state was responsible for those goods where it had a national monopoly, the cooperative could obtain the resources it needed that were 'outside the state plan' from other areas:

- supplies from the state that were surplus to the cooperative's approved requirements;
- materials bought on the retail market;
- materials brought in by customers seeking putting-out contracts.

There was an admitted severe problem with waste materials, where shortcomings in pricing and management had created large idle stocks and wastage. Transport companies were to sign contracts directly with cooperatives, and cooperatives could purchase means of transport if the state had any to sell them.

The second area of overall plan reform was the important question of putting-out (*gia cong), the basis for many well-established relations between SOEs and industrial cooperatives. These were encouraged, and the government sought to improve them by advocating longer-term contracts of up to three or even five years. Again, the legislation recognised production units' right to produce extra products to meet consumption needs, and to utilise production facilities and sources of waste materials to do so (NXBST, 1976: 44).

Finally, the decree identified a number of areas where specific policies either needed attention or, where unimplemented, greater efforts. Cooperatives were to be supplied with loans to purchase fixed capital and construct buildings at rates of interest equal to those paid by SOEs, or possibly lower. Banks were also to supply loans for circulating capital, and these were specifically allowed to cover production based upon own resources and disposed of directly by the cooperative.[56] Goods sold by cooperatives could be at freely negotiated prices, so long as they were not on the state 'list' – the basis for these was to be products of a similar type that did have a state price. Such negotiated prices had to be permitted by the bank when settling accounts.

The decree also sought to strengthen central control by extending the field of action of the central ministries. The industrial management ministries, such as light industry, engineering and metallurgy, staples and food and construction and chemicals (a department) were to manage small and artisanal industry within their own branches.

The local level – the province and the district – was seen as 'determinant'. The People's Committees of provinces and cities were to take on board the thinking of the Party and state, and reinforce their direction of small and artisanal industry. Here the provincial Cooperative Associations were to play a key coordinating role in advising the provincial offices.

As what appeared to policy analysts as a loyal and powerful organisational structure, Cooperative Associations thus appear to have generated the same optimism as the SOE unions had in the state sector (pp. 75 and 86). Signed by Nguyen Duy Trinh in 1976, the decree represents reasonably clearly the attitude to the sector. Confronted with considerable *de facto* autonomy, and equipped with a set of policy options that was limited essentially to organisational solutions, policy-makers nevertheless presented a rather supportive attitude to the mass of small-scale producers. It is clear that they should give the state priority access to their output, but equally clear that this was conditional upon both the state supplying inputs and the provision of adequate living conditions for cooperative members.

The decree moves away from the idea that the state, and especially state industry, had absolute priority. It does not, however, really move much distance towards encouraging production units to enter into deals outside the control of the relevant authorities. The establishment of Cooperative Associations is an example of an organisational solution. But it is interesting to note the considerable *de facto* freedoms.

Such units did not need much encouragement to get out there and start dealing directly with suppliers and customers: 'fence-breaking' was an organic part of 'aggravated shortage' well before it was given that name. And this was quite clear from the Vietnamese literature.

Conclusions

'Economic logic' and reform

By the late 1970s those Vietnamese reflecting upon the state of Vietnamese industry had to accept, more or less explicitly, the important role played by the interaction between different allocative mechanisms. After all, they themselves spent large proportions of their incomes on the free market, especially at the margin, and were well aware of the overall environment within which industrial producers of all types had to operate.

Even those who were among the more advanced and perceptive observers of the situation, however, could not see an easy way through to unravelling the political and economic compromises that dominated the situation, above all in the north.

At root, this was because the political situation was such that those who wished to implement what they understood to be socialism lacked the power and force necessary to impose upon the economy the terms of transactions needed to implement the neo-Stalinist programme. Vietnamese neo-Stalinism, it appeared, was insufficiently nasty – Stalinist – to force through what was needed to make central planning work.

However, without the capacity to enforce these desires, the state could either keep on trying, or give up, or both, relying willy-nilly upon voluntary, and thus ultimately market-oriented, methods. *Stalemate.*

De facto *freedom, rigidity in much but not all formal policy, signs of liberalisation as boredom with organisational solutions set in – the grassroots*

The quotations from the panel cited earlier (p. 53) show clearly, as does the tone of their remarks, that it was the commitment to traditional socialism and the DRV programme that maintained the system (the DRV model) intact. Aid helped, and less of it would push more 'fence-breaking', but 'aggravated shortage' was part of everyday reality. Driven by a desire mainly to increase consumption, a wide range of relations had arisen beside and interwoven with the plan to utilise assets and inputs in ways that supported local interests. Missing from this picture are stories of relatively private accumulation; central to them is the desire to increase local consumption. One reason for this was the clear powers to attack 'capitalism' that remained (the 'certain revolutionaries' mentioned on p. 61).

So what was about to be greeted as 'fence-breaking' was in fact nothing of the sort. Such fences had long been rickety and highly permeable. The term therefore can be thought of as referring not to something in itself radically new, but to a further development of existing practices not uncommon in many centrally planned systems. What was new, however, was the way in which it marked a break with the past in formal policy terms, leading to 25-CP and the breakthrough legalisation of SOE transactions in list (see note 13) goods.

Notes

1. For example, Wiles (1962, 1977), Ellman (1979) and Wadekin (1982).
2. This section is largely based upon EPU (1975), a planners' textbook; I would also like to record my thanks to many Vietnamese SOE cadres who explained this system to me at the time, as well as to the panel formed in 2004–2005 to provide a clearer referential basis. What is often confusing is the existence of apparently familiar categories – e.g. prices, costs, profits – whose meaning is different in the capitalist systems with which most readers will be familiar.
3. The system was based upon conventional double-entry book-keeping. It included records of assets in so-called balance sheets – but without a proper system of capital accounting. As commercial accounting became valuable in the 1980s, the opinion of the dean of the National Finance University was that it was not difficult for an accountant trained in traditional methods to switch (personal communication).
4. It was the breakdown of this system as the state-set price system could no longer generate adequate revenues to pay for both investment and cash purchases that was at the root of the 'fiscal crisis of transition' (p. 33).
5. These were the production development fund, the welfare fund and the bonus fund.
6. Personal communication from staff of the State Prices Commission. It is striking that the commission should have produced such a strong and well-articulated position on a number of issues. Links between this group and the

NEU/EPU in Hanoi can be traced through such men as Doan Trong Truyen, head of the commission until 1984, and especially Phan van Tiem, head from at least 1986 and one-time head of the NEU Price Faculty.

7. As the state sought to restore its finances from the late 1980s and into the 1990s, treatment of depreciation charges became contested. While through the 1980s they had increasingly been made subject to SOE control, this was now reversed. A similar trajectory occurred with the treatment of SOEs' 'own capital' (*von tu co*), where arguments were increasingly deployed to shift control over it from SOEs to higher levels. See Chapter 9 and TCTK (1994: table 54) for data.
8. Use of the system where SOEs' transactions were accounted for in this way paralleled the way in which an SOE's functional departments (such as finance, organisation, etc.) were treated by its superiors as 'their' agents within it. The reader may conclude that under the 'textbook' system SOEs had so little autonomy that treating them as independent agents is unrealistic.
9. The odd role played by money is often described by reference to its 'passive' character (Podolski, 1972).
10. One striking element of the effects of marketisation was precisely in this area. There are a range of research projects that could look into this aspect of economic change in the 1980s, such as just how machinery was adapted to permit its use in making things that could be sold on the market: two examples I observed with interest were the wall clocks (labelled 'Westminster Chimes') one could find by the late 1980s in the houses of minority families who had done well on the market, and the production of bicycle spares. Both often came from military factories, well equipped with machinery.
11. The 'envelope' culture continued on into the 2000s, with public officials receiving envelopes (containing money) in return for attending meetings and other tasks.
12. What follows reflects various presentations that I attended during my time at Hanoi University in 1978–1979, a 'seminar' interpretation to put against textbooks such as EPU (1975).
13. 'List' goods were those over which the state sought a monopoly control (e.g. Fforde and Paine, 1987: 134–5 gives a list from the early 1960s). See pp. 10 and 136 for 25-CP's treatment of them.
14. While some refer to decree 279-CP (2 August 1979) published in *Nhan Dan* (1979l), this may refer also to 344-TTg (24 September 1977) on the use of metals. Decrees from the late 1960s had encouraged use of by-products and waste for 'non-list' activities.
15. This was probably the Hanoi soap factory (*Nhan Dan*, 1980l). By 1985 high-quality locally produced soap was available in Hanoi since the factory had managed to get access to southern palm oil (p. 149).
16. My own experience of Vietnamese official meetings suggests that the obligation to listen should not be viewed as a light one.
17. Again, the reader should recall that this interview predated both 279-CP and 25-CP.
18. Formally, *all* enterprises under state bodies, at whatever level, were referred to as SOEs and were conceptually the same from a legal point of view. This

differed from some other countries. In China, for example, statisticians distinguished between 'national' and other SOEs, with the former typically referred to as 'state' and the rest as not (Fforde, 1999). 'State' (*nha nuoc*) thus included commune-level administration. There was no link between terms such as 'national' – *quoc gia* – and the status of such SOEs. Thus 'state business' (*quoc doanh*) could be carried out by a district SOE as well as by a central SOE.

19. For a discussion of the law of value in the context of the nature of SOEs during the decade from 1992 see Fforde (2005d). The 'law of value' is a term used by Marx, and more importantly by Stalin, to refer to the economic and social effects of the exchange of commodities or production for the market – for profit. Stalin's 'Economic problems of socialism in the USSR' surprised many at the time (the early 1950s) by arguing that the law of value operated within the Soviet economy, specifically in areas such as trade with the peasantry on their private plots (in Vietnam the 5 per cent land). That such an obscure terminology should mean this can be understood by reference to Marx's theory of surplus value, whereby separation of workers from the means of production allowed capitalists to pay them less than the value of their work, with value understood here in terms of the embodied labour in commodities rather than market price. The point here is that profit-oriented exchange was doctrinally accepted within Stalinist thinking, which may come as a surprise to some readers.

20. See Abrami (2002) for a detailed study of activities related to these, with comparisons to China.

21. Thus, confusingly, 'industry' (*cong nghiep*) meant SOEs, while small and artisanal industry was *tieu thu cong nghiep*.

22. The change was supported by wartime decentralisation.

23. Politburo decree 105-NQ/TW (p. 105) explicitly stated, however, that the association was 'a political organisation of co-operators in small and artisanal industry and not an organisation of production or economic management' (NXBST, 1980: 186).

24. These were an 'intermediary' form set up to encourage Vietnamese capitalists to remain in the country. The previous owners retained 'shares' in the company, which entitled them to a share of profits, but these were usually very low and for all practical purposes the companies were operated like ordinary SOEs.

25. The preamble to 81-CT/TW on the 'Reinforcement of control [literally 'leadership' – *lanh dao*] over artisanal production' ('*Ve viec tang cuong lanh dao san xuat thu cong nghiep*') reviews the general position at the time and the positive role played by the untransformed artisanat in economic development prior to 1959–1960. This is available in NXBST (1978: 7–13).

26. This was 124-NQ/TW 'On the problem of stimulating the reform and development of artisanal industry in accordance with socialism' ('*Ve van de day manh viec cai tao va phat trien thu cong nghiep theo chu nghia xa hoi*') (NXBST 1980: 45 et seq.).

27. The '*Lien minh cong nong*' – this was the classical explanation of class alliance forming the legitimising basis of the DRV state. Wags argued that by the 2000s this had been replaced by a '*kinh-ninh*' alliance of business (*kinh doanh*) and the security apparatus (*an ninh*).

28. An example of Kim Ngoc's law operating in reverse – see note 12 on p. 47.
29. This practice meant that SOEs would receive input supplies from the plan and then 'put them out' to such producers, who would return processed products to the SOE.
30. Two useful references are NXBST (1978) and Doan Hai et al. (1979).
31. Fforde (2005b). I thank Joerg Wischermann for collegial discussion on these issues.
32. Which is not to say that they did not study events elsewhere – Dang Quoc Tuyen (1990) is one among many examples.
33. Marx believed that he had proved that the core of capitalism's inner logic was the relationship between capital and labour *in production*. Thus communism was defined as the 'planned production of use-values' and neo-Stalinist thinking focused upon construing the plan as a plan of *production*. It was therefore difficult for Vietnamese economists trained in traditional socialist ideology not to focus upon ways of better organising production when they faced problems. By contrast, Marx was very critical of what he called 'bourgeois economists' who thought that the core logic of capitalism was to be found in markets and exchange – in how economic resources are *distributed* to competing ends. This stress upon markets and price involves a focus upon incentives. The old joke goes that socialism is the opposite of capitalism, and so while under capitalism there is discipline in production and chaos in consumption, under socialism there is chaos in production and discipline (the queue) in consumption. Much of the economic history this book presents tends to show that the main analytical puzzles to understanding what happened in the DRV and the SRV up until 1989–1990 are to be found in questions to do with incentives: what determined what happened to economic resources as different allocative mechanisms offered different opportunities to those who determined where they would go.
34. I do not seek to do more than point to major themes. We lack decent political studies. Important participants ignored here Tran Phuong, whose long article in *Nghien cuu kinh te* is said to be an early statement of a traditional reformist position – but I, like others, find it impossible to understand (Tran Phuong, 1966/1967), and Bui Cong Trung, who was an early advocate of a market-oriented approach working at the Economics Institute in Hanoi (Bui Cong Trung, 1959).
35. At the time Nguyen Tri was a professor at the Industry Faculty of the NEU. He died poor, smoked too much and told jokes. The best, whose possible significance as usual I realised only years later, concerned a shop with a sign in the window listing the large number of foreign languages spoken there. A customer, trying out one of them on the staff and finding that nobody working in the shop spoke it, asked what the sign meant, and was told 'Oh, that refers to the customers, not us'.
36. Thus Nguyen Cao Thuong (1980) saw sources of higher output seen as being independent of the distributional environment.
37. While it is true that the potential ideological force of market economics was offset by its anathema to neo-Stalinists, it is probably fair also to add that the debate was carried out in a relative vacuum, though with knowledge of similar problems in China and Eastern Europe, as well as the USSR.

Most North Vietnamese economists were trained in Central and Eastern Europe, China or the USSR, where traditions of intellectual opposition to the neo-Stalinist model were of course variable but often strong.

38. This institution changed its name to the NEU around 1986 or so. It was and remains the main elite cadre school for planners, business people and so on in Hanoi. I was a visiting researcher at the Industry Faculty in 1985–1986. De-Stalinisation had yet to occur and personal relations were still closely policed. Some of the most interesting economic analysis of the 1980s came from people associated with its Price Faculty, led for some time by the outstanding Phan van Tiem, later head of the State Prices Commission. Other personnel included Tran Xuan Gia and Le Xuan Nghia.
39. This, of course, echoed Le Duan's opinions.
40. This was not, however, an integral part of party policy; agricultural cooperatives' artisanal activities were a prescribed part of the new management system (Fforde, 1989: Chapter 9).
41. Artisanal workers' wages (presumably monthly) were cited as follows: clothing 15–30 dong; publishing 15–20 dong; metalworking 20–40 dong (Nguyen Lang and Nghiem Phu Ninh, 1972a: 101).
42. Note here the logic of the argument: only SOEs and cooperatives should be allowed to participate in the market.
43. The stipulation that output targets should not be issued without supply to the unit of adequate means to fulfil them was to become an important issue in the application of the 'three-plan' system after 1981 (Chapter 5).
44. I would like to thank Nguyen Lang for this reference. Here, if anywhere, should the dragon's teeth have been sown.
45. The earliest plenum cited during the debates of the 1970s and early 1980s tended to be this one, although the Party's directives of the late 1960s appear to mark a still earlier stage of the process (e.g. Le Thanh Nghi and Pham van Dong, 1972, cited in Nguyen Nien, 1974a; Doan Trong Truyen, 1977). EPU (1975) dates the start of reform slightly differently.
46. This was entitled 'Thoroughly grasp the line and direction of economic management during the new stage, struggle to realise victoriously the economic tasks before us'.
47. I have seen a small number of excellent and extremely interesting articles in the *Legal Studies* journal (*Luat Hoc*) – for example, Nguyen Nien (1973, 1974a, 1974b, 1977, 1985).
48. In the 1980s the old Government Council (*Hoi dong Chinh phu*) was renamed the Council of Ministers (*Hoi dong Bo truong*). The latter name is used throughout this book to refer to both.
49. By department is here meant the ministerial-level organisations, such as the Chemicals Department, rather than sub- or intra-ministerial levels.
50. Only two orders applied to the territorial economy: total investment in housing and social projects and the corresponding increase in capacity. This was a 'first step'.
51. This shows up to some extent in the official statistics – reported individual employment fell from a peak of 56,000 in 1965 to a low of 32,000 in 1968, and then rose to a new peak of 72,000 in 1971. But at the same time there

were substantial variations in the size of the cooperative labour force, which also rose sharply between 1968 and 1971 (Fforde and Paine, 1987: table 37).
52. Here note use of '*tu*' – a strong marker of autonomous behaviour (note 17 on p. 47) – as a *technical* term.
53. This term later grew to refer to 'business'.
54. This vocabulary was later used to describe similar behaviour by SOEs operating according to the 'three-plan' system (Chapter 5).
55. Fforde and Paine (1987: table 43) put total sectoral output at 1.1 billion dong at 1970 prices, which agrees well enough with the data quoted above. But the employment data are nearly double those given in Fforde and Paine (1987: table 37), which put total sectoral industrial employment at 434,000 in 1975. Furthermore, the footnote to this table specifically states that the data include people in agricultural cooperatives as well as registered private producers. Such puzzles are commonplace (p. 10).
56. Literally 'self-produced, self-sold' (*tu san, tu tieu*) – rather pithy.

4

Vietnamese neo-Stalinism and its feet of clay – from reunification to August 1979

The origins of the 1979 Sixth Plenum – what went wrong?

The first trap

The trap that traditional socialism faced in Vietnam after 1975 should now be obvious. Two factors constrained and limited the development of market forces within the state sector. First was the belief in a better future, defined as socialist construction that would take Vietnam to levels of strength and well-being comparable to the USSR; this was construed as being respect for the norms of central planning.[1] As we have seen (p. 61), at the grassroots level this gave power to 'revolutionaries' who could and would report market activities, a real threat to those responsible for such activities. Second was the role played by the supplies of real resources to those in SOEs, both cadres and workers, through the rationing system. A substantial part of these were aid imports.

However, what 'aggravated shortage' meant was that various practices (such as 'putting-out') could lead to ways for interests within (and above) SOEs to exploit their access to state-supplied materials. In this way informal language would refer to the beneficiaries of such relationships (families, cooperatives, groups and so on) as 'bastard offspring' (*con rung*).

The forces that could open the first trap were therefore clear: reduction in ideological pressures, perhaps due to changes in Party doctrines, or changes in popular sentiments which would encourage further marketisation at the base. With a population that could display considerable cynicism and capacity for manoeuvre for personal advantage, just what – *really* – was stopping far more 'fence-breaking'? What if the authority of the DRV programme fell away? What if the level and quality of flows into the state allocation system did the same?

Whether the VCP could avoid this trap would depend, therefore, upon what happened to doctrine and popular sentiments, to imports, to procurement and to rations. Its position, so far as it rested on the plan, was deeply dependent upon imports, and upon the ability of the system to get its hands on rice from farmers. Risky.

The political economy of Vietnam just after reunification

In 1975 the VCP found itself in a position to establish a unified and independent Vietnamese nation-state. After over a century of foreign domination, nationalist energies were now free to express themselves in reconstruction and development. But while the end of the war clearly liberated considerable human and economic resources, the north could no longer expect to receive the same economic assistance as before, in terms of either volume or composition. And the fall of Saigon meant that links between the southern economy and the West were abruptly cut.

Development policy faced two quite separate sets of problems.[2]

First, the transition from war and national division confronted policy-makers with vitally important but essentially short-term questions. Moving to a peacetime footing involved big shifts in a wide range of economic activities. Any changes in the availability and pattern of foreign assistance, with cutbacks in current aid likely to be offset by increased supplies of development finance, were a major part of this. South Vietnam, previously administered under quite different principles from the DRV, had to be run on a day-to-day basis after many years of conflict.

Second, however, a government strongly committed to national economic development (here defined as 'socialist construction') had to look further ahead, towards the creation of a sustainable and long-term pattern of socio-economic advance, of which steady economic growth and industrialisation had to be an essential part.

Policy had therefore simultaneously to face the different issues associated with the short- and the long-term needs of the Vietnamese economy. These problems were, naturally enough, hard to disentangle on a month-to-month basis; what is more, an understandable desire for a rapid transition to peacetime construction, coupled with an equally comprehensible post-war optimism, would tend to encourage policy-makers to downplay short-term problems.

Furthermore, central authority in the DRV was weak and had been so for many years; as is clear from the previous discussion, the economic management apparatus had never been in a position to exercise the strong control prescribed by Soviet textbooks. In this as in other areas communist Vietnam differed from pre-reform China (Fforde, 1999). The post-1975 decade can thus be viewed as one of a slow but incomplete resolution of the tension between the strong desire for economic growth and the burning issues of the moment.

But, as we have seen, state industry, the core of traditional socialism in any neo-Stalinist system, was viewed by a range of policy analysts as facing entrenched problems rooted in the institutionalised and settled interactions between the different allocative mechanisms of plan and market that were the defining features of 'aggravated shortage'.

Origins of crisis – the second FYP, 1976–1980

During the immediate post-war period (1975–1977) the SRV authorities focused upon national reconstruction and administrative unification of the country. Since this was understood to mean attempting to implement the DRV's socio-economic programme throughout the area, large-scale industry was nationalised throughout the south and a collectivisation campaign begun. Formal unification took place in 1976 with the establishment of the SRV; at the same time the Party changed its name from the Vietnam Workers' Party to the VCP.

For northerners, in many ways after reunification money had more value in the south. However, the abrupt drop in imports to the south from the West meant that the authorities had, immediately after the fall of Saigon, to divert supplies southward within the state material supply system. These two factors alone turned the balance of goods availability against the planned sectors, further encouraging people to seek ways of gaining access to valuable unplanned output.[3] Furthermore, the end of the war had itself directly reduced aid supplies to the north as donors downgraded Vietnamese needs. This further exacerbated the difficulties facing the authorities. The end of the struggle reduced popular inhibitions against illegal or less than moral behaviour, cutting further the effective labour supply to state factories and other socialist institutions while expectations of a better life rose.

Despite these difficulties, and notwithstanding experiences during the first FYP, investment policy remained highly optimistic. The authorities still saw state industry as the main site for accumulation. Aid finance was directed into large-scale and generally high-tech projects whose viability rested upon highly dubious assumptions about their local economic environments and the prospects for rapid development of forward and backward linkages. In the euphoria of the immediate post-reunification period it is possible to observe a 'leap' mentality in the statements of many top policy-makers (e.g. Le Thanh Nghi, 1977b). There was no fundamental rethinking to reflect lessons learnt from what had happened to central planning in the DRV.

The 1976 Twenty-fourth Plenum argued for rapid extension of the DRV's social and administrative structures to the south. A series of government decrees in late 1976 confirmed this position, as did the 1976 Fourth Congress (DCSV, 1977).

Implementation of this direction, acting as it did against local interests, would require strong party discipline and control (see p. 30 referring to Le Duc Tho's position). The evidence suggests strongly that this was lacking. SOEs were too happily engaged in market and related activities, and policy analysts were too tolerant of these.

The practices linking SOEs and non-plan activities were often highly personal. In a very poor area, with extreme shortage premia and where allegations of 'anti-socialist' behaviour could be fatal, well-chosen gifts could be very valuable. An important area at the margin between markets and plan were the small-scale industrial cooperatives. This was well expressed in the idea that they were often the 'bastard children' (*con rung) of the state planning system.

The south and tiep quan – Party control and its problems

The VCP was creating major problems for itself by trying at the same time to restore some order in the chaotic northern economic management system while using that same system to manage the south. And this was made harder still by the aid cuts. But the central issues were power and the ability to establish control over the situation through a state that was, clearly, an unreliable and disobedient instrument.

What Leninist methods would permit sufficient control over small-scale production so as to push resources into the plan?

Party organisations in small-scale industry

The position of local Party cadres in the small-scale industrial cooperatives was an indicator of the extent of the Party's disciplinary powers and ability to enforce the distributional norms of the neo-Stalinist programme. Without priority supply of inputs from the state, and producing goods in ready market demand, such cadres faced particularly strong temptations from the 'outside economy'. As we have seen (p. 61), this was an old issue.

In 1979 the Central Committee of the Party published a pamphlet on the role of the Party in small and artisanal cooperatives (TWD, 1979). This contained an order of the Party secretariat issued in April 1978 and two supplementary guides to its implementation. These were intended to guide grassroots Party organisations as southern industry was subject to socialist transformation.

The legislative basis for industrial organisation reform was said to be 134-CP (3 August 1976), discussed on p. 108 (TWD, 1979: 5). This required 'Reinforcement of Party leadership at all levels and strong efforts to construct and strengthen Party cells [*chi bo] in small and artisanal cooperatives' (TWD, 1979: 6). But many cooperatives apparently had no Party members at all, and total membership was less than 5 per cent of the workforce (TWD, 1979: 8–9). Party members of poor quality had to be 'expelled immediately'.[4] But the decree had to be realistic – if cadres had to be sent into the cooperative from outside, and were therefore not members, the cooperative was not to be made responsible for their livelihood.

The guides to implementation of the order contain far more information and also attempt to justify Party policy towards industrial cooperatives. One quotes statistics to the effect that 25 per cent of small and artisanal output in the north was occurring in agricultural cooperatives in 1977 and as such was an important contributor to 'the new division of labour in the countryside'; furthermore, working conditions in some 25 per cent of northern industrial cooperatives were said to be similar to those of workers in SOEs (TWD, 1979: 28). In the south gross output had risen to 1.7 billion dong by 1977. Socialist transformation had gone slowly, for by 1978 only 7.9 per cent of small and artisanal workers had joined cooperatives (TWD, 1979: 29).[5]

During the initial stages of cooperativisation in the north (1959–1963), Party organisation in the industrial cooperatives had been negligible. Initially cells had been started by demobilised or wounded soldiers or

Party members sent in by the local commune. Party-building had been a part of the later movements to reform cooperative management, develop production and improve socialist production relations.

There were problems. The system of Party control was on the whole thin and weak. While the number of Party cells was growing steadily, the number of Party members was still 'too low'. Most cooperatives only had some three to five Party members, and while some 25 per cent of cooperatives had Party groups, 30 per cent had no Party members at all.

The document traced the breakdown of the Party's expansion drive to 1970, and blamed local cells for their hesitancy, small-mindedness and fear of responsibility (TWD, 1979). While many Party members had been well tried during the war, many had been gravely weakened by their proximity to petty production; this had bad effects upon their thinking and style of work. Some had looked to their personal interests, 'Running after incomes, producing slipshod and poor-quality work, going "outside" [*chan trong chan ngoai*], ganging up with the masses to violate policy and not really identifying with the cooperative' (TWD, 1979: 33).

There were incidents of Party members paying themselves high incomes and embezzling cooperative property. Lack of internal unity among Party members, especially the key cadres, in any given cooperative was widespread: 'In a number of cells leadership is slack to allow people free rein in their activities within the cooperative, including running after "outside" commodities [*hang ngoai*]' (TWD, 1979: 34).

While the mass of cooperative cadres had been brought up in the cooperatives, they were generally of a poor political, cultural and educational background. Most cooperative managers were old and had great practical experience, but they lacked the political and managerial capacity needed for modern production development. There were, however, very few young cadres, with a great shortage of accountants. Most Party and mass cadres were new and lacked experience. Similar difficulties seem to have applied in the south (TWD, 1979: 34–5).

There were, it was reported, two reasons for this poor state of affairs. First, planning was 'slow' and cooperatives' dependency upon materials supplied by the state's putting-out organs meant that they could not expand production.[6] The sector's organisation, which was the responsibility of the system of Cooperative Associations, had not been clearly fixed. And the reform of a number of state policies aimed at stimulating the sector had been delayed. Under such circumstances it was hard for the Party to develop its activities within the industrial cooperatives. Second, however, it had to be said that many Party cells 'do not understand the line and viewpoint of the Party centre with regard to small and artisanal industry. Many organs and units do not seriously implement policies promulgated by the Party and state' (TWD, 1979: 36).

This situation shows the extreme difficulties facing any attempt by the Party to secure tight central control. 'Aggravated shortage' saw a range of relationships that permitted SOEs and interests close to them to use plan materials to their own 'local' advantage. The internal Party discipline that should have been able to limit this and ensure that resources were channelled into implementing the plan was lacking.[7]

Grassroots views

The opinion of the panel about relationships with artisans and cooperatives confirmed this state of affairs vividly. They reported that before 1979 SOEs had two sorts of relations with artisanal industry and agricultural cooperatives.

First, wherever an SOE had been set up, it tended to develop 'alliances' (*ket nghia) with cooperatives and artisanal producers in the locality. The goal was to establish mutually beneficial relations, mainly in the form of supplies of labour, staples and foodstuffs (outside the plan).

Second, the SOE would actively establish direct exchanges of output and raw materials with the artisanal establishments and the cooperatives. In one example:

> Of course we had to be careful and act under the name of the SOE – saying we were 'helping the collective' when we reported to the superior levels, as well as giving them presents – such presents usually were rice, alcohol and meat and not envelopes as nowadays – for if we were not careful we could be accused of violating the plan and socialism itself.

Small and artisanal industry on the eve of the economic crisis

The problems facing this sector are of great importance to understanding what happened to SOEs. It was, as many Vietnamese commentators stressed, a major contributor to recorded industrial output (pp. 77 and 89).

The sector provided important products, such as certain consumer goods and agricultural means of production (especially hand-tools).

It was highly visible, and a focus of attention for many local Party members with good war records who wished to take up some sort of responsible (and perhaps profitable) post. The sector was therefore both 'close to the masses' and in many ways rather 'Red'. For the local Party membership, 'their' industry must have often meant the cooperative sector.

The sector, furthermore, was of low priority. State industry had always been the key leading sector. An industrial cooperative with politically reliable leaders trying to make a living for its workers and supply needed goods to the local economy could, therefore, argue effectively for greater *de facto* freedoms. The state was clearly incapable of organising an effective system of material supply to industrial cooperatives. The goods produced were perhaps not, in addition, of absolutely vital national significance. The clear indications that top policy-makers could permit this sector rather greater freedom in the acquisition and disposal of resources should not therefore be too surprising.

This pragmatism was especially marked in the Party secretariat, and here there is evidence of considerable impatience and dissatisfaction with the ineffectiveness of the state apparatus. Some time in 1979 the then secretary of the Industry Department, Nguyen Lam, wrote a short book on the subject of consumer goods and regional industry (Nguyen Lam, 1980a); he followed this with the article in *Tap chi Cong san* (*Communist Studies*) already discussed (p. 26) and took a liberal view of economic matters and advocated far greater reliance upon markets (Nguyen Lam, 1980b). This position did not quickly command support. The experiences of the small and artisanal cooperatives, however, were a stimulus to such thinking, and resonated strongly with local interests.

Con rung, the 1989–1990 holocaust and the background to the 1990s

Though I do not have much evidence to go on, it appears to me from a range of discussions and indicators that the effects of the loss of Soviet-bloc aid were profound. Many of the artisanal and small-scale cooperatives existed to act as the '*con rung*' of SOEs, as sites where resources obtained from the position of SOEs within the residual central-planning system could be placed so as to generate higher benefits to those who mattered. They either had better rights to participate in markets, as we have seen, or faced lower bribe costs. Arguably, in the natural development of things they would have acted as sites for the 'primitive accumulation' of still more private commercial activities as time went on, one of the ways in which an emerging non-state – and eventually private – sector would have been recorded by surveys and official statistics.

The party daily *Nhan Dan* in March 1990 published an article that discussed the collapse of artisanal cooperatives – reportedly 50 per cent in of those in Hai Hung province were no longer in operation, and 130,000 cooperative workers in Hanoi had only 'confused' work (Ngu Phong, 1990). The author was highly critical: it was 'not clear' just which state organ was responsible for the situation. Further, he extended the area of attack to include criticism of decree 10 (1988) that had seen perhaps 50 per cent of rural cadre jobs lost. 'Why weren't people outside the Party asked their opinion? Extermination of the cooperative sector was "hurried" – just like the old problems...'

But this is to run ahead of the story.

The run-up to 1979

By 1977 the political effects of the breakdown in relations with China were mounting. In March 1978 there was a major clampdown on free markets that badly hit the overseas Chinese in south Vietnam. The July Fourth Plenum discussed relations with China and the crisis in the southern collectivisation drive. In late 1978 the final split with China occurred. The last Chinese experts were soon withdrawn and Vietnam signed the Treaty of Friendship and Cooperation with the USSR and sent armed forces into Cambodia. Phnom Penh rapidly fell, and Vietnamese troops remained in Cambodia until 1989.

By the end of 1978 high-level Party reports had already taken a strong position, criticising the failure of the southern collectivisation drive. The Fifth Plenum was delayed, and only held in February 1979. The Chinese then invaded Vietnam's northern provinces in retaliation for the Vietnamese activities in Cambodia. This was a crisis of many dimensions, but would result in major industrial policy changes.

Macro-economic performance and the origins of the 1979–1980 crisis

As economic problems mounted there was a sharp slowdown in output growth in 1977, largely made up of an absolute decline in agriculture and a violent deceleration in trade, transport and communications. State employment had grown absolutely, by some 38 per cent, during the

Table 4.1 Capital and output in state industry

Year	1975	1976	1977	1978	1979
Billion dong					
Gross output of state industry	7.29	8.21	9.03	9.52	9.09
Absolute change		0.92	0.82	0.49	–0.43
State investment in industry	0.82	0.95	1.14	1.24	1.31
Ratio of investment to change in output		1.03	1.39	2.53	?

Source: TCTK (1980)

period 1975–1979. Industry had received around 35 per cent of all state investment, and of this over 70 per cent went to the so-called 'Group A' (means of production) branches (TCTK, 1980).

The inability of the model to utilise this newly installed capital equipment shows up in the rising incremental capital-output ratio in state industry (Table 4.1).

The economy was already facing serious difficulties before the Chinese and Western aid cuts of 1978–1979. The interpretation of 1977 is crucial, for in that year, *before* major Chinese and Western aid cuts precipitated the rapid 1979 industrial collapse, capital investment was ineffective. Shortages of other inputs were preventing industrial output growth. As during the first FYP, state investment was often increasing capacity, not output; competition between allocative mechanisms, between plan and market, ensured that labour and other inputs were unavailable.

The economic crisis of the late 1970s and its political economy implications

The crisis was essentially, as it had been before 1975, to do with the consequences of the attempt to impose neo-Stalinism. This was most evident in the distributional tensions that were mounting as economic reunification and the socialist transformation of the south proceeded. By 1978–1979 the gathering crisis in northern agriculture joined a sharp fall in procurement in the Mekong to place great pressure upon food supplies. The process was exacerbated by the termination of Chinese economic assistance in 1978, just before the Vietnamese military went into Cambodia and the SRV joined the CMEA (Council for Mutual Economic Assistance). At the same time Western (hard currency) aid was cut off in reply to the Vietnamese presence in Cambodia.

The underlying systemic tensions within the DRV's economic system therefore interacted with both the consequences of national reunification and the particular exogenous shocks of 1978–1979 to reduce sharply both relatively and absolutely the volume of goods available through the system of material supply. Economic agents responded by reallocating resources into locally more advantageous areas. The crisis was manifest in a shift away from 'planned' activities.

This meant that the institutions of the socialist state – never particularly clear – began to dissolve. The collectivised peasantry of the north rapidly expanded their 'own-account' activities at the expense of their cooperatives; newly collectivised peasants in the Mekong began to return to private farming as levels of procurement slumped abruptly; the state's trade monopolies (both foreign and domestic) were attacked, often successfully; in state industry initial sharp output falls in certain sectors were followed by the rapid and spontaneous growth of illegal direct – 'horizontal' – relations between SOEs and their suppliers and customers.

Soviet-style planning, based upon the direct allocation of resources to priority sectors, lost more of its intended meaning. This struck at the resource base that fed the bureaucracy and state employees, some of whom were not benefiting from the growth of market relations. Those who had 'alliances' with sources of market incomes, or who had cash to spend, found their interests diverging from those who did not.

Conclusions

During 1979 the VCP faced acute problems. Of these economic questions were perhaps not the most important – but they were crucial enough. The combined effects of the stalled collectivisation drive in the south, the rapidly rising distributional difficulties as Chinese aid stocks and hard currency ran out and the continuing international tensions pushed strongly for tactical concessions. These culminated in the August 1979 Sixth Plenum.[8]

Notes

1. See the late Huynh Kim Khanh's work, and especially his stress upon the attempts of the VCP to link the socialist and the nationalist efforts (Huynh Kim Khanh, 1982); also Thayer (1983). Compare with e.g. Nguyen Duy Trinh (1976).
2. Compare with Beresford (1989).
3. That is, the volume of resources controlled by planners fell both absolutely and relatively.
4. This derived from 22-TT/TW (5 September 1977) (TWD, 1979: 8).
5. There were reportedly around 31,700 people in the 221 extant cooperatives, implying a total labour force of around 400,000.
6. 'Dependency' upon such materials of course gave considerable potential for mechanisms such as 'hooking' (*moc ngoac) to gain access to market value.
7. Studies of artisanal activities such as Luong (1997), Abrami and Henaff (2004) and others offer the reader opportunities to explore histories of these issues in particular contexts. My and others' work on agricultural cooperatives (Fforde, 1982, 1989; Vickerman, 1986) showed very similar issues there, confirmed later by Kerkvliet (2005; see also Kerkvliet, 1995). Fforde (1982, 1986) stresses the origins of the lack of effective Party control to the failure of the 1950s' land reform to create a sufficiently loyal Party base in the rural areas (also Kleinen, 1999).
8. In what appears to have been a coincidence, a report to the plenum on light industry had been under preparation for two years prior to the meeting as part of the regular series of reviews of strategic topics (personal communication).

5

The transitional model of the 1980s: a new solution?

The 1979 Sixth Plenum

Continuity and change

The August 1979 Sixth Plenum had wide political importance. The plenum's resolution[1] and underlying philosophy stressed the need to break through the log-jam. The resulting liberalisation necessarily attacked the direct interests of many central economic organs. The policies that followed the plenum exhibited, however, a certain degree of continuity with earlier legislation, and in some cases extended to new areas freedoms previously granted to others. The parallels between the 'three-plan' system and the treatment of industrial cooperatives are striking. Policy towards marketisation of SOEs – technically the growth of horizontal transactions in 'list' goods – was of enormous importance. The plenum resolution stressed the importance of consumer goods production and local industry. The decision to move in this direction was preshadowed by a series of *Nhan Dan* editorials during June (*Nhan Dan*, 1979g, 1979h, 1979i).[2] Since Chinese aid had supplied an important proportion of consumer goods, it is not surprising that this should have received priority. But the debate hardly mentioned the aid cuts at all, least of all attributing current problems to them. This helped to focus political attention upon the shortcomings of the economic management system.

In early June a *Nhan Dan* editorial took an uncompromising line. It stressed that the 1976 Fourth Congress had called for 'A full utilisation of all productive resources and all forms of production to produce more consumer goods and overcome the shortages of everyday items' (*Nhan Dan*, 1979g). Since then, it was reported that Vietnam had constructed a consumer goods industrial sector that included 2,000 SOEs and 3,000 cooperatives. But development had been extremely slow. For this a number of broad objective and subjective reasons were cited, but the particular points where action should be taken were:

- a lack of desire to produce consumer goods;
- the continued separation of agriculture from industry;
- the low priority given to small and artisanal industry;
- leftist errors in socialist transformation.

These are direct criticisms of the over-optimism of the second FYP, with its implied high levels of investment and limited scope for increases in consumption (if not implied falls); a focus of investment upon large SOEs (which would, it was assumed, be central to the growth of military industry); and over-hasty pressure against the market and for southern collectivisation. Very similar criticisms drove the very early rounds of reform in China (Fforde, 1999). They do not directly imply any shift to encourage markets, but, granted the conclusions reached above about just how the economy was operating, this was a strong implicit element. For example, support for small-scale industry would increase the possibilities for SOEs to form 'alliances' with units that we have seen were permitted greater freedoms in their relations with markets. But this is to risk 'policy fetishism' and attribute too much to formal policy.

What was actually happening to SOEs?

In a rare and perceptive analysis of events published in 1981,[3] two Vietnamese economists asserted that the root cause of spontaneous decentralisation (or 'fence-breaking' – *pha rao) was the chronic shortages of materials, power and fuels (Dam Van Nhue and Le Si Thiep, 1981: 24). This had broken the restraints of the existing economic management system. SOEs had been 'turned loose' and had to fend for themselves.

Their strategies had taken two main directions: changes in allocative mechanisms and output diversification. These were, however, related. SOEs had set about obtaining materials by purchasing them in the free market, or by going directly to other SOEs and other regions; they had also entered into direct contracts with customers in a position to supply needed materials.

SOEs had carried out a massive expansion of extra-plan activity in minor lines. This had taken a great variety of forms and varied greatly in scale. The intention behind such activities also varied. Sometimes SOEs had sought to increase cash incomes, or the income in kind paid to workers; alternatively, disposal of minor products enabled the SOE to obtain inputs used in the production of major lines (Dam Van Nhue and Le Si Thiep, 1981: 24).

There is abundant evidence from the micro level to support these observations (Chapter 6). A particularly striking example was the northern soap industry (p. 72), an area where allocative tensions were inhibiting output growth. Other clear examples came from paper and textiles. These are discussed further below. Before that, however, we need to discuss the detail of policy change relating to SOEs. The focus of policy was essentially conservative, though tactical concessions, by legalising market participation, protected those involved (see quotes from the panel on p. 61).

Towards the transitional model: partial reform?

By mid-1981 the various contradictory aspects of the recentralising package were in place. These covered a number of different areas, which are conveniently classified under the headings of agriculture, industry, foreign trade, internal markets and resource allocation. Apart from the elements of the August 1979 Sixth Plenum resolution itself, public documentation prior to 1981 referred almost entirely to agriculture. As has been seen, during early 1980 the political climate changed, and this was marked initially by attacks upon free market activity; these were associated with 26-NQ/TW of June 1980 (p. 28). But pro-market thinking as a *systemic* issue could not come to the fore.

The 'new course' – construing a transitional model

While the 'new course' remained somewhat confused, various Vietnamese documents are available outlining its contents. Of these a pamphlet issued by the Ministry of Labour is of particular interest (BLD, 1981). The booklet is relatively early, and claims to refer only to policies introduced between the Sixth Plenum and June 1981.

The document deals almost immediately with issues relating to markets and resource allocation. Crucial to this was the principle of 'economic advantage' in official purchases of agricultural output. This was understood to have two dimensions: first, cooperatives should be adequately remunerated and have the right to exchange goods on the market – in other words, state purchasing agencies should pay more attention to economic interests in their relations with agricultural cooperatives; second, entire regions should be treated in the same way – 'A locality that produces better and contributes more agricultural materials should enjoy a higher level of consumption than another region' (BLD, 1981: 18).

But while this principle was used to support a number of measures, the ambiguity behind the 'new course' meant that little was cut and dried. Almost the only area where things were made clear was in the treatment of foreign trade (BLD, 1981: 19–20). Interestingly, the document did not assert the right of production units to have direct contact with foreign markets, but stressed instead that unions and specialised companies could have such access, albeit subject to the guidance and direction of the Ministry of Foreign Trade.

The conflicts of interest between localities and central government were acknowledged; but there was no simple way of resolving them. The document therefore took the same basic approach as much else in the 'new course' – it asserted that each side had to respect the other, and sought refuge in the notion that the 'list' would allow resolution of the conflicts. But even this was unclear – the locality had to respect the centre's rights over goods that it managed or for which there was a 'partial mobilisation indicator' (i.e. a levy placed on the region), while the region had the right to determine the production, price and allocation of other goods (BLD, 1981: 19).

The document went at some length into the complicated details of accounting for goods transferred between the centre and so-called 'Level II' organisations – provinces, cities and special zones – and then also to levels below that again (BLD, 1981: 39–48). This reveals the enormous difficulties involved in coping with the wide price differentials that were opening up, and which had varying impacts upon the cash incomes of different levels of the state apparatus.[4]

The document relies heavily upon 25-CP in its description of the 'new course' in industry. It mentioned explicitly the SOE's right to retain 'list' output to use as a basis for direct relations with producers to acquire inputs. Other decrees reinforced the attempt to manage direct relations and increase the proportion of output controlled directly by the state (e.g. 64-CP, 23 February 1981 – see below). Much effort went into explaining the changes in the profit and pricing systems.

This document shows the complex nature of policy logic and its inconsistencies. Without a clear commitment to shifting towards a market economy, and facing a need to manage a situation of near collapse of the existing system through tactical concessions, control and negotiation had to coexist in a situation where planners, to gain extra cards, had to find ways of securing resources from a state economy that was spontaneously commercialising. Yet to do so would involve attacking the tactical concessions associated with the Sixth Plenum, and central to these was 25-CP.

Legalising SOE commercialisation: 25-CP

Council of Ministers' decree 25-CP ('A number of policies and measures to continue to develop the rights in production and trade and to financial autonomy of SOEs') is a document of great importance to the history of industrial organisation.

Do Muoi, deputy chairman of the council, signed it on 21 January 1981, and it was published in the official gazette a few days later. While the decree undoubtedly reined in the burgeoning unplanned activities of many SOEs, it also encouraged the more conservative or less well placed to explore such possibilities. It was thus two-sided in its basic meaning. While recentralising in intent, it also marked a clear step in the abandonment of the old 'pure' neo-Stalinist programme.

The decree formally based itself upon the Sixth and Ninth Plena of the Central Committee, and also 26-NQ/TW on distribution and circulation. I have stressed the shift in policy emphasis between the Sixth and Ninth Plena (p. 28) and their quite different economic contexts. 25-CP should therefore be seen as one of the various recentralising measures adopted from around the summer of 1980. The decree makes fascinating reading, especially in the context of the established rules of discourse.

The precise wording of the title deserves comment, since it appears well chosen to limit the extent to which unplanned activities were permitted. This compares with the blanket exhortation covered by the phrase '*bung ra' (explode) – see p. 23. But the title was also ambiguous.

First, the words used here translated as 'trade' (*kinh doanh) had then no precise English equivalent. A more accurate gloss would be 'non-production activities' – under capitalist conditions, perhaps 'business'.[5] Second, the words used to refer to the SOE's rights in production and trade, *quyen chu dong*, in effect have a meaning close to 'rights to play an active role in production and trade', so that 'autonomy' borders on an incorrect interpretation. Finally, however, the title does use 'autonomy' (*tu chu*), but only when referring to SOE finance. The decree's title therefore is better understood to refer to SOEs playing a more active role in the determination of production and trade, which – implicitly – should remain subject to central authority (p. 56).

The decree defined three categories of SOE.

First were those that had 'economic importance'. These had to be guaranteed supplies of materials and generally provided with the conditions for them to operate stably. They had to be managed centrally.

The second category was those SOEs for which the state could not guarantee adequate material and technical conditions. Such units had to use their own initiative to provide work for their employees. They had actively to seek out alternative sources of supply, change output and generally seek out valuable horizontal relations with other SOEs or cooperatives.

Finally, if the SOE could find no way of carrying on its activities, it could temporarily close down. But it had to make proper provisions to deal with its equipment and workers, and must not lose its key cadres and workers (BLD, 1981: 18–19).

The key to understanding this is the role played under 'aggravated shortage' by the conditionality and negotiation that accompanied the varying ability of the state's material supply network to deliver means of production to any given SOE.[6] This meant, of course, that membership of the second category of SOEs offered encouragement to those wishing to development horizontal – market-oriented – relations.

Inputs availability formed the basis for the multi-plan system. Here the decree was quite clear:

> Apart from the plan issued by the state, the state encourages Enterprises actively to produce more, both of their principle and their minor products, and also to expand other work of an industrial nature (with regard to production Enterprises) or expand trade (with regard to trading Enterprises). This depends upon the Enterprise having spare capacity and the ability to 'self-supply' [*tu cung ung*] with the necessary material conditions. (BLD, 1981: 19)

The decree stated that this meant the SOE's plan had three parts: the part, issued by the state, *for which materials were guaranteed*; the part the SOE carried out itself (*tu lam*); and the part made up of minor or non-list (*san xuat phu*) output. Market-based activities were thus labelled as part of the plan, a rhetorical win of great significance.

While this system subsequently came to be called the 'three-plan' system, for obvious reasons, and these three elements were referred to as 'Plan A', 'Plan B' and 'Plan C', the decree did not do this. The three parts

The transitional model of the 1980s: a new solution?

were seen as the constituent parts of a single plan, which had to be reported to higher levels. But higher levels only approved the first two elements (BLD, 1981). Here, the nomenclature of the 'three plans' is used for convenience.

The novelty here was the notion that SOEs could legitimately produce 'list' goods 'outside' the state's formal traditional planning system, which remained preserved in Plan A. This was to operate on the basis of a computation of input needs based quite conventionally upon the economic-technical norms fixed by the state or branch, and set so as to enable the SOE to meet its plan indicators. These indicators were thus to be set with reference to the state's ability to guarantee delivery of the inputs needed to meet them (BLD, 1981). Furthermore, planners had to tell the SOE beforehand the level of supplies they could deliver to permit it to set about finding additional inputs. This suggested, of course, that such additional inputs could – if not should – be used to support production of goods for delivery to the state; in other words, a net diversion of resources from the burgeoning network of unplanned 'outside' activities back into the planned system. But whether this intent would be realised, of course, would depend on factors outside planners' control.

These changes implied a *qualitative* change in the nature of relations between individual SOEs and their economic environment. Their increased power is marked not only by positioning them as entities that negotiate with planners, but by *formally recognising them as such*. Here the idea that Plan A was dependent upon planners' actually delivering what the plan said they would deliver is of particular interest.

We have seen this discussed earlier in the case of cooperatives (p. 108), but here it is strongly marked. The issue would return as the direction of policy shifted back to support SOEs late in the decade. But what is happening here is the *formal* recognition of what appears to Western eyes as a *voluntary* contracting relationship. The leading thinker Dao Xuan Sam was early to broach the vast set of issues associated with this notion, which is of course closely related to the evolving and disputed meanings of SOE autonomy, not to mention 'civil society' (pp. xx and 82) (Fforde, 2005b).

This was further clarified by the decree's understanding of the nature of Plan B, for the 'part of the plan that the SOE carried out by itself' was defined as follows:

> When the state plan cannot yet mobilise all of the Enterprise's production capacity because the state cannot guarantee adequate

> input and raw material supplies, the Enterprise may, if it is able to cope itself with securing the missing input and raw material supplies needed to produce extra goods within its allocated tasks, construct the part of the plan that it carries out itself. (BLD, 1981)

Here the phrase 'within its allocated tasks' refers to 'list' output.[7] The definition of the 'plan to produce minor output' confirms this, for it is understood to mean 'The part of production organised by the Enterprise in a supplementary manner, which does not lie within its allocated tasks' (BLD, 1981).

25-CP makes it clear that the introduction of Plan B was *not* simply intended to increase planners' control over production. For example, it stipulated that the SOE could ask for changes during the plan period. Furthermore, if a customer asked for services or output outside the original (three-part) plan, then the SOE did not have to ask for permission to meet the demand. It only had to let the superior level know what it was doing: 'On the basis of the general [i.e. three-part] plan, the SOE Manager has the right to supplement the SOE's concrete production-trade plan, so long as this is on the basis of respect for state law and an adequate implementation of the state's plan targets' (BLD, 1981: 20).

Furthermore, the state bank was authorised to lend funds to support Plan B activities, while SOEs could use their profits to build up capital such as circulating capital.

The key was the attitude taken to what was done with the SOE's output – 'output disposal' (*tieu thu san pham*) – and here the decree was quite unambiguous:

> Output belonging to the parts of the plan put out by the state and carried out by the state must all be sold to the material supply or state trading organs for distribution according to the state plan. Priority for the sale of minor products belongs to state trading organs. If state trading organs neither accept the goods nor carry out their purchase contracts the Enterprise has the right to sell to purchase-sale cooperatives or dispose of them itself. (BLD, 1981: 20–1)

However, in Plans B and C, if it was judged necessary for the SOE to keep back some output to exchange for materials (including imports) to continue production, then the SOE had to ask permission from the ministry or People's Committee. Also, the SOE was forbidden to keep back more than 10 per cent of its minor output for internal distribution among its workers and cadres. The decree stated that the SOE itself should not determine the proportion of goods of all sorts that it retained for direct horizontal exchange or internal distribution.

The main intent of 25-CP was thus to control SOEs' allocative relations – who they bought from and who they sold to – rather than production within the factories. This conclusion is further supported by the discussion of plan indicators, which kept the existing system of nine indicators for SOEs with 'relatively stable production conditions', but reduced the number to five for others (effectively those not entitled to 100 per cent supply from the state and so likely to pursue Plan B activities). These were as follows.

- The value of realised output (including the value of exports).
- The volume produced of principal products (including exports).
- The value of the wage fund.
- Profits and obligatory contributions to the state budget.
- Principal materials supplied by the state.

The idea was that the choice between these two quite different systems should depend upon the degree of 'relative stability of production'. The decree does not attempt to define what this might mean operationally, but it is quite clear about the relative priority of Plans A and B: 'If the enterprise implements its own plan but does not implement the part put out by the state, and does not have a good reason for doing so, it will be penalised materially...' (BLD, 1981: 20–1).

The pressure upon SOEs to acquire resources directly (i.e. horizontally) but then dispose of them to the state reflected the generally adverse incentives facing planners in trying to secure SOE output.

The decree stipulated that earnings from different plans had to be distributed to all the SOE's workers and cadres to 'avoid those working on Plan A earning less than those in Plan B, and those in "list" products earning less than those in minor lines' (BLD, 1981: 22). The SOE was allowed to use contracts with workers to implement its various plans.

In all this, bearing in mind the behaviour entailed by 'fence-breaking' (*pha rao*), it is natural that the decree reminded managers of their responsibilities. This throws some light upon the real standards by which such people were to be judged. They were specifically allowed to sign the relevant contracts and do the various deals associated with the different plans. They had the explicit right to use the SOE's capital and acquire additional funds and credits to expand production and trade. But the SOE manager would be judged by the material output and profits contributed to the state, as well as by increases in the incomes of its cadres and workers. He or she had the right to recruit and dismiss workers, to reject workers sent by superior levels and so on, 'as stipulated in the Enterprise Statute'. But the decree stated also that the Council of Ministers made the relevant economic ministers or People's Committee chairmen responsible for the 'direct guidance' of their SOEs in implementing the decree (BLD, 1981: 23).

Conclusions

It was the way in which policy, through 25-CP, now formally treated SOEs as relatively autonomous units with which planners should negotiate that was fundamental. The rules of this negotiation varied according to how the relationship with the SOE varied. The three-plan system defined these (with some effort) with reference to an intellectual structuring of the different ways in which SOEs acquired and disposed of inputs and outputs, i.e. allocative mechanisms (p. 10).

By saying that they were all 'plans' this stopped differentiating them in terms of whether and by whom they were managed, controlled or planned through the idea that Plans B and C were the SOE's 'own plans'. It also ignored differentiating them in terms of the fixed assets used to produce them. These were not at all always those supplied to the SOE by the plan, for there were already signs of the emergence of capital 'of' SOEs – called, of course, 'own capital' (*von tu co).

Central to this was, rather, the core issue of the transition from plan to market, viewed in terms of the end point – markets. The distinction between the plans was fundamentally in terms of allocative mechanisms: were inputs and outputs acquired through some plan, or rather according to local calculations of interest and decisions that were made based upon those?

The stroke of brilliance, however, was to label the essentially commercial activities of Plans B and C as 'planned'.

But, as 25-CP, the Sixth Plenum and fence-breaking surfaced into documentary sources, what was happening as SOEs explored commerce (and plan) for opportunities? It turns out that there is much micro-level public information on this. Around SOEs, as these relations built up, were an increasing range of opportunities and calculations. Initially, similarly to other countries, markets seemed ill developed (note 16 on p. 47).

Notes

1. See *Nhan Dan* (1982e). The decision of the 1979 Sixth Plenum can be found in *Nhan Dan* (1979l); also NXBST (1980).
2. For example, editorials on 2 June 1979 on ways of stimulating consumer goods production, on 5 June 1979 on local industry and on 14 June 1979 on economic levers (*Nhan Dan*, 1979g, 1979h, 1979i).
3. Two noticeable points about this article are, first, its concern to describe what was actually happening at the grassroots level before setting about analysis and prescription; second, its willingness to discuss the aims and intentions of production units as autonomous entities.
4. The document reveals very clearly indeed the recollectivising intent of the 'new course' in agriculture. This was quite consistent with Party policy from the middle of 1980, and stressed the active and controlling role to be played by the cooperative in agriculture (BLD, 1981: 60–76).
5. By the late 1980s the term indeed became synonymous with 'business'.
6. Thus can be seen how one of the basic characteristics of the real operation of the DRV model in Vietnam was now simply being legalised.
7. That is, goods on the list of commodities subject to direct allocation through the plan (note 13 on p. 113).

6

Just how important was policy? Spontaneous decentralisation, 1979–1980

Exogenous shocks, 1978–1979, and their immediate local effects

Prelude – the changing balance of incentives

The economic shocks of the late 1970s gave a sharp added energy to the underlying allocative tensions within the economy. The central economic organs of the state, which had been attempting rather vainly to overcome the systemic diversion of economic resources away from priority sectors, found that their position had severely deteriorated. The volume of resources they controlled directly had fallen sharply. Furthermore, the sharp reduction in state cash income from sales – of both directly imported goods and output based upon them – raised the state's fiscal (cash) deficit and helped push up free market prices. In the north a gathering process of agricultural decollectivisation increased food supplies on free markets, further shifting incentives against the plan (Fforde, 1989: Chapter 12; Ngo Vinh Long, 1985a, 1985b). This had little directly to do with policy.

The economic crisis was therefore taking the form of an abrupt drop in the relative economic power of central state economic organs and their ability to supply their own producers with the inputs needed to operate installed capacity. This was true in both the north and the south.[1] Expressed in this way, it appears that the crisis was simply an intensification of the underlying tensions within the Vietnamese economy that dated from the first FYP and the early 1960s. It is not therefore surprising that there was a strong element of continuity, and, while the extent of the crisis and the initial policy reforms were rather novel, there was a strong sense of *déjà vu* about both many aspects of the debate and the strategies adopted by individual production units. SOEs, planners and others had been there before.

The differential impact of import dependency

The Chinese aid cuts had profound effects. The historical pattern of Chinese aid had increased the vulnerability of the central economic organs in Hanoi to pressure for relaxation of control. There were a number of reasons for this.

During the first FYP regional policy in the DRV had sought to decentralise industry, and to this end the Thai Nguyen and Viet Tri industrial complexes had been set up to move steel and chemicals outside the existing major cities of Hanoi and Haiphong. The new factories in Hanoi had concentrated upon consumer goods, and nature had created an enclave dependent upon imported raw materials. Chinese aid furthermore had, with exceptions such as the Thai Nguyen iron and steel complex, contributed greatly to increasing industrial capacity in consumer goods sectors. Hanoi thus had a significant number of factories producing extremely valuable consumer goods that were dependent upon Chinese assistance. These included the Dong Xuan clothing factory, the Sao Vang rubber goods factory, the Rang Dong thermos and lightbulb factory, the March 8th textile factory, the Hong Ha office goods factory and the Hanoi soap factory. The Van Dien phosphate factory was probably also important in supplying fertiliser to the city's rural districts. Many of these installations were capable of rapid output diversification, and goods such as thermos flasks, bicycle spares made of metal and rubber and soap were in great demand on the free market.

By comparison the USSR's assistance was less significant, and in Hanoi its most visible contribution was the large No. 1 machine tools factory, which, interestingly, formed the basis for the grassroots report on industrial management to the 1982 Third Plenum during the initial stages of the recentralisation drive.

Hanoi was among the first localities to encourage its factories to utilise new sources of raw materials, and in 1978 this seems to have early taken the form of various light metal goods – bicycle handlebars and iron beds (*Nhan Dan*, 1979b). The balance between regional and central industry in the city was to shift during the early 1980s in favour of the former as local investment mounted. A factor acting against central economic organs was the precise timing of the 1978–1979 economic crisis, in that it occurred too soon for the major investment projects launched by the centre during the second FYP to have come to fruition. During the early 1980s the city took a number of active steps to encourage development of its own industry.

Ho Chi Minh City's position was somewhat different from that of Hanoi. The same conflicts existed between central and regional authority, but these resulted more from the pattern of nationalisation since 1975. Resource flows from the north to support economic activity after international economic links were cut in 1975–1976 tended to enhance the position of the centre; but from then on the lack of established supplies equivalent to the long-standing relations between factories in the north and the Chinese and Soviet aid donors meant that the city's authorities had greater scope in finding their own sources of supply as attempts were made to re-establish trading links. In addition, the absence of the relatively secure rural hinterland that in Hanoi took the form of the collectivised surrounding districts meant that Ho Chi Minh City had to place greater emphasis upon mutually beneficial exchange in its relations with suppliers, which again acted against the centre. Almost no economic assistance from socialist countries went to the city's industry.

A basic difference between factories was their origin: in the north, whether they dated from the French period or had been built with Chinese, Soviet or Central European assistance; in the south, whether they predated 1975.[2] Managers and workers were strongly influenced by donors' work practices and style of organisation. It was said that the old French factories often worked particularly well because it had been the practice of the French to set up systems that allowed them to delegate authority so that they themselves had merely to make occasional inspections. Operating within a basically capitalist environment with functional accounting systems, this had often encouraged the Vietnamese staff to take the initiative and get things to work without relying upon superior levels to sort out difficulties as they arose. It is striking that this comment should have been made in the mid-1980s, some 30 years after the French departure. Apart from public utilities such as electricity, the most important factories taken over from the French were probably the Haiphong cement factory, the Hanoi alcohol factory and the Nam Dinh textile mill (Fforde, 1983: 62–3).

Spontaneous decentralisation, 1979–1980 – grassroots experiences

The Sixth Plenum of August 1979 and the changing balance of incentives to a large extent acted in the same direction, encouraging economic agents of many different types, including SOEs, to increase economic activity and exploit opportunities. This led to a fascinating and vivid pattern of economic change (see the list of rhetorical questions on p. 20). The pattern was varied by region: while nationally 40 per cent of SOE output was either Plan B or Plan C, in Hanoi this was 20 per cent and in Ho Chi Minh City the percentage was far higher (p. 173).

Grassroots reports

Discussing the main changes of 1979 and the Sixth Plenum, the panel reported that the economic situation was not something they recalled with any clarity: the principal memory of 1979 was the Chinese attacks. The main aspects of economic life were as follows.

This was the year of the greatest material difficulties. Workers bought their rice with ration coupons, but had to eat it mixed with manioc, maize and wheat. Foodstuffs were extremely scarce. Second, due to the Chinese attacks Vietnam returned to a war footing. In the north they dug trenches and evacuated the population from urban areas. Young workers were called up.

Third, Chinese aid goods were now no longer available, but supplies from the USSR soon arrived in large volumes, including consumer goods such as cloth, watches, electric fans and so on. According to one manager, the USSR bought all their tea and supplied them with rice, petrol and tractors for the SOE. This improved conditions in the SOE.

Finally, at the end of 1979 the government issued 279-CP 'On policies to stimulate and circulate goods not managed by the state and supply materials and goods produced from local materials and waste and by-products [*phe lieu, *phe pham]' (p. 171). One manager said that because of this decree a number of denunciations from conservatives in the SOE were ignored. The strong 'fence-breaking' of earlier years was accepted and even praised: 'Had this decree come out a year later I should have gone to prison.'

Experiences of northern factories built with Chinese assistance

Those SOEs built with Chinese assistance had suffered earlier than others from the effects of the withdrawal of aid. A number of these are of particular interest.

Exploitation of buoyant consumer demand – the Rang Dong thermos and lightbulb factory

Chinese aid had supported a number of large light industrial projects in the north during the first FYP. For instance, the Rang Dong thermos and lightbulb factory in Hanoi was inaugurated in January 1963. Both its major products were in strong consumer demand, and it was well placed to capture shortage premia if it was allowed to do so.[3]

In 1978, as Chinese aid was cut back, the factory found itself suffering from its dependency upon the Chinese for spare parts and raw materials. It began to seek ways of improving its input supplies in 1978, although this mainly involved attempting to use its own resources to upgrade its equipment (*Nhan Dan*, 1979e). The factory's main focus through 1979–1980 was on obtaining a better deal from the state trading organs that bought its output, and also upon finding ways of improving workers' incomes. The basis for the latter was a greater utilisation of piecework schemes, which helped push incomes up sharply during the last quarter of 1980 (*Nhan Dan*, 1981c). The factory had thus been able to cut costs and increase its contribution to the state budget.

But around this time the factory was accused of illegally disposing of its output. The defence offered was that the factory had indeed been disposing of output directly, but that this was supra-plan and 'own-plan' output. The latter had risen sharply, so that by the first quarter of 1981 around half of its thermos flasks were disposed of directly. But this was not simply a matter of sales on to the free market. The ways in which the SOE exploited its new ability to dispose of high-value goods reveal much about the pattern of incentives created by conditions of 'aggravated shortage'. Furthermore, criticism of the SOE indicates those areas where pressure was mounting for restraint.

The SOE had kept records of much of its activities. According to the accountants' return, there were three main recipients of its output. Under the old system the Household Goods Company of the Ministry of Internal Trade had responsibility for purchasing these goods. Increasingly through 1980, however, the SOE had disposed of them quite differently.

First, it had allocated amounts to supply organs which delivered to it materials, transport and energy. Second, the owning ministry (the Ministry of Light Industry) had obtained lightbulbs and thermos flasks, which it had then allocated through the Association of Porcelain and Pottery Enterprises to unexpected demands from organs and factories inside and outside the branch and the army.

Third, the SOE had itself sold many on the retail market, and carried out 'internal distribution' (*phan phoi noi bo) to its own cadres and workers. Through 1980 each worker received on average four thermos flasks. The SOE had been widely distributing its products in response to 'letters of introduction' from cooperatives, state organs and individuals.[4] Prior to the 1981 Tet festival the SOE had made money through a batch sale to the Hanoi General Retail Company at prices way above the industrial wholesale price. It had used the proceeds to buy rice and chickens for the workers to eat over Tet.

Areas where the SOE's behaviour was said to be quite specifically illegal were in its establishment of a storehouse for keeping these goods and in its use of volumes of cash well above the legal maxima. The SOE was clearly able rapidly to generate cash holdings that it could use freely. A *Nhan Dan* (1981c) article reported difficulties with quality, admittedly long a problem for the SOE, and suggested that these had worsened as patterns of disposal widened.

Problems with inputs supplies: materials

The Sao Vang rubber goods factory and the Hanoi soap factory were also Chinese-assisted Hanoi consumer goods factories.

The former had long presented a strong argument for permitting output diversification. The waste from its main output lines could be used to produce valuable consumer goods such as bicycle spares; it was, however, easily identifiable and there were not many sources of supply. Possibly because of this, controls were relatively tight, but the factory had been allowed to diversify into minor products as early as 1972 (*Nhan Dan*, 1979u). While it had received favourable resource allocation through the plan during the period of the state industrial enterprise statute (circa 1977), it suffered as Chinese aid was cut.

A 'model' SOE, stressing the orthodox system of norms and wide use of piecework, found itself having to scratch around for waste materials and under rather strict supervision. Input substitution in 1978 permitted it to manufacture car tyres, and the availability of waste materials appears to have facilitated diversification into high-value consumer goods such as tables and chairs.

By late 1979 it was still being restrained. The authorities permitted it to sell scraps for 5 xu a kilo, but only to the Bat Trang porcelain enterprise and the city transport branch (*Nhan Dan*, 1979u). Despite this, however, the factory managed to make a lot of money through 1979 by selling minor output. It was asserted, moreover, that this had required almost no additional inputs and was based entirely upon a more efficient use within the factory of waste materials. It is more likely, however, that there had been a reallocation of raw materials towards higher-value uses. Supply of a new machine in 1980 reportedly helped to boost output, but may have strengthened the hand of the SOE's superiors in inhibiting free disposal (*Nhan Dan*, 1980g). The machine permitted economies in both labour and material use.

The Hanoi soap factory confronted buoyant demand and a chronic shortage of one particular input. Since the domestic substitute for imported oil was palm oil, and this was only available in the south, this focused interest very acutely upon the economic basis for inter-regional exchange. In 1979 the factory received only some 16 per cent of planned oil supplies, and, as stocks fell, in 1980 the situation deteriorated further. By the end of August 1980 they had obtained only 6 per cent of the year's planned volume (*Nhan Dan*, 1980l). The factory had got as far as carrying out some 'extra-plan' purchases from peasants in the south, but had faced from some southern provinces a blanket refusal to permit such deals. The factory had, however, been able to establish business relations with two northern provinces, Thanh Hoa and Hoang Lien Son. By 1981, however, the factory had been able to establish new sources of input supply (*Nhan Dan*, 1981d) and was able to exploit soap's high value by selling it to the mines in return for foreign exchange (*Nhan Dan*, 1982a).

An interesting example of the diversification of input suppliers permitted by creative strategies was the method adopted by the Dan Sinh textile enterprise. To justify setting up a separate plant that had a quite independent accounting system, the SOE presented it as a way of employing women who could not work the full shifts required by the main plant due to poor health or family hardship. The plant was well stocked with machines. It provided the basis for the establishment of direct relations with the Nam Dinh Textile Association, the March 3rd textile enterprise and a number of southern SOEs for the purchase of thread (*Nhan Dan*, 1980h).

Labour relations

Local experiences

There is much interesting information on the state of labour relations, tending on the whole to confirm considerable potential for increased labour effort in response to higher real incomes.

Among the many intriguing examples of SOE behaviour in the face of difficult labour relations, that of the Ha Bac oil factory is particularly interesting. Along with a number of other SOEs, such as the Nam Dinh textile factory, the Sao Vang rubber factory and the Hai Chau bread factory, it was cited as an early user of output contracts to boost worker incentives (*Nhan Dan*, 1980p). But it was clearly encountering great problems with its workers.

The factory belonged to the Ministry of Staples and Food, and was mainly involved in pressing peanuts to produce oil for export (*Nhan Dan*, 1980o). For many years it had used piecework as a basis for calculating wages, and this had tended to make workers ignore production costs in favour of output maximisation. The factory's utilisation of coal and electricity and the time spent on repairs were all well above the official norms. There was little attempt to use waste products such as shells. Furthermore, the way in which norms had been calculated had lacked incentive effect, and if output reached 30 per cent above norm the factory recalculated and raised the norm. The workers were generally fed up, there had been stoppages and thousands of hours had been lost. State wages had lost most of their value:

> People calculated – a small gain, such as 7 dong, was almost nothing compared with the value of a tiny scrap of waste material 'taken for sale outside' [**dem ban ngoai*], or taken home for the family's livestock, or even beside the possibility of taking time off to 'work outside' [**lam ngoai*]. (*Nhan Dan*, 1980m)

A new method was devised to pay people more: it involved increasing their production autonomy by introducing group contracts based upon a new set of labour and input norms calculated in money terms. These formed the basis for contracts between groups of workers, led by their foremen and negotiated between them and the factory manager. There was no explicit suggestion that workers would find it easier to dispose of output on the free market, for bonuses were apparently payable in cash.

Part of the value of supra-contract output went to the workers, part to the factory's welfare fund and part to cut the cost price. But, combined with efficiency and output gains, labour incomes had risen substantially, from 51 to 83 dong a month.[5] This sharp percentage gain was probably inadequate to explain the changed labour effort, however, and this may have come from undeclared 'internal distribution' (**phan phoi noi bo*). Workers' access to shortage premia thus increased labour effort; the contracting system internalised costs and raised efficiency; and output rose. Labour supervision was apparently no longer necessary, again implying that the material incentive system was far more effective.

Other examples of the use of contract payments to boost the value of workers' incomes came from a number of construction companies. The No. 3 provincial construction company in Thanh Hoa reportedly experienced a 72 per cent fall in days lost to 'illness' between September and November 1980 in response to a sharp jump in wages to around 350 dong a month. Interestingly, in a comment on the relatively high wages paid before the changes, this was said to be around a 75 per cent increase, implying that earnings had previously been around 200 dong. This compares with typical earnings in the late 1970s of 50 dong a month.

But other units where this system was introduced through 1980 failed to produce such sharp income jumps. The No. 6 Haiphong construction site was praised for paying its top skilled workers up to 5.4 dong a day (*Nhan Dan*, 1980n) – this cannot have meant more than around 150 dong a month. Indications of hidden interactions between the contract system and conditional leakages on to the free market came from the Bac Thai construction materials production company. This time, however, 30–40 dong gains in monthly salaries had helped cut 'losses' (i.e. pilfering) by a reported 90 per cent (*Nhan Dan*, 1981a).

The most striking reports of labour problems came from the coal mines in the north.[6] The departure of the Chinese labour force in 1978–1979 badly hit many, as the new labourers found the work extremely taxing and the sector suffered from common problems of the low value of 'inside' wages. A long article in *Nhan Dan* (1980f) discussed the problems of the Quang Ninh coal area. Both the Uong Bi and Hong Gai companies were reporting high levels of absenteeism, and the Vang Danh coal mine of the Uong Bi mining company was losing 16 per cent of its workers on average. The Hong Gai company lost more than 1 million days from absenteeism during 1979. To overcome these difficulties, some bonus schemes were pushing total monthly earnings up near 700 dong (*Nhan Dan*, 1980f).

The development of regional economies

Provinces

The development of regional industry during this initial period was closely related to the buoyancy of agricultural production and marketing during the winter of 1979–1980. It also varied substantially from province to province. In the traditionally poor and overpopulated centre, Quang Nam in Da Nang province soon showed itself to be quietly adventurous but unwilling to been seen going beyond a middle-of-the-road position. Local industry included textiles and silk, and there was also some light engineering capacity (*Nhan Dan*, 1979a). The province completed agricultural collectivisation in the late 1970s, well before the Mekong delta. Local industry had been able to supply machinery to local agriculture – for instance, each cooperative reportedly received two forges and a feed-preparation machine (*Nhan Dan*, 1979c).

From this base, the province was able to implement development strategies that reveal a rather eclectic approach to organisation. Indeed, the day after *Nhan Dan* published a piece by Le Duan on the regional economy (*Nhan Dan*, 1979o), the paper printed a long article on the province's experiences with the development of regional industry (*Nhan Dan*, 1979p). This confirmed the province's engineering capacity, and stressed support for its traditional industries. Artisanal workers had been collectivised, and the resulting cooperatives integrated through putting-out contracts with SOEs or trading companies. However, many workers still spent time on their own, and 'When the cooperatives have work they collect around them, and when they do not they freely search for raw materials and dispose of the output' (*Nhan Dan*, 1979p). This pointed up the province's main complaint, which was the shortage of raw materials.

By early 1981 the province, again keeping a position in the middle of the road, was reporting successes with the introduction of output contracts in local industry (*Nhan Dan*, 1981b). There was, however, no suggestion of workers selling payments in kind on the free market.

In the heavily populated northern deltas, local economic development in 1979–1980 revealed much about the patterns of economic competition that grew up around scarce resources. South of the Red River delta, the poor province of Nghe Tinh had suffered badly from US bombing. The capital, Vinh, had been a major centre of regional industrial development during the first FYP, but was almost razed to the ground. Its population growth was fairly high, and per capita rice production fell slightly during the period 1976–1984, from 193 kg to 188 kg. Furthermore, it was the home province of many top leaders, and famed for its revolutionary spirit. It had little to fear from experimentation.

A long article in *Nhan Dan* in November 1979 pointed out the inefficiency of the existing way of organising artisanal industry. There were reportedly over 100,000 artisans in a total provincial population of around 3.1 million (*Nhan Dan*, 1979q; TCTK, 1983: 13). The 'existing potential was not well utilised' – hard, concrete examples showed this. For instance, the administrative supply system did not really deliver much to the members of the forestry teams of the artisanal cooperatives. By comparison, workers in the forestry SOEs were treated as state workers and supplied 'properly' through the subsidised supply system. The province had not been allowed to use the abundant supplies of wood lying about in its forests. Output of wood-based products therefore, it was argued, suffered greatly.

The article referred to the 'new policy', which had greatly improved things. In one example the state, previously supplying materials as part of putting-out contracts, now could no longer do so (*Nhan Dan*, 1979q). This had happened to a provincial clothing cooperative (Thong Nhat). The province had therefore encouraged the cooperative to 'organise its workers to use scrap material fully, and other supplies, and also to go to textile SOEs to buy cotton and thread'. In a short time this had enabled the cooperative to sell some 2,500 quilts to the state.

Another example was metalworking, where work had been given out for household-based production. As an indication of the effects of the growing free market at this time, however, the article complained of spontaneous diversification by artisanal cooperatives in response to sudden availability of different materials, and investment in machines to facilitate this (*Nhan Dan*, 1979q). The more skilled artisans had been asking for permission to stop work so they could 'work freely' (*lam tu do).

North of Nghe Tinh lies Thanh Hoa, which also possessed a diverse economy by virtue of its substantial mountains and uplands and was particularly revealing. The province had a fertile area producing rushes, Nga On, facing sharply falling yields (*Nhan Dan*, 1980j). The basic reason for this, according to the article, was incentives. The province had had reason to look after the sector, and had ignored it. Rushes were mainly used to make sleeping mats. The price on the free market was many times that offered by the state's purchasing organs, so the good rushes were sold on the free market by the people who grew them (*Nhan Dan*, 1980j). Furthermore, two separate organisations were responsible for buying rushes and setting up putting-out contracts for sleeping mats – a foreign trade company and an agricultural products company. They operated quite different systems, especially of prices. The article, referring it should be remembered to a rather conservative area, advocated three solutions: better incentives and organisation of rush-growing; giving the foreign trade company a monopoly and making it simplify its procedure; and giving the sector priority supplies of staples (*Nhan Dan*, 1980j).

Among Red River delta provinces, the two situated on the coast south of Hanoi – Thai Binh and Ha Nam Ninh – are of interest in that they have no border with the two major industrial centres of Hanoi and Haiphong. Both were facing major worries over their food supplies. Over the period 1976–1984 per capita staples output rose from 266 kg to 309 kg in Thai Binh and 234 kg to 270 kg in Ha Nam Ninh. Both had relatively slow-growing populations (1.9 per cent and 1.4 per cent annually respectively). Neither province had much to play with. With rising populations threatening a renewed erosion of the subsistence margin, their strategies are of great interest.

Through 1979 Thai Binh seems to have made considerable attempts to develop its sources of raw materials supplies for artisanal producers and to have reorganised production, in many cases by returning artisanal workers to agricultural cooperatives (*Nhan Dan*, 1979m). Earlier, the province had been successful in investing in weaving frames, and this was meant to be coordinated with a spinning mill that the Ministry of Light Industry had built in the province. They were ready to move up to 20,000 workers out of agricultural production into carpet-making, organised within the agricultural cooperatives (*Nhan Dan*, 1979d). The supply of raw materials was seen as the main constraint upon output growth here. Like others, the province started to set about finding resources for itself in 1978–1979. This was linked to development of provincial consumer goods production, which reportedly grew at around 10–15 per cent annually during the late 1970s (*Nhan Dan*, 1979f).

In 1978 gross output value of industrial consumer goods was put at 86 million dong (*Nhan Dan*, 1979f). The province had greatly increased the activities of its purchasing office, located in 15 provinces and cities, which was actively buying cotton, wood, steel, iron, aluminium, cement, lime and equipment such as 'old and broken machines'. It had spent around 2 million dong to date. Within its borders the province had been increasing the industrial crop area under its own control, growing rushes and jute in specialised areas. It was well aware of the consequences of ineffective purchasing strategies, since it had had to use 'emulation' (*thi dua) to encourage families to supply crops. Even so, 'Because the prices were wrong and the organisation was weak the province had only got one-quarter of expected supplies, and the rest had leaked out to other provinces' (*Nhan Dan*, 1979f).

What is striking about these strategies, however, is their relative dependence upon input supplies and greater efficiency (*Nhan Dan*, 1979m).

Ha Nam Ninh adopted a similar broad strategy, working through its own trading branch to seek out raw materials supplies (*Nhan Dan*, 1979j). It bought from the centrally managed textile factory in Nam Dinh. Unlike Thai Binh, however, it seems to have been actively encouraging cooperatives to look for a part (around one-third) of their input needs. This was exacerbating tensions between various allocative mechanisms.

As usual, the free market's ability to express the existence of shortages was important. In Nam Dinh a state store was almost empty of bicycle spares while a street market near to it was well stocked. A provincial cooperative (Van Trang, in Nam Ninh district) was producing these goods, but the state could not buy them. This was said to be because the province, while it had five organs for buying materials, only had one company responsible for putting these out to producers, and the committee of the provincial artisanal Cooperative Association, the committee of the purchase and sale cooperatives, the Industry Office and the Foreign Trade Office were busy buying materials for direct sale to producers. Units were taking hundreds of tonnes of materials for exchange against goods in other provinces. The situation was deeply confusing:

> Branches and production units are directly organising the exploitation of raw materials, reducing middlemen and intermediaries, cutting transport costs and quickly using the materials to produce valuable goods... this is good. The organs supplying materials to producers need to liaise quickly with the state trading organs so that the sale of materials can be linked to the purchase of products so as to ensure centralisation of commodities in the hands of the state. (*Nhan Dan*, 1979j)

Out of this, however, does come a picture of increasing levels of activity. Exports rose in both provinces (*Nhan Dan*, 1979k).

But by 1980 Ha Nam Ninh was starting to run out of steam, and local supplies of raw materials were inadequate to support further gains. In the first half of the year it could only meet around one-third of its producers' needs (*Nhan Dan*, 1980i). This was very much to do with the inability to maintain land yields in the area growing rushes used to make sleeping mats. This was blamed upon the inadequate supplies of consumer goods – especially staples – to the workers there, and the simple choice between using the land to grow rice or rushes (*Nhan Dan*, 1980k). Furthermore, it was accepted that payment according to ration was not a sufficient material incentive to rush-growers. The outlook was poor. Workers were selling rushes on the free market, and using the worst-quality supplies to meet putting-out contracts with the state. This was also happening in the area responsible for producing export products (*Nhan Dan*, 1980k).

The problems facing these provinces were magnified by the extent of free market activity, and here the experience of provinces near to Hanoi tends to confirm the overall trajectory of the northern economy at this time. The fundamental poverty of the region should not be forgotten. There were many such stories, although Ha Son Binh, containing the important town of Ha Dong just outside the capital's boundaries and a major and traditional commercial centre, was largely ignored by the official press during this period. I do not know why.

Haiphong

Modern Haiphong (the second largest city in the north) was set up as an administrative region in 1972 when the city was merged with Kien An province. This provided the city with an extensive rural hinterland, and the area saw its per capita staples output rise from 152 kg to 187 kg between 1976 and 1984. The city appears to have pushed rather hard for decentralising reforms, and was a strong supporter of the 'output contract' system in agriculture. Indeed, it was reportedly its earliest advocate (Huu Hanh, 1980). This evident ability to initiate new policies was also apparent in local industry, for by late 1979 its implementation of the Sixth Plenum had already taken the form of a resolution of the city's People's Committee (*Nhan Dan*, 1979s).

This resolution was an effective condemnation of national neo-Stalinist policies. Its main thrust aimed to stimulate local production of industrial crops, but it sought also to develop local industry, especially pottery, glass and bicycle spares, and to stabilise output of rubber and plastic goods. But local state industry was not oriented towards agriculture.

The city had started to produce over 200 new lines, especially household metal goods, bicycle spares and toys. Some parts of the city had allowed a sharp rise in individual artisans and artisanal groups, and output from waste and by-products had doubled. However, among rising numbers who had sought registration for private sector activity, service and repairs had been more important than producers. Furthermore, there was competition between cooperatives for technical workers, who often wanted to work for themselves.

The city continued to permit this expansion of activity through early 1980. It was extremely active in issuing regulations and lists of goods subject to its management, but it eased private goods circulation and tried to improve producer incentives (*Nhan Dan*, 1980a). It allowed SOEs to dispose of output freely 'if the state trading organs did not buy them' (*Nhan Dan*, 1980a). Output growth continued, and gross industrial output was up around 9 per cent on the year over the winter of 1979–1980. The city's producers had started to establish links with suppliers in other provinces, and this had helped it to start production of new products such as pens, bicycle pedals, paper and rubber sandals. This apparently sustainable but rather controlled growth process was marked by the asset census of late 1980 (*Nhan Dan*, 1980q). In early 1981 the city's small and artisanal cooperatives were over-fulfilling the plan for disposal of output to the state trading organs.

Haiphong appears to have been less concerned than Hanoi about the development of markets. Two reasons for this may have been the greater preponderance of local industry and the relative absence of the 'unproductive' bureaucrats staffing Hanoi's government offices, whose incomes were a major source of effective demand. The city seems to have started by increasing activities that involved the exploitation of local waste materials in 1978 and early 1979 (*Nhan Dan*, 1979b). By late 1979 attention had shifted to the performance of the consumer goods sector.

In the early stages commentators seem to have taken a relatively neutral view of developments. The city had undoubtedly permitted a considerable resurgence of private sector activity. Previously, to obtain a permit for economic activity or to produce a new product, the producer had to wait two or three months and had to complete 15–20 forms with ten to 15 stamps and 30–40 signatures. In recent months this had much improved. The producer's registration document no longer contained any limits on the goods produced, the labour force, the time taken to produce the good or the area of output disposal (*Nhan Dan*, 1979r).

There had been changes in the policies regarding taxation, accumulation funds and staples supplies. Some branches had seen their monthly staples allocation raised from 11 kg to 16 kg. Cooperators' monthly incomes had gone up from 40 to 60 dong (*Nhan Dan*, 1979r). Many SOEs had been establishing new allocative relations and advantageously selling cooperatives their surplus materials – for instance the woollens and netting enterprises (*Nhan Dan*, 1979r). On the roads many private traders could be found buying and selling plastic sandals, bottles and waste paper. But there were already problems, above all to do with increasing competition for raw materials. The better artisans felt that 'outside' work was preferable to 'inside' ('the outside foot is longer' – *chan ngoai dai hon chan trong).

Many SOEs were keeping back surplus materials to sell at a high price or make minor products themselves. As a result of the input shortages, very many producers were increasing their searches for new products and abandoning unprofitable putting-out contracts. Needless to say, under such conditions 'the question of taxation and purchase pricing is not clear' (Nhan Dan, 1979r). The city tried to argue that it was closely guiding this explosion of extra-plan activity (Nhan Dan, 1979t). To support its own position, it had opened up trading links with mountainous and southern provinces.

Towards the end of 1979 the output response in some local industries was spectacular: the city's gross industrial output in October was reportedly 10 per cent up on September, and there was a similar rise in November. Over an undisclosed period, paint output went from 250 to 900 tonnes and plastic sandals from 200,000 to 1 million pairs. There had been a sharp rise in such activities as the opening of minor plants by SOEs to produce extra-plan output. A number of shops had opened to carry out 'domestic export' of cultural objects. Most of these changes had occurred during the early autumn. They continued to expand rapidly during the winter of 1979–1980 (Nhan Dan, 1980b). Exports seem to have grown markedly, especially in carpets (Nhan Dan, 1980c, 1980e) and embroidery (Nhan Dan, 1980d).

Conclusions

Two main conclusions follow from this.

First, there is a clear and vivid narrative of spontaneous decentralisation from within the state sector. It responds to a combination of economic incentives, changes in the political atmosphere and intense interaction between SOEs and other elements of local economies. It is sometimes actively guided by the local state (Abrami, 2002).

Second, all of this was discussed in the official Party press. The preceding pages draw almost entirely upon Nhan Dan, the official VCP organ. This suggests, apart from the politics of it, which some attribute to the high-level protection given to journalists by the tensions at the peak, especially those between Le Duan and Truong Chinh, that the same 'go and find out' attitude epitomised by Ho Chi Minh (Duiker, 2000) was in play. There was relatively abundant information. Opinion was divided, though, and this is hardly surprising.

The main beneficiaries of fence-breaking activities were usually consumers and, in SOEs, mainly workers. Pay-offs to higher levels were simply pay-offs, and managers at this stage were not yet significantly moving to control new assets. Class formation was therefore extremely limited. What was happening was largely emerging from SOEs within which shared interests were rather keenly felt.

Grassroots comments

The opinion of the panel concerning 25-CP was as follows. All agreed that it was a step forward and formalised further 279-CP of 1979 (see p. 171). 25-CP legalised market activities of SOEs.

In industry the sign of renewal (*doi moi*) was 25-CP, and in agriculture order 100. The ideological meaning was the institutionalisation of a transitional model.[7] Because the government had 279-CP in 1979, but by 1980 the conservatives had returned through 26-NQ/TW (p. 28) that required close controls over private staples trade, 25-CP restated that trade in non-state-managed products was legal and accepted the three-plan system. All agreed 25-CP meant that SOEs had greater peace of mind and better conditions to develop.

The implementation conditions of 25-CP were that each SOE had to register its 'outside plan' activities and give priority to implementing targets supplied by the state. To put it another way, the SOE had to implement Plans A and B before it could implement Plan C. But in SOEs there were many 'flexible' ways of changing what happened – for example they could use some of the raw materials (inputs) for Plan A in Plan C to produce minor products.

One manager reported that it was mainly because of Plan C that worker welfare improved, and many workers asked to be moved to the workshop producing 'minor' products. Also, at this time managers had to be more alert and creative, rather than just doing what their superiors told them.

Comments on their experience of spontaneous marketisation during the period 1979–1980 were as follows.

First, it was very important to follow closely the documents of the Party and state, paying attention to the text and words so as to find 'openings' to fence-breaking. Second, it was important to proceed silently; hastiness would have been dangerous because there were still very many conservatives in the SOEs and they would have immediately reported to superiors. Third, anything done needed to be directly reported to the superior level. It was important only to ask for a general direction, while in implementation one had to be 'creative'. If there were criticisms, one should reply that the superior had given permission and the error was that the lower level had been too 'strong', but this had been in the interests of the collective which made it less serious.

Fourth, it was necessary to have a 'team for renovation' (*doi moi*), and within it there should be transparency regarding financial matters. In one opinion, if the manager was not open ('as nowadays') then he would certainly have gone to prison. This was because at that time the crime of 'embezzling socialist assets' was treated very seriously. If the superior level checked and found fence-breaking but no embezzlement then they would be sympathetic because the error was in the interests of the collective; if people had pocketed things as they do nowadays it would have been very dangerous. The panel were proud that they had been clean when they broke fences. According to two other managers, an additional issue was that when the superior level was asked for 'guidance' there needed to be a present. If there was a profit as a consequence of the fence-breaking then part of this should be shared with superior levels (even if only a little), in which case they would approve at once. If such a present was given it needed to be clear as far as the collective (*tap the) was concerned, unlike nowadays, when there appeared to be no limits.

The emerging pattern of accumulation and the issue of decapitalisation: class formation

The data suggest strongly that it is not very meaningful to speak of emerging classes in the period prior to 1980–1981. While managers and others are clearly poised to establish their position and exert their influence to increase their control over assets and business generally, the focus at this period seems more upon measures to improve welfare – to increase suppliers to workers and consumers (Tran The Duong, 1994).

Conclusions: the impact and meanings of 25-CP

25-CP appears in this analysis to be far from being classic reform policy. Rather than looking at it as a change in policy stance aimed at reform, it is better seen situated in a textured historical process with roots going back to before the war. Further, it was highly political, responding mainly to *conservative* pressures.

According to the panel 25-CP formalised the three-plan system and continued to open up after 279-CP. To put it another way, 279-CP in 1979 was a first loosening, after which 26-NQ/TW tightened up, so that 25-CP was a reloosening of SOEs.

This suggests that 25-CP has two significant meanings for my analysis.

First, it *formally* established the SOE as the focus for negotiations with planners over the balance between plan and market at the micro level. This meant that the liberalisation process would have a strongly micro and 'bottom-up' flavour.

Second, it had nothing directly to say about the treatment of assets and hence the likely class structure of any future market economy. Managers and others were obviously well placed in this historical change, but so far how this would play out was not yet clear. This implies that the nature of the Vietnamese market economy, and especially the question of who would control its economic assets, was not yet decided. The events of 1989–1991, and decisions taken then, would determine who the economically powerful would be through the decades of market-oriented growth that would develop the country. Thus, while the trap of 1979–1980 determined the fate of traditional Vietnamese socialism, it was the trap of 1989–1990 that strongly influenced the nature of Vietnamese capitalism.

Notes

1. One important reason was the similarities in the effects of the Chinese aid cuts in the north and the severance of economic relations with the West in the south. I am grateful to Professor Nguyen Tri for stressing this point to me – that the crisis was above all else a crisis faced by *central industry*.
2. This was stressed to me a number of times in discussions at the NEU/EPU Industry Faculty in 1985–1986.
3. Its manager became Minister of Light Industry in April 1980 and from then on appears to have played a major role in setting up a number of enterprise unions. He lost his post at the time of the Sixth Congress.
4. Flasks do not fit easily inside envelopes (see note 11 on p. 113).
5. These are old dong; by the early 1990s 150,000 of them were worth about $1.
6. See also Greenfield (1993).
7. The Vietnamese word used for transition here was *chuyen doi* rather than that used for the transition to socialism (*qua do*).

7

The attempted recentralisation, 1980–1985

Reaction and its failure

One of the most important elements of the Vietnamese transition in general, and of SOE commercial renaissance, was the way in which powerful processes had sufficient momentum to continue when policy shifted from a 'reformist' to a 'conservative' stance. This was very often the case in the period discussed in this chapter. With the 'genie out of the bottle', and with the VCP long accustomed to compromise in various ways, including tolerance of markets that went well beyond what was doctrinally set, it is hard to imagine how conservatives could have successfully imposed strong plan control after 25-CP. Yet the attempt was made.

I am not at all sure what the wider macro politics of this were, but they seem linked to the struggle at the peak between Le Duan and Truong Chinh. Having accepted the Sixth Plenum and *bung ra*, Le Duan was obviously vulnerable, as he had been during the rural 'contracts' controversy of the late 1960s, to accusations that he had abandoned socialism. Certainly Truong Chinh does not seem to have been openly 'reformist' until 1986, when he was seeking support from SOE interests (the 'state business interest' – Fforde, 1993) as part of his thrust to regain the Party secretaryship. Such conflicts at the peak help explain the openness of the official press. But for me the overall picture remains obscure, not least I think because of the common desire to interpret Le Duan's position as essentially conservative when in fact it was under his leadership that all this happened.

What is important here is to examine the direction of policy as the transitional economy developed. This relates to my argument that it was the limited nature of the transitional programme in Vietnam that was central to the way in which the SOE-focused thrust of the 1990s emerged, and so to the delayed arrival of the private sector and the tensions of the mid-2000s as SOE business interests found themselves hanging on to state support in face of rising competition from the private sector and foreign-invested businesses.

Defending the DRV: SOE policy immediately after 25-CP

The 'new course' – 146-HDBT

The Fifth Congress of spring 1982 confirmed the continuing political dominance of the recentralising tendency. In the summer the Council of Ministers promulgated the second of the period's important decrees on SOEs, 146-HDBT. It confirmed the general intention to limit 'unplanned' activities, and the ongoing attempt to use legalistic methods to divert resources into the state's still largely unreformed system of direct material supply.

The decree, entitled 'On the reform and modification of 25-CP...', stressed the broadly successful results of 25-CP. Under conditions of great 'imbalances' in the national economy, it had sharply raised SOEs' activities in increasing the utilisation of existing economic resources – labour, equipment and materials – and maintaining and increasing output. This had helped stabilise numbers employed as well as workers' living conditions. Budgetary receipts had also benefited.

146-HDBT's main intentions were:

- to improve the planning system to stimulate production 'and centralise sources of commodities in the hands of the state';
- to regularise the purchase and disposal of materials and products while improving enterprise accounting in order 'to get rid of production and trade based upon the unorganised market';
- to distribute enterprise profits in such a way as to ensure adequate budgetary receipts by the state and ensure that while enterprises and workers were properly paid there was a reduction in the wide differences in incomes between enterprises and branches (*Cong Bao*, 1982c: 382).

Given the economic context of the decree, its intention is very clear. Many SOEs were unwilling to supply goods to the state when unplanned relations offered better incentives. 146-HDBT sought to use legislation to force them to ignore such opportunities and enforce limits upon the prices and conditions of these deals. At the same time it saw such enforced accounting as a way of raising tax revenue, and while it saw this as a way of boosting the state budget's share of SOE profits, widening differentials were resisted. The call for higher profit deductions as a way of cutting the wide variations in incomes clearly reflected a desire to increase subsidies. The decree thus sought to defend the core institutions of the neo-Stalinist state by attacking uncontrolled horizontal relations and diverting resources by administrative means into the 'priority' areas.

The decree preserved 25-CP's threefold categorisation of SOEs. The state guaranteed supplies to 'priority' units. The rest could seek out resources for themselves, and here their right to borrow foreign exchange was made quite explicit. Alternatively, if they either could not operate at all or could not produce economic results, they could change their output or temporarily shut down.

146-HDBT also maintained the state's commitment to supplying materials as part of the plan, which formed the basis for deliveries to the state. It explained what was meant by the 'principle materials supplied as part of the state plan'. These were 'materials supplied by the state's material supply organs, by SOEs, cooperatives, state farms, state forestry SOEs...' to the SOE in accordance with the state's plan indicators and at state-directed prices. This meant that 'priority' units could continue to operate under the old unreformed system.

The decree also preserved 25-CP's supportive position regarding Plan B activities, but discussed them in far greater detail. Potential sources of 'unplanned' supplies were the idle stocks of other SOEs; agricultural, forestry and marine products belonging to units of the state economy, cooperative units and individuals who had fulfilled their duties towards the state; and materials that the locality and the SOE had permission to import (*Cong Bao*, 1982c: 383).

146-HDBT clarified the conditions under which SOEs were to carry out 'unplanned' activities, stressing that they had to comply with the state's system for managing and pricing materials (*Cong Bao*, 1982c: 383). It gave considerably more concrete explanations of the meaning of this, which asserted the rights of superior levels to intervene in a number of significant ways. For example, it did not explicitly sanction outright direct sales of goods between SOEs outside Plan A:

> Surplus and unused materials can be transferred between enterprises in a spirit of cooperative assistance and must be accounted for at 'state wholesale prices' [*gia ban buon Nha nuoc*],

> plus allowances for rational preservation and transport expenses agreed upon between the two parties. (*Cong Bao*, 1982c)

Purchases of technical materials had to be at directed prices set according to principles established by the Ministry of Finance, the State Price Commission and the Ministry of Materials. If agricultural, forestry and marine materials were those belonging to the state's 'unified management' (i.e. were 'list' goods), the SOE had to buy them at prices within the state's directed price frame that was established by the relevant delegated management organ according to time and place. SOEs could pay negotiated prices for 'non-list' goods.

> Enterprises are strictly forbidden from purchasing on the free market those goods subject to the state's monopoly. They must contribute to proposing measures for stopping instances of the purchase and sale of state materials without permission. (*Cong Bao*, 1982c)

146-HDBT confirmed the gathering importance of localities in controlling such activities by stating that while SOEs were free to operate in the free market for 'non-list' materials, they had to respect the regulations and guidance of the provincial or city People's Committee. Applications for foreign exchange had to be based upon a proper plan and approved by the unit's 'owning' organ.

The decree put pressure upon the great freedom to carry out Plan C activities conferred by 25-CP. SOEs were specifically forbidden from organising minor production based upon use of waste materials or by-products that the state had planned to allocate to another unit (*Cong Bao*, 1982c: 384). Any SOE wanting to carry out minor production had to register the goods concerned, along with their unit costs (*gia thanh) and selling price. The minor goods output plan was to be an integral part of the SOE's overall plan, and had to include the principle goods output as well as the material purchases plan and the financial plan. It had to be approved by the directly superior management organ of the unit.

In principle, all output had to be sold to state trading organs and other state economic units. But now this was to be in accordance with the product allocation plan of the organ that had approved the SOE's production plan. This organ was responsible for signing and implementing output disposal contracts for the SOE (*Cong Bao*, 1982c: 384). SOEs could freely dispose of 'non-list' consumer goods that state trading organs did not take, but had to follow registered and approved prices and pay state taxes on them. 146-HDBT limited somewhat the right to retain output produced from 'own-procured' materials, or minor output, to exchange for materials by maintaining that the unit had to get approval at the same time as its plan was approved. Furthermore, 'When it unexpectedly needs materials not laid down in the plan, the enterprise must also get approval from its superiors' (*Cong Bao*, 1982c).

The decree also clearly stipulated that SOEs were not allowed to retain minor output for 'internal distribution' (*phan phoi noi bo*) to their workers and cadres – in practice, an important source of sales on to the free market and a key mechanism for raising real wages. Units were only allowed 'to buy back some minor products for bonus sales'; even these purchases had to receive the permission of the relevant minister and the president of the local provincial or city People's Committee.

146-HDBT's stipulations regarding costing and output pricing and profit distribution reinforced these heightened controls on distribution. This touched upon deep-rooted problems, since the essential passivity of money relations within the neo-Stalinist system, which did not really attempt to reflect social values, now had to coexist with the spectrum of opportunities and values offered by 'unplanned' activities that the 'three-plan' system sought to contain and control. The plan's price system was set at levels that differed by perhaps a factor of ten times from free market prices, which were in any case neither an accurate measure of alternative values nor, under inflationary conditions, stable.

This meant that SOE accounting was extremely complicated and ambiguous. A full-scale price reform, however, would have disturbed the balance between the existing allocative mechanisms, resulting in sharp shifts in relative incomes. The gathering crisis in this area provided a focus for the underlying systemic tensions between allocative mechanisms, which culminated in the Eighth Plenum and the failed wage-price reforms of 1985. Many SOEs clearly saw little reason for keeping the prescribed accounts, which often appeared solely as a means for extracting resources from them under unfavourable terms. Yet this led to an area of numbing complexity – pricing. This, though, was at the heart of the state's struggle to secure revenues from SOEs, the fiscal base of neo-Stalinism, and its collapse was at the root of the fiscal crisis (p. 33).

Accounting, costs, prices and profitability

The decree made a clear distinction between unit costs (*gia thanh*), SOE wholesale prices (*gia ban buon xi nghiep*) and industrial wholesale prices (*gia ban buon cong nghiep*).

146-HDBT introduced detailed revisions to the system of deductions from the norm profits that formed the basis for calculating the plan's internal accounting margins between the two sets of wholesale prices. These were mainly to do with the SOEs' permitted profit retention for payment into the bonus and welfare funds, and differentiated between meeting the Plan A targets; over-fulfilling Plan A targets; and Plan B activities. These were very hard to understand, and give the impression of an attempt to catch an eel with bare hands.

With SOE profits effectively out of planners' control, since they were so dependent upon Plans B and C, planners were put in a difficult position. The decree stated that SOEs in heavy industry, wood, sea-fishing, construction and transport were to retain an amount equal to 24 per cent of the realised wage fund for their Plan A activities if they met that plan's target; if they over-fulfilled the plan they could keep up to 60 per cent of the profits earned on the plan over-fulfilment. For SOEs in light industry and food and staples processing the corresponding retention and bonus rates were respectively 20 per cent (of the realised wage fund) and up to 50 per cent of profits on over-fulfilled output (*Cong Bao*, 1982c: 385), but 20 per cent of 'bonus' profits had to go into the SOE's production development fund. The SOE had to deliver all remaining profits to the state budget (*Cong Bao*, 1982c: 386). Plan B activities were treated in the same way as Plan A over-fulfilment – the two groups of SOEs were allowed to retain 60 per cent and 50 per cent of 'realised profits calculated according to the norms in force' earned in this way. Profits made from foreign exchange loans were also treated in the same way. But the state set the rate of exchange, and the SOE could not put foreign exchange into the bonus or welfare funds. 146-HDBT did, however, set a higher retained profit rate for minor Plan C activities: SOEs in all branches could keep up to 70 per cent of realised profits on these activities.

It seems highly unlikely that these fine stipulations had much real force. Scope for cooking the books was vast. For example, bearing in mind that Plan A and B activities were both in 'list' goods, and so using the same fixed assets, how could capital costs be charged? And how could anything be monitored by outsiders?

These measures were given a blanket circumscription by the stipulation that there should be a super-profits tax if the sum of the payments from all sources to the bonus and welfare funds in any given quarter exceeded an amount equal to six months' outlay on the SOE's wages. The SOE had to pay a part of the excess into the state budget, and the proportion was to be fixed subject to the guidance of the Ministry of

Finance (*Cong Bao*, 1982c: 386). Bonuses for export plan fulfilment were excluded from this provision.

Given that the most interesting thing for many SOEs at the time was finding out ways of exploiting market opportunities, this decree cannot exactly have been the most attractive thing to land on managers' desks.

Grassroots comments on 146-HDBT

The panel commented that through 146-HDBT the state again 'bound' SOEs, significantly tightening the pressure to implement the central plan. While 25-CP had granted SOEs autonomy regarding the third plan, 146-HDBT stipulated that the superior level had to approve all the plans for products not on the SOE's 'list' (note 13 on p. 113).

As one manager put it:

> This was the ebb and flow of renovation – the state loosened up, then, afraid of losing socialism, tightened up again, then they saw that the economy did not develop and there was a crisis of shortages, so they again loosened up, and then again tightened. This pattern made life very hard: 'above the anvil, below the hammer'.

The process was construed as something inherent in the process of economic change, as understandable and unavoidable as the weather (Humphry, 1983).

Debate, conflict and policy development: interpretations of the new legislation – the 'new course'

Parallel to the relatively liberal treatment of the issues in the daily press could be found published documents that presented themselves as guides to or interpretations of these decrees. These articulated positions within the Party-state apparatus of various types and directions, and show clearly how limited was the extent of reformist thinking at the time. Traditional socialism was caught between the pressure from below and the weight of the Soviet-bloc aid programme, which was supporting the central-planning system. This aid had to come in via FYPs, material balancing and so on. This inevitably reinforced the conservatives as well as adding to the relative value of participating in the plan, confusing discussions about the pros and cons of plan and market.

A number of documents reveal the way in which the new legislation was interpreted in various quarters. Two of the most interesting are the middle-of-the road pamphlet issued by the Ministry of Labour (BLD, 1981) and discussed earlier (p. 133) and a cunningly radical series of 'questions and answers' in book form issued by the Party's Truth Publishing House in 1982 and prepared under the guidance of two economists from the CIEM (Duong Bach Lien and Le Trang, 1983). One of the most valuable insights these provide is into contemporary policy. Party propaganda took a forthright position:

> In the recent past, because of slackness in management during a situation where industry was very short of materials, energy, spares etc., a number of cadres have shown a strong tendency to run after profits and the market... Many bad methods continue and in some places things have deteriorated to dangerous levels – such as the use of various ruses, such as avoiding adequate deliveries of products to the state, not paying state incomes to the state, freely setting up bonus and 'bringing-on' systems in the unit, unprincipled increase in cost prices, violation of basic socialist economic management regulations – in essence, operating in accordance with the principles of the guild. To stop all this, it is necessary... to implement 146-HDBT. (Van Dac, 1983: 47)

As an economic solution to these difficulties, this source stressed the key central role to be played by the plan; the strictly limited and supplementary role played by 'own procurement', and the need to respect the state's rights to output; proper and accurate accounting; and public disclosure of the distribution of income within the SOE (Van Dac, 1983: 47–8).

'Reformists': the Ministry of Labour's position

The Ministry of Labour pamphlet (BLD, 1981) approved of legislation encouraging the use in industry of output contracts as a way of raising output. It stressed that the old system 'based upon rank and time' was ineffective, but there was no need for a single uniform new system for all units (BLD, 1981: 112). The top priority was to raise output and product quality.[1]

This document followed 25-CP very closely. It stressed areas related to output disposal. The previous chapter examined the key legislation here – 64-CP (23 February 1981). The ministry fully endorsed the pressure to centralise resources in the hands of the state, and also mentioned other policies designed to prevent the establishment of illegal (cash) funds, gold and foreign exchange. Cash had to be put in the bank (BLD, 1981: 85–7). *But* the ministry also pointed out that the SOE manager had the explicit right 'actively to search for supplementary sources of raw materials' (BLD, 1981: 99). Support for Plan B activities was, of course, consistent with 25-CP.

'Reformists' and the gathering reformist discourse

This was a subversive exercise in judicious justification, an excellent example of reformist tactics with the pen. It commenced by linking the rights granted to SOEs to the decree (93-CP, 8 April 1977) that had issued the enterprise statute; as has been shown, however, these rights did not extend to the establishment of direct horizontal relations aimed at avoiding the constraints of the direct administered supply system. 25-CP had thus had to recognise and legalise these through the creation of the so-called 'three-plan' system. The economic conditions that had made these necessary were those of the period from 1978 onwards, characterised by generalised imbalances and the state's inability to supply needed inputs:

> At that time, for many reasons, there were many sources of materials in society that enterprises could not exploit because the systems in force were inappropriate and only slowly reformed. (Duong Bach Lien and Le Trang, 1982: 6)

Inputs shortages coexisted with surpluses that could not be used because of the shortcomings of the economic system. Labour discipline was weak; output and quality were falling sharply.

The immediate response of policy-makers was reportedly 279-CP (according to this source issued after the 6 August Plenum) on ways of stimulating output of 'non-list' goods. And after this a number of producers started to dispose of 'outside plan' goods or '279 goods' quite outside the state's system of marketing and pricing. Here, therefore, we see clearly the hostility towards the behaviour described above: 'Not only small-scale enterprises, but also a number of large enterprises ran after "outside plan" goods to have high incomes' (Duong Bach Lien and Le Trang, 1982: 7).

26-NQ/TW (p. 28) on the reform of distribution and circulation had sought to improve this situation and reportedly had a strong effect upon industrial output. SOEs that relied upon agricultural, forestry and marine inputs did particularly well – sugar, tobacco and food notably so. This largely resulted from relations established *directly* between producers and customers. But the existing management system was still a great constraint upon output growth: the wage/price system was largely unreformed, and the financial and profit distribution systems entirely so. Subsidies were widespread and accounting had little real role to play.

The underlying administrative-bureaucratic philosophy of economic management relied heavily upon vertical rather than horizontal relations, and this limited the autonomy of base units and so their ability to set up supplementary balances for the state plan (Duong Bach Lien and Le Trang, 1982). This had hit many SOEs from 1978, and especially in 1979–1980, precipitating declines in both output and worker incomes.[2] The nature of the situation was particularly marked in the case of agricultural processing SOEs, which were unable to obtain inputs produced in the country and so had to shut down (Duong Bach Lien and Le Trang, 1982: 9). This, they said, was the background to 25-CP and 26-CP.

The document asserted that both decrees were concretisations of the relevant clauses of the enterprise statute; they were not a new system, but temporary measures to meet the needs of the time. Their focus was planning, economic accounting, profit distribution and output disposal. Their basic principle was a simultaneous recognition of both the state's rights to centralised management and SOE autonomy.

Much of the remainder of the piece argues for the positive value of the state's attempt to carry out a number of broad elements of industrial management reform as outlined in 25-CP:

> Increasing the rights of the base in planning at present does not weaken the centralised and united nature of state planning, and is not in contradiction with the principle of democratic centralism... The reform of planning work aims to allow the state to grasp all the principle products of the enterprise, determine all its production activities, its output disposal and its financial and pricing activities. (Duong Bach Lien and Le Trang, 1982: 18)

Then, showing how the reformist narrative was forming, the study went on to confront 25-CP's legalisation of self-procured inputs with the orthodox position that 'under socialism, the state manages all principle means of production'. It does not deny the necessary role of the state's direct allocation of resources, but simply points out that the state had not been able to carry out that function in the past. The economy was full of economic slack – waste materials, idle stocks, goods in store that had not been paid for and primary products that producers held after they had met their duties for delivery to the state. Thus, while the state did not yet know how to manage and exploit these resources properly, it had eventually passed laws allowing units of the socialist economy to do so (Duong Bach Lien and Le Trang, 1982: 21).

The overall effects of 25-CP were said to be strongly positive, reinforced by 26-CP. In 1981 around 30–40 per cent of output had come from 'supplementary' output (i.e. Plans B and C) organised by branches and SOEs (Duong Bach Lien and Le Trang, 1982: 24). A number of well-known SOEs by then operated almost totally outside the state's material supply system – for example, the Hanoi Freshwater Enterprise, the Ha Nam Ninh Biscuit and Sweet Enterprise and the Hoc Mon Oil-pressing Enterprise; others, such as the Soap-powder Associated Enterprise, the No. II Tobacco Factory, the Hanoi Soap Enterprise and the Hanoi Engineering Enterprise had relied extensively upon own-procured inputs (Duong Bach Lien and Le Trang, 1982: 25).

Results had been good throughout the country, but there were some important regional variations. In 1981 Hanoi had kept the proportion of Plan A activities at 80.5 per cent of total output – average wages had jumped 75 per cent but labour productivity had gone up 9.1 per cent. Budgetary receipts had risen. This compared with rather more violent shifts in Ho Chi Minh City, where in 1981 the state could only supply around 40–60 per cent of inputs required by planned output, and around 50 per cent of the 1980 outturn. Despite this, the city had managed to increase industrial output from all components by 27 per cent in 1981 compared with 1980 (Duong Bach Lien and Le Trang, 1982: 26). The central economic ministries had been able to cope: the Ministry of Engineering and Metallurgy was expecting to meet 30 per cent of its output from 'own-procured' inputs in 1981, which had allowed it to plan for a 10 per cent rise in output (Duong Bach Lien and Le Trang, 1982: 27).

These successes would, prima facie, suggest that 146-HDBT should have sought to strengthen the stimulus given by 25-CP to the development of horizontal relations. That it did not is primarily blamed upon the 'shortcomings' allegedly introduced by 25-CP, which naturally enough were closely bound up with the effects of burgeoning horizontal relations upon the position and power of the central economic management organs. Since, as is argued here, this was the basic reason for the introduction of 25-CP in the first place, this should not be so surprising. This is rhetoric.

Most disturbing (though clearly seen as a very positive sign by hard-line reformists) was the failure of the new regulations on prices and incomes to cope with the massive differentials that had arisen as selected units happily captured shortage premia. These were clearly focused upon workers, suggesting that surpluses at this stage mainly went to consumption rather than into managers' pockets.

In some cases SOEs had set up welfare and bonus funds equal to 40–50 months' wages; there had been instances of 100 months' wages (Duong Bach Lien and Le Trang, 1982: 29). Confronted with such incentives, SOEs had sought to maximise 'pure profits' (*loi nhuan don thuan*), 'gone in the wrong direction' and gained large incomes by exploiting price differences. This, it was said, had had bad effects upon output quality. Worst of all, SOEs had pushed up the material utilisation norms to obtain extra supplies from the state that they could then use in other 'unplanned' activities.[3]

The study pointed to a number of advances in 146-HDBT which reveal the recentralising trend. First, there was the introduction of the 'price frame' as a way of loosening the previously rigid centralised price system. This was principally intended for use with primary inputs, and allowed prices to vary over time and space. But in practice the effects of this measure must have been to permit some added control over previously free dealings while giving greater flexibility in more conservative areas. Second, there was the reduced freedom of SOEs in the exercise of the right to borrow foreign exchange; this had now to be part of the SOE's unified plan and approved by its superior. The latter, not the SOE, was responsible for losses (Duong Bach Lien and Le Trang, 1982: 35).

The clearest indication of the intent of 146-HDBT (as presented by reformers forced to justify it but taking, as can be seen, many opportunities to condemn it) comes from the study's explanation of its role in three areas: output disposal, cost and price accounting and profit distribution.

The study explains that the SOE was not free to dispose of its output. 146-HDBT had made this very clear – it had to get permission:

> The basic content of this regulation is that the state allows the enterprise to take part of the output from its supplementary plan and its minor plan to form the material and commodity basis for it

to barter with other units to obtain inputs; it does not allow the enterprise to retain output, either from the part of the plan put out by the state as a legal plan indicator, or the supplementary plan of the enterprise, to pay bonuses in kind, to barter for consumer goods for its workers and cadres or to sell as a bonus [*ban thuong] to other units. (Duong Bach Lien and Le Trang, 1982: 36)

Similar considerations applied to minor output, and the SOE was not allowed to keep any part of it for material bonuses. In the past this had been a major cause of vast differentials between workers, both in the same SOE and throughout branches; since average real wages had not risen much, this had created great tensions (Duong Bach Lien and Le Trang, 1982: 37). Furthermore, it had cut state incomes. Thus 146-HDBT had merely allowed SOEs to buy back minor output for sale to workers and cadres:

> 'Bonus sales' in reality are an 'active regulation'. After buying back a part of minor output at an approved proportion and at industrial wholesale prices – i.e. after financial contributions to the state – the enterprise has the right to sell those products to its workers and cadres at the prices paid for them, or at lower prices or as material bonuses. (Duong Bach Lien and Le Trang, 1982: 38)

Apart from these severely restrictive measures regarding output disposal, 146-HDBT also squeezed the SOE in the areas of price and cost accounting. To prevent pressure for upward pressure on SOE wholesale prices and insulate the state from the higher costs of 'own-procured' inputs, the SOE now had to account for inputs separately. Each sub-plan had its own accounts. 146-HDBT also cut back the higher 'norm' profits that 25-CP had allowed for the supplementary plan (Plan B) – these were now set equal to those on the plan issued by the state (Plan A). Previously the SOE had received a bonus of two to four times norm profits (Duong Bach Lien and Le Trang, 1982: 39). Finally, industrial wholesale prices for output coming from each of the two plans were now to be the same.

The effects of these upon the formal incentive structure were seen as deliberately adverse:

> Thus in reality, the deductions from the supplementary plan for the enterprise's funds will be less than before as a result of the change in norm profits; the incentive for enterprises to carry out supplementary plans will decline. (Duong Bach Lien and Le Trang, 1982: 39)

The final area cited was profits. The study points out quite clearly that the intent here was to shift incentives in such a way as to favour heavy industry against light industry, and to bring rewards for Plan A over-fulfilment level with those for Plan B (Duong Bach Lien and Le Trang, 1982: 41–2). As a further check on the too successful, the decree placed absolute limits upon the size of payments into the bonus and welfare funds.

A justification for this was that although greater use of such methods was satisfactory while the wage system was still unreformed, they tended to encourage excess consumption at the expense of accumulation (Duong Bach Lien and Le Trang, 1982: 45). In addition they created excessive differentials between SOEs, which had to stop. But since the limit placed upon payments into these funds was now equal to six months' wages, and all extra was to go to the state, this implied that the large number of SOEs reportedly paying in over 50 months' wages would find themselves facing a very sharp fall in incomes. Hidden in all this was the fact that the high level of cash generated by such behaviour was in practice frequently used to finance 'unplanned' transactions which showed up in the Plan B activities that these decrees sought to bring within the 'passive money' system of state-controlled accounting.

The study also pointed out that 146-HDBT, by defining its sphere of operation as solely industrial SOEs, sought to stop strictly non-industrial units in distribution, circulation, services, medicine, education and administration from getting involved in production. Construction and transport branches could, however, 'use the basic spirit of the decree' (Duong Bach Lien and Le Trang, 1982: 47).

Conclusion

This text is a clever hatchet job, effectively attacking what it has been tasked to support. Its line of argument, and its clear empirical foundation, point to characteristic elements of reformist argument at the time.

146-HDBT and 25-CP appear similar in their underlying intention. They sought to control and restrain SOE autonomy by changing both the formal incentive structure – prices and 'norm' profits – and the terms under which they had legal access to 'unplanned' allocative relations. 25-CP imposed 'order' upon a situation that, from the point of view of the authorities, was basically out of control; 146-HDBT moved on from that tactical concession to tighten the screws and, in traditional neo-Stalinist manner, use administrative methods to override immediate material incentives and concentrate resources in so-called 'priority' areas. But the discussion shows very clearly the underlying dynamic of an expansion of economic activities that focused upon markets at the expense of the plan. This had been very rapid, drawing upon earlier practices, so that by 1981 nearly half of SOE output was unplanned (p. 173). This was well known and increasingly expressed within an intellectual framework that valorised autonomous SOE activities and justified practices and perceptions which situated the SOE as an autonomous entity that negotiated with the state and the plan.

Grassroots response, 1981–1984: the debate, perceptions and rationalities

The pattern of grassroots and regional responses to the recentralising legislation varied greatly. The extent to which spontaneous liberalisation had developed was very important, and so, since this was illegal until 25-CP, information is coloured accordingly.

I have already discussed the evidence for the development of horizontal relations during 1979 and 1980. When one reads the evidence from the official press one impression is the almost gleeful delight in exploiting the opportunities available by bending and breaking the rules: the positive aspects of confusion when linked to autonomy were frequently reported. Perhaps the most striking example of this was a construction enterprise which was employing 1,200 of its employees solely to rear pigs for sale 'outside', capturing shortage premia.[4]

Grassroots comments

The panel made a clear division of this period into two. From 1981 to the start of 1982 things were good as a result of 25-CP. By the end of 1982 through to 1984 things got worse because of the constraints of 146-HDBT and 156-HDBT. 1984 was particularly difficult because of inflation and severe staples shortages.

Gathering political tensions: 156-HDBT, 306-BBT and the road to the Sixth Congress

Overview

In my opinion the politics of 1982–1984, especially in central circles, remains particularly badly under-researched by foreigners. This is in part because it is straddled by the important events of 1979–1980 (the Sixth Plenum) and 1985–1986 (the 'price-wages-money' débâcle and then the Sixth Congress itself). The pattern of industrial reform suggests that the origins of the U-turn represented by 306-BBT are particularly interesting, and I tend to the view that this suggests that the 'state business interest' (Fforde, 1993) was even then particularly strong, and sufficiently so to get its way well before the congress – *and indeed before the death of Le Duan*. This suggests in turn that the broad 'pro-market' economic policy changes associated with the Sixth Congress were not in fact very important, which is suggestive given that the years 1987–1989 saw very little done really to encourage growth of a private sector. The picture that emerges is one where state business interests are very powerful.

1985 was a crucial year. 156-HDBT, the last recentralising SOE decree, was implemented early in the year, and to this was added the so-called 'price-wages-money' measures which cranked inflation up to hyperinflationary levels. In these chaotic conditions in early 1986 there then appeared 306-BBT, strongly supportive of SOE autonomy *vis-à-vis* planners and so marking a U-turn in the formal policy stance in the run-up (but not the immediate run-up) to the December 1986 Sixth Party Congress – the *doi moi* congress. Le Duan died mid-year, replaced by Truong Chinh as stopgap general-secretary until the congress, which saw Nguyen van Linh come to power and introduce de-Stalinisation.

156-HDBT, 1984

The last of the three recentralising decrees on industrial SOE management was 156-HDBT, entitled 'On some problems in the reform of state industrial management'. To Huu signed the document, dated 30 November 1984, which appeared in a number of sources early in 1985. The version used here can be found in the journal of the Ministry of Light Industry (Ministry of Light Industry, 1985). The immediate basis of the decree was the Sixth Plenum of the Fifth Congress, which, held in the summer of 1984, had concentrated upon 'Pressing problems in the reform of economic management'.

The decree is considerably longer than either 25-CP or 146-HDBT. As well as the familiar ground of the 'three-plan' system, it covered important questions associated with the attempt to strengthen the central economic management organs. These included the establishment of a number of enterprise associations, product groups and other umbrella organisations aimed at 'productionist' solutions to the basic problem of raising the economic efficiency of the state sector. The decree appears in many ways as a major statement of policy intent, and therefore contains comments upon the relation between industrial organisation and both the Party line and the role of local Party organisations (Ministry of Light Industry, 1985: 18, 26).

The decree stressed the need to utilise the state plan as a means for concentrating resources, and the necessity for the 'rationalisation' (*sap xep lai*) of production. This term, although never clearly defined, featured with some regularity in the policy documents of the period. Here it included:

> the rearrangement of products and the 'adjustment' [*dieu chinh*] of commodities to meet socio-economic needs; the rearrangement of production bases with regard to both technology and equipment; paying attention to balancing [*dong bo*] the production chain [*day chuyen san xuat*]; rearranging the labour force; rearranging economic components [*thanh phan*] in industry in close alliance with socialist transformation in production and circulation to ensure the leading role of the state. (Ministry of Light Industry, 1985: 18)

This obfuscation reflects both the dominance of conservative thinking and the way in which the relative failure of the recentralising effort was preventing – as had happened with other policies in the past – its advocates from producing concrete and implementable policy. As a further example of this basic confusion, the decree stated that:

> From the very beginning of 1985, the state plan must centralise principle production conditions for those key goods that serve production, exports, mass consumption, national defence, and goods that create important sources of income for the state budget, above all those enterprises that produce a lot and have high economic results. (Ministry of Light Industry, 1985)

This cannot be taken as an operational system of economic priorities and reads more as a list of desirable outcomes, which is not at all the same thing.

The decree asserted the Council of Ministers' right to establish a national list of priority SOEs and key products throughout the entire national economy, but also said that ministries and provincial and city People's Committees could set up their own lists of priority SOEs and key products 'in their own branch or region and in accordance with their ability to supply materials' (Ministry of Light Industry, 1985).

The priority areas were Hanoi, Ho Chi Minh City, Haiphong, Quang Ninh, Vinh Phu, Bac Thai, Quang Nam-Da Nang and Dong Nai.[5] But its treatment of non-priority units was somewhat perfunctory, and far less clear than in 25-CP. They were, however, still encouraged to seek out resources for themselves and also to develop new products. Non-priority SOEs that could not function in the foreseeable future should shift to branches where they could; recently established units that had developed spontaneously and did not function with positive economic results should be wound up.

The decree introduced some changes in the understanding of the nature of the SOEs' plan. As a single united plan, it had to be balanced in both volume and value terms. In the first instance it was to be sent up from the SOE under the guidance of the superior economic organ, so as to reflect the base's exercise of its rights to collective mastery. The legally binding plan indicators the state issued to the SOE were to be based upon the state's own balances at both central and regional levels, as well as the SOE's abilities to obtain stable supplies of materials. The state undertook to encourage SOEs to exploit fully the opportunities available to them, which took four forms: their own resources, resources obtained through business associations, exports aimed at securing imports and loans in domestic and foreign currency from the bank (Ministry of Light Industry, 1985: 20).

But the detailed sequence of steps intended for the formulation of plans suggested that this part of the state still saw itself as essentially planning by administrative order. In the second quarter of the year the SOE's superior organ was to inform the SOE of its basic direction and tasks for the coming period in both material and financial terms. It had also to give it guide numbers regarding its ability to supply materials, energy and services and output disposal; this accompanied information on technical norms and standards, as well as market and price information and the names of the units that would be responsible for supplying inputs and receiving output. The SOE was then to use this information as a basis for contacting customers and suppliers and signing the contracts that would form the basis of plan formulation.

In the third quarter the SOE would actually construct its plan and submit it to its superior level for approval. By December at the latest the superior level would approve the plan and issue legal plan instructions to the SOE. The decree stated that the SOE did not have to get approval for output outside the legal indicators, but had to inform its immediate superior. The system of plan indicators for all SOEs was now as follows:

- the value of realised output (including the value of exports);
- products within the planned system (*san pham giao nop*) as fixed by the state and according to signed contracts, within which exports were clearly noted;
- the reduction in cost prices: for existing products, the fall on the year; for new products, the fall relative to planned cost prices;
- profits (*loi nhuan*) and obligatory contributions to the state budget, now including the enterprise's accumulation of foreign currency if it either exported or participated in exports;
- principal materials supplied by the state, whether central or regional, in accordance with the legal plan indicators (Ministry of Light Industry, 1985: 20).

This system of indicators was to be applied to all output of 'list' goods, no matter what the source of the materials; but for 'non-list' goods they were only guiding indicators.

The decree was greatly critical of the state of economic accounting: 'A very weak link in essence only carried out formally and not reflective of production-trade results' (Ministry of Light Industry, 1985: 21). The key phrase was 'management by the dong', and the main task was to ensure that all necessary production expenses were included in costs. But so long as profits were to be based upon the orthodox system of norms, this meant that reforms had to stress the need to improve the system of norms as well as accounting *per se*: 'In 1985, all enterprises must calculate cost prices on the basis of the system of technico-economic norms in force' (Ministry of Light Industry, 1985).

But this immediately raised the old question of how to account for resources that the unit had procured for itself. Here 156-HDBT maintained the dual-pricing system of earlier legislation, for materials supplied by the state were to be accounted for at state guidance prices while other inputs were to be included in cost prices at 'real purchasing prices' that had to be within the price guidelines fixed by the relevant organ as laid down in the price management statute.

The SOE could retain output produced from own-procured resources (i.e. Plan B) or minor output to exchange it for materials for production, but this had to be approved by its superior as part of the plan. It could repurchase some minor output at industrial wholesale prices for sale to its employees if needed. Again, this had to be part of the plan and have the approval of the minister or the president of the provincial or city People's Committee. The 'winnowing-out' of goods on to the free market was to be avoided at all costs (Ministry of Light Industry, 1985). If the contracted customer did not take delivery – for which the customer was responsible, not the SOE – the unit had the right to dispose of the goods to another organ or SOE. The customer had to compensate the producer for losses incurred as a result of this. SOEs had the right to open shops to sell examples of new products or minor products, so long as they had the permission of Internal Trade – the state bodies responsible for managing such activities.

They could also start up services to repair their products.

The shared rights of the SOE were related to 182-CP (26 April 1979), and the SOE manager was enjoined to call meetings of employees for them to participate in management (Ministry of Light Industry, 1985: 27). Each SOE should organise an enterprise council to advise the manager.

Conclusions

The tedious level of bureaucratic detail in 156-HDBT (and I have abridged much), compared with the vigour and energy associated with 'own-account' activities, is very evident. It was largely a dead letter, without authority or power – the main game was elsewhere.

In this context I recall visiting the CIEM in the early 1990s and being told to listen to a delegation from China, who were outlining in similar turgid if not Kafkaesque detail to 156-HDBT the state of Chinese reforms to official housing allocation procedures. Since by this time the Vietnamese were well along the road of simply coping with the shouting and screaming attached to the fights over shortage premia as state housing and some urban land was allocated out in various highly obscure ways ('get it over with'), the Vietnamese at the meeting were soon yawning, despite the obvious enthusiasm of their visitors.

Yet for some SOEs, as well as for people dependent upon state rations and lacking cash incomes, marketisation had very negative aspects. The fiscal crisis of the state in the late 1980s (p. 33) was a major aspect of this. In the rural areas teachers had been reliant upon state rations, while local medical staff depended upon the cooperatives. The shift of resources back towards families and away from the cooperatives badly hit primary health care. Survival of primary school education in rural areas compared with the very negative effects upon primary health care resulted mainly from local values, which appreciated education and so made it relatively easy to mobilise resources into teacher income supplements (de Vylder and Fforde, 1996: Chapter 6).

But in SOEs it was to a great extent the tensions and chaos of the mixed transitional system that provoked strong feelings of the fundamental irrationality of neo-Stalinist thinking. These, combined with the resources to push politicians to support state business interests, gathered strength through the first half of the 1980s – I think especially in the period 1982–1984 (p. 177).

The manager's lament: chaos and its offspring

Giao gi lam nay
Chi dan danh day
Co gi cho nay
Het roi ngoi day

'Whatever you're given you have to use – order the men to work/play. Whatever you've got, I'll take the lot... Sorry, we're out of stock – why don't you sit down for a minute and rest: you must be tired and you never know, we might get some in and while you're waiting you might think up another argument for why we should let you have what we have got – not that we have any...' (My far from literal translation.)

Het tien xin cap
Het hang xin cho
Ton that khong lo
Lo lai khong chiu

'If there's no money, ask for some more! If there's no materials, ask for some more! Waste – don't worry! You don't bear losses or profits.' (NCKT, 1985: 13)

On to the incendiary pile was now placed a large quantity of (black market) petrol in the form of reactionary anti-market reforms that led to hyperinflation.

1985: 'price-wages-money' and the start of chaos

The failed 'price-wages-money' measures of 1985 saw the attempt to reimpose controls over private trade, collectivise the Mekong and push through a wage-price reform and a currency reform that would re-establish a planned order in the economy. This failed, and added to distributional tensions. Unresolved through a more powerful shift to a market economy to underpin a *stabilising* use of state power, the inevitable result was hyperinflation. Tran Phuong, the powerful deputy Premier in charge of economic affairs, lost his job as a result. The exercise greatly eroded the authority of those who asserted that central planning would – could – work in Vietnam.

At the level of the SOE, however, these measures were in some ways very distant. Comments from the panel were that they were unaware of the wider 'macro' meaning of these measures, but at the level of the SOE they created major shocks.

Managers had much to worry about, especially if the SOE had cash in the bank – ten dong were now only worth one dong. Workers were turned upside down with inflation at three-digit levels. After the currency reform prices fell for about a month, after which they grew very strongly; from a situation where worker welfare was very difficult, it became even harder. Society was deeply unstable because people had put money into savings accounts and now lost much of it. Worst hit were the retired.

As one member of the panel put it, 'price-wages-money' was a policy mistake, a crime committed on the people, and so far nobody has been held responsible for it.

It was the peak of the use of administrative commands to lead the economy.

Conclusions

A turning point had now been reached. At last the wheel could turn again and policy move to supporting SOE autonomy and commercial renaissance. The shift was extremely political as VCP leaders sought support from state business interests.

306-BBT and 76-HDBT: the policy U-turn prior to the Sixth Congress

As already discussed, the precise political origins of the policy U-turn of early 1986 are not known to me. That it predated the *doi moi* Sixth Congress by more than a few months suggests that the political power of the state business interest was by now considerable. Note that this policy U-turn was expressed in a Party document, unlike its three predecessors (25-CP, 146-HDBT and 156-HDBT), which were state documents. There were no other significant economic decrees at this period, suggesting that the state business interest was the main goose worth cooking.

Its stance, supportive of market-oriented liberalisation, was further developed by the last decree of the transition period, 217-HDBT of December 1987 on the eve of the extinction of central planning in 1989–1990 (p. 198).

306-BBT was a draft secretariat resolution.[6] It was intended, though, that:

> In the immediate future, the Political Bureau will promulgate this draft resolution for implementation by all levels and sectors. By the end of 1986, [it] will be reviewed to draw experience, to perfect the document, and to promulgate the official resolution. (Joint Publications Research Service, 1986a: K 9)

This is of course somewhat strange and suggestive, though exactly of what is not clear. The resolution's text articulated the emerging critique of the 'centralized bureaucratic, red-tape, and subsidy-based management systems' (Joint Publications Research Service, 1986a: K 7) that was to be central to the rhetoric of the Sixth Congress. It supported SOE autonomy, as was clear from its title ('Draft resolution guaranteeing basic economic units' rights to autonomy in production and business') (Joint Publications Research Service, 1986a). It strongly supported SOEs' rights, but nuanced its language:

> guaranteeing the grass roots units' right to autonomy must be aimed at switching the operations of enterprises to the socialist accounting and business system on the basis of using plans as the center... the laws of value and the relations of goods and money must be correctly implemented and production must be combined with circulation through the implementation of various uniform and suitable economic policies and economic contracts. (Joint Publications Research Service, 1986a: K 8)

The draft resolution also supported cooperatives' rights to autonomy vis-à-vis planners (Joint Publications Research Service, 1986a: K 9), foreshadowing decree 10 in 1988.

Interestingly, senior leaders presiding at the cadre conference held on 17–20 April to discuss the resolution included Nguyen Lam, who perhaps felt that the position he had taken in 1980 (p. 26) was now vindicated.

While the resolution returned to supporting SOE autonomy, in contrast to 146-HDBT and 156-HDBT, its focus upon state management structures was nuanced. Workers' rights were stressed, as were those of 'socialism'. Yet the underlying issue of the relationship between the state and business was unresolved, and lay at the root of the political problems of the 1990s and 2000s.

Failure to introduce radical political reform in 1990–1992 meant that the question of the political basis for the VCP in a market economy was not addressed, and indeed would not be until new commercial forces had arisen to match the state business interest, which would not happen until the early 2000s (Fforde, 2004a, 2005a). Some implications of this are sketched out in the two concluding chapters. But 306-BBT shows that renewed support for emergent state capitalism *predates* the Sixth Congress.

The return to strengthening SOE autonomy is clear. See for example what was coming from *Nhan Dan* in an editorial of mid-May:

> Enterprises must exercise their autonomy in planning when carrying out planning at the grassroots level, balancing themselves [*tu can doi*] on various sources of resources, deciding on the need to supplement or revise planned tasks regarding the manufacture of above-quota goods [Plans B and C], expanding relations on economic cooperation or integration, and enhancing the role of economic contracts. (*Nhan Dan*, 1986)

Notably, Truong Chinh supported the resolution in June 1986 (Joint Publications Research Service, 1986a). Through 1987 references to 306-BBT argued that it had been too limited in its scope, focusing upon SOE autonomy rather than reform of the state (e.g. Nguyen van Linh's speech at the late 1987 Third Plenum – SWB, 1987) and the *Nhan Dan* editorial on the same plenum, which stated that 'Administrative agencies at all levels... must... completely assign the function of production and business management to basic economic organisations and units' (*Nhan Dan*, 1987).

While the complexities surrounding such a major policy shift are clear, it is also certain to me that this did mark a U-turn. *But the state then refused to implement it.*

76-HDBT

76-HDBT of June 1986 was a state document intended to implement 306-BBT, but it tried to put a brake on the direction implied by the resolution. This was confirmed by criticisms of its 'limitations in concretising 306-BBT' reported in Tran Duc Luong's (1988: 19) discussion of the far more clearly liberalising 217-HDBT in 1987.

The decree took the form of nine accompanying regulations that focused upon the key state economic management organs. Since it appears that the regulations were written by these organs, it shows the varying degrees of conservatism at the time.

In *planning*, although the scope and extent of planning indicators was reduced, the most important SOEs remained subject to plans for the value of production, physical output of main products and their destinations (including defence and exports if they existed) and budgetary contributions (KHH, 1986: 14).[7] In matters related to *labour and wages* the position was liberal, with SOEs now free in principle to hire labour directly and to refuse to recruit workers allocated to them by higher levels (KHH, 1986: 19). But wages funds had to be situated within the overall plan (which had to be approved by superior levels) (KHH, 1986: 20).

Regarding *finance* the position was also more liberal, clearly stating that SOEs had the right to create and expand their own capital so as to expand production and business (KHH, 1986: 22). Own capital was defined as that derived from depreciation funds left back to the SOE, plus deductions from its profits via the production development and welfare funds (of the 'three funds'). The *state bank*, however, facing hyperinflationary conditions, sought to retain strong controls over SOE cash holdings (KHH, 1986: 26), requiring them to open bank accounts and put their cash in these. The *Prices Commission* continued its push to increase autonomy in price-fixing for SOEs, giving, after general stipulations that they should follow state price-fixing instructions, a long list of instances where they could set prices freely (KHH, 1986: 30). Crucially, where the SOE had used self-procured – and so high-priced – inputs to deliver according to the plan, it had the right to a state subsidy (KHH, 1986). In *foreign trade* SOEs were granted rights to retain 10 per cent of net foreign exchange earnings (KHH, 1986: 35).

The decree also maintained that application of 306-BBT would be an experiment of limited scope, which is not what initial interpretations of it implied, and 306-BBT did not in fact refer to itself as an experiment. Yet the source cited refers to experimentation and who were to be responsible for it; for example, central branch ministries were to choose one or two units (KHH, 1986: 42). The document was signed by Do Muoi. A suitable conclusion to reach from a comparison of 306-BBT and 76-HDBT is that various elements of the Politburo were now clearly moving to support SOEs, but that these were still opposed by others close to central state organs, of which the SPC remained the most conservative.

Grassroots comments

The panel placed 306-BBT into the following context.

The period of 'hard pain' in the birth of the market economy was not long – about four years (from August 1982 to April 1986). This period saw a strong pressure for recentralisation exerted by central ministries. At the level of the SOE, all managers in the panel reported that their Plan C activities were reduced and some of the associated workshops were actually closed. In the opinion of one:

> It is lucky that Le Duan, the general-secretary, died, for if not things would have been awful and Vietnam now would have continued with centralisation like Cuba. The 'price-wages-money' measures were simply yet another highly centralised form of state management that failed.

As for 306-BBT:

> 306-BBT was a reloosening as far as the SOEs were concerned. It simply continued the cycle started with 279 in 1979. Confronted with a situation where the country was close to collapse and the people were deeply unsettled, the state had to continue with loosening up through 306-BBT.

This resolution permitted the SOEs of the panel to recover. The 'under-the-table' activities were once again formalised. One member of the panel reported:

> At the start of 1986 I was denounced by some people in the SOE on the grounds that I had violated socialist management principles, but once 306-BBT came out everything was OK; without it I could have been sacked and even been sent to prison.

This last quote suggests that 306-BBT was an attempt to secure political support from the state business interest 'over the heads' of central state organs, and was successful, since compliance still relied heavily upon whether local cadres would or could be attacked on grounds that they had deviated from traditional socialism.

Doi moi *before* doi moi...?

These decrees show that the Party's formal industry policy had shifted back to a liberalising stance *before* the Sixth Congress.

The Sixth Congress, as is well known, introduced *doi moi* and committed the Party to moving towards a market economy. The crucial question, though, was that of who would control assets in that economy, and how. It would seem relatively clear from the discussion so far that this question had to a great extent already been answered: SOEs would continue to play their central role in Vietnam's development. But what relationship would they have with the state, for marketisation processes would have to lead at some point to capital wanting to move beyond individual SOEs, and at that time it was (after the politics of 306-BBT) hardly likely that tensions between the interests of the collective and those who controlled capital would be resolved in favour of the workers? It was not too hard, therefore, to imagine that the crucial long-term political issue would be just how the new commercial classes would be formed, and what relationship they would have with the SOE-based commerce that had played such an important role in the 1980s.

The Sixth Congress of 1986

According to the panel:

> By the end of 1985 and early 1986 the situation was not only very difficult but was getting both harder and more tense. At the start of 1986 the Party distributed the draft political report of the congress. Its content was extremely conservative. It was lucky that Le Duan died [mid-year] and Truong Chinh replaced him. The political report that Truong Chinh then guided the editing of was extremely reformist and quite different from that drafted by Le Duan. This made everybody happy, both the leaders and workers in the SOEs.

Like other congresses, the SOEs organised meetings to greet the results of the congress, and then organised Party members to study its resolutions.

The Sixth Congress confirmed the shift (to a market economy) and granted rights of autonomy to the base. At this stage the term 'renovation' (*doi moi*) was used and became the strategic line of the Party and government of Vietnam.

217-HDBT encouraged even further (p. 198) the rights to autonomy of SOEs and reduced the legal power of Plan A. At this time SOEs had far greater potential for rapid development. It was only at this time that the members of the panel realised that they themselves were not likely to find it easy to adapt to a market economy.

Conclusions: the attempted recentralisation

I have dealt in some detail with the events from 1979 to early 1986, especially the policy record. This shows clearly the recentralising intentions, their failure in a traditional communist state and so – which is my point – the sheer strength of the commercial renaissance that was overpowering them.

Commercial renaissance drew upon 'aggravated shortage', and was then powered through in the face of official opposition after the economic crisis of the late 1970s. It emerged from and within SOEs, and was therefore utterly 'Red' in that managers and other key individuals were all insiders, good Party members. The comments from the panel show clearly that it was as Party members that they were most vulnerable to attacks from 'revolutionaries', who were curbed at times by the adroit rhetoric of those writing policy, who managed in 25-CP to define SOE market relations as part of the plan, a brilliant stroke.

The fact that 306-BBT predates the Sixth Congress suggests that the state business interest was pushing hard for political support.

Absent from this history is much to do with a formally private sector. The narrative instead shows SOE links with 'outside' economic agents as mediated through the *con rung*, themselves usually also insiders but of lower formal status, since they were cooperatives, groups and so on rather than SOEs. It follows from this that any immanent class formation was taking place *within* SOEs, and workers were largely benefiting from commercialisation: there are frequent references to increases in wages paid from 'outside' activities, so such surpluses were at this stage tending to be shared. This was in part due to the ongoing ideological hostility to markets, which made managers vulnerable. But also one should not forget the strong links between managers and other cadres through the Party, and the shared experience of wartime and fence-breaking.

Notes

1. The two 'models' for the new methods were reportedly the Con Dao Fishing Enterprise and the Pho Yen Ball-bearing Enterprise.
2. It is interesting to note in this passage that there is no explicit mention of the Chinese and Western aid cuts.
3. In the text, the phrase actually used is 'in other parts of the plan' (Duong Bach Lien and Le Trang, 1982: 30).
4. I am afraid I have lost the reference for this. My own site visits in 1985–1986, and then from 1987, showed that such investment practices very often focused on areas that provided inputs to workers' reproduction needs, and thus were often food-oriented. Food aid did not stop until around 1990.
5. It is worth noting that only one of the three cities cited (Ho Chi Minh City) and two of the five provinces (Dong Nai and Quang Nam-Da Nang) were in the south.
6. The reader may recall that Nguyen Lam only left the secretariat at the Sixth Congress (p. 32).
7. 76-HDBT, 26 June 1986, appeared in *Cong Bao* on 15 July 1986 but I refer to the KHH text here.

8

From the 1986 Sixth Congress to the emergence of the SOE-focused model of the 1990s

Policy logic – failure hidden by success?

The late 1980s is a period of increasing intellectual coherence,[1] followed by hiatus after the market economy emerges and many of the fundamental policy issues of the 1980s vanish. There is then a return to a focus upon SOEs and their 'guiding role' (*vai tro chu dao) which laid the ground for many problems in the late 1990s and 2000s. This points to the limits to both the reformist thinking of the 1980s and the success of the transition: in other words, the consequences and nature of the intentionality behind policy. Central to this are the implications for politics and government of a situation where business primarily means state business, and where the regime is over-dependent upon state business. This, as we have seen, was far being the main concern of policy in the 1980s. The game had fundamentally changed.

Analysis of this through the 1990s and into the 2000s requires an assessment of the overall political economy of the situation. While prior to 1990 or so I rely upon existing analysis (de Vylder and Fforde, 1996), for the later period this is still unfinished. Preliminary work supports the view that the return to the state sector of the early 1990s created a trap for the regime, but the implications of this require a wider analysis than I can present here. In hindsight, the *limitations* of policy in the 1980s, its failure to confront core issues such as the nature of state property and the political role of major institutions such as the SPC and the MOs (especially the trade unions), are relatively clear.

Phan van Tiem (1992), perhaps the best macro-economist working in the 1980s and certainly the best monetary economist, provides a short teaching text surveying the problem of inflation and its history. Inflation is extremely interesting as its causes reveal, and touch deeply upon, fundamental political issues of state power, what influences it and which social groups win and lose when state power is used to drive up prices (a prerequisite of hyperinflation). The text says very little about this.

The intellectual coherence of the late 1980s' reformism shows up clearly in the written sources. Many senior policy-makers and their advisers believed that they understood what was happening, and that reform was increasingly viable. State power, in this construal, had potential for progress. It was also personally apparent, as I lived in Vietnam from mid-1987 to 1992, working in Vietnamese, and was strongly impressed by, if not drawn into, the vigour of the reformists' world. The counterpoint to this analytical vitality was a rhetoric that could draw upon the experiences of SOE managers, consumers and others. Theatre, such the brilliant play 'Toi va chung ta' ('Me and Us'), also worked within the metaphors and juxtapositions of this discourse. The early 1990s, once central planning had vanished, saw this language largely disappear, although, unsurprisingly as it drew upon the deep resources of the language, echoes were to remain to drive new movements and debates.

But, if there was increasing intellectual coherence, there was still economic chaos.

Industrial policy at this stage continued its self-definition in ways that marked its origins in the late 1970s, if not earlier: the dialectic between loosening and tightening in the relationship between SOEs and the state. This had inherently limited it but made it robust, as this was the reality of state industrial organisation in the decade after 1979. It was the failure to move beyond this thinking that committed Vietnam to an SOE-focused growth model in the 1990s, with profound effects upon possibilities for both political change and the emergence of a 'true' private sector, probably more competitive and creating more jobs – this had to wait until the early 2000s (Fforde, 2004a, 2005a).

A radical current in debate?

Yet reformists were far from having established a hegemony, and much of the debate regarding economic matters remained deeply conservative. Interesting new currents were starting to appear. One, presented by Dao Xuan Sam, sought to move away from the limitations of the attack on the centralised administrative supply system and the call for 'socialist economy and business'. Here his crucial innovation was a stress upon the contract (e.g. Dao Xuan Sam, 1986), and the need for a contract's validity to be independent of the hierarchical relationship between the contracted parties (p. 137). This was a strong assertion of the validity of peripheral autonomy, but it also went far further, above all in its implicit disregard for a central ideal: if contract enforcement was to be fair, in the sense that both parties were materially liable for failure to implement it, this would apply to many more types of economic relations and notions of hierarchy would have to change profoundly.

Like the earlier distributionist position, this based itself upon a critical assessment of the actual operation of the Vietnamese economic management system. This time, however, attitudes had altered as a result of the failure of the recentralisation drive:

> The use of economic levers based upon the system of functional branches is well established, and rests on the desire to ensure a high level of unified centralisation. In reality, however, it results spontaneously in ever-increasing drift and slackness. This is because each functional branch gives priority to its own goals, and all are in opposition so that they neutralise each other, hindering production and trade. This greatly restrains each economic organisation – branch, region, base units, each with their status as producers and planned traders in commodities. They may lose their rights and weapons [*vu khi*] in trade relations, and in particular in the struggle to master the market. This is the main regrettable reason why each new factor must overcome the system as a necessity, because it is only in this way that it is possible to attain one's own mastery of production and trade so as to master the market in accordance with the resolutions and major policies of the Party. An over-centralised used of economic levers through individual functional branches is a characteristic of bureaucratic-subsidisation. (Dao Xuan Sam, 1985: 77)

The Sixth Congress

The 1986 Sixth Congress introduced the slogan of *doi moi* (renovation). Developments in the USSR were moving towards *glasnost* and *perestroika*. Reports at the time focused upon the congress's ideological shift towards acceptance of a socialist commodity economy (e.g. Furuta,

1988; Williams, 1987). The official documents indeed stressed this. But what would be the role of the VCP itself in a market economy while the view was in the other direction – towards SOE interests and 'getting the state out of production'?

The congress was strongly critical of the old system of administrative subsidy and supply, juxtaposing this with the new system, which had four main differences:

> First, under the old system the base unit was situated within relationships where they were supplied with materials and delivered outputs that were directly balanced by the superior level with mandatory prices. In the new system, they are placed within relationships of buying and selling with other business entities... [in other words] base units act within markets where they have legal status as commodity producers.
>
> Second, in both the old and new systems, base units follow a plan under the unified management of the state. [But under the new system the base units' plans] are based upon economic contracts. Under the old system the basis for plan discipline was administrative, the implementation of orders from above. Under the new system, plan discipline is the discipline of economy and law based upon economic contracts.
>
> Third, under the old system base units essentially were not independent financial units, did not autonomously calculate results, benefiting from profits and bearing the costs of losses... Under the new system base units must be financially independent, must themselves cope with calculating costs and revenues, benefiting from profits and bearing losses, and must themselves bear responsibility to do their duty regarding the state, ensuring that they balance the three interests.
>
> Fourth, in both systems base units must act legally subject to state monitoring and control. But the basic difference with the new system is that under the old system base units simply implemented so that inevitably the superior level had to protect them before the law if they had followed orders. But in the new system, economic base units really have independent legal status... [and] all enterprises are equal before the law. (DCSV, 1987: 78–9)

This quote shows the focus upon SOE status. As 306-BBT had shown as well, the renewed push was to increase their autonomy in an economic world regulated by markets and law. But what was to be the *political* basis of 'economy and law'? What authority would the state deploy and where would it come from? It is striking how the focus of the quotation above is upon base units (mainly SOEs) as the most important entity in the state economy. This of course assumes that they are simply the collectivity made up of their cadres and workers. There is no emergent 'class issue' within them.

In a more detailed discussion of the economic thinking of the Sixth Congress, senior official Tran Duc Nguyen looked at four issues: first, the meaning of the 'pre-stage'. He stated that:

> Reality eliminated the point of view that stated that with the advantages [we had] in terms of aid from fraternal socialist countries as well as the great strides in modern technology the transition period in our country would not be long. (Tran Duc Nguyen, 1988: 9)

The context of SOE reform was the need to meet four central goals:

> To produce enough consumer goods and to have positive domestic savings; to make the first step in creating a rational economic structure so as to develop production; to construct and improve at a step new production relations suited to the nature and level of development of the forces of production... in which the state economy will play the guiding role; and to obtain positive social change. (Tran Duc Nguyen, 1988: 13–17)

If the terminology is translated, this means two things. The state business interest was to see SOEs granted still greater autonomy from planners, but this was to take place without reference to what might be going on *within* SOEs. This is part reflected the fact that SOE 'own capital' was still largely being used to benefit consumption, with SOE workers' incomes benefiting significantly and their managers still not starting to separate out in terms of capitalist class formation. Or, to put it more directly, such issues remained latent.

Reforms after the Sixth Congress

After the Sixth Congress and before the loss of Soviet-bloc assistance there were a number of important policy measures. The most important were not directly related to SOEs, but were of some indirect importance.

In the rural areas cooperatives' cadres saw their power further reduced by decree 10, which got rid of the system of work points, so that control over product now reverted back to the farming household, at least for rice. Rhetoric hostile to emergence of capitalism in the rural areas was expressed in the decree's mutterings about 'red landlords', and large number of rural cadres subsequently lost their jobs, though a rump remained because the cooperatives were only rarely actually disbanded (BNN, 1991; n/a, 1989; DCSV, 1988; Fforde, 2001). SOEs now found, since decree 10 had stopped superior levels issuing plan targets to cooperatives, that they had a harder task in securing inputs from the rural areas (Nguyen Sinh, n/d).

At the same time internal trade barriers were greatly reduced, easing up the local market and, among many important results, granting access throughout the country to low-price and reliable supplies of rice, especially from the Mekong. Accompanying these moves to free up agriculture, SOEs gained improved but far from free access to foreign suppliers and buyers.

But while the state was pushing to open up national product markets and support SOEs, this can be contrasted with VCP views in other areas, such as the strong criticisms of agricultural cooperatives' cadres made in the preamble to decree 10 (DCSV, 1988). These were both classist in Leninist terms and also leftist (Boudarel, 1983; Greenfield, 1993, 1994). Yet SOEs were discussed as areas without such tensions.

The balance between the SOE and its superior level – 1987's 217-HDBT

217-HDBT: content

217–HDBT was well publicised (UBKHNN, 1989). A speech by Tran Duc Luong introduced the system of which 217–HDBT (14 November 1987) was the central pillar. This was an attempt to create a new economic management system, and to do so there were two central issues: first, reform of the management system at the level of the base unit, and second, reform of state economic management (Tran Duc Luong, 1988: 7). The former was primary, since it was the 'cell' of the national economy, the place where goods were produced, workers' incomes generated and surpluses generated for both the unit and the state. Only through its autonomy could it guarantee these tasks. But, on the other hand:

base units operate within a unified national economy under the direction, government and coordination of the supreme conductor, the state of proletarian dictatorship.

Our system's strength and superiority derives from the harmonious blending of these two basic factors. (Tran Duc Luong, 1988: 8)

The decision had been taken to focus upon SOEs. Latent in this was the desire to avoid early liberalisation of conditions facing the private sector, yet at this time private trade remained still severely limited (city streets were not to see return of trade and petty services until the very end of the decade), focusing upon SOEs' limited options and so the long-term political and commercial game. In other words, one can see here already the closing down of the option of political liberalisation to accompany an opening up to the private sector. In terms of timing, Tran Duc Luong (1988: 14) reported that they were expecting to have implemented these measures 'basically' by 1990.

This was of course to be caught up by the macro-economic stabilisation measures and the loss of Soviet-bloc aid. As Tran Duc Luong noted (1988: 20–1), the basic structural issue was that SOEs received their inputs from two sources: the plan and their own efforts. 217-HDBT was an attempt to realise a balance between these two in ways that preserved overall harmony. This was perhaps a chimera, solved in the breach by the *force majeure* of the loss of Soviet aid, but what is most clear is the ways in which 217-HDBT was seeking to support SOE autonomy. In this it responded to the spirit of 306-BBT in ways that 76-HDBT had not done.

Central to this was the shift in the relative authority and power of SOEs *vis-à-vis* state planning, for the basis of planning was now the SOE's plan rather than what its superior sent it (NXBST, 1988: 62). Further, any plan issued to it was related directly to the ability of the state to supply the inputs required to meet it (NXBST, 1988: 64). There was to be a gradual replacement of legally binding targets with state purchase orders and auctions and a reduction of the number of 'list' goods to a minimum level (NXBST, 1988: 69). The list went on: SOEs had the right to sell assets if their requests had not been replied to after 30 days; superior levels had the right to move materials and money between 'their' SOEs but had to have their agreement. The entire system of materials supply was thus to shift to one of purchase and sale based upon economic contracts.

In what was the high point of SOE independence in this area, they were granted 100 per cent of basic depreciation (NXBST, 1988: Clause 20) and full rights over their capital, including retained profits (NXBST,

1988: Clause 21). My reading of this is that SOE 'own capital' was recognised as belonging to the SOE.

There are various intriguing aspects of this legislation. First, there is no clear statement of ownership; rather, an SOE is construed as an entity containing a range of interests, somewhat like a village, with these interests structured in various ways by the Party, MOs, management and other local interests of various sorts, yet capable of carrying out economic calculation and entering into economic contracts. Second, there is a clear push to support SOE autonomy, and this self-reflectivity is defined as a radical change from the direction taken in the early 1980s (as I have argued): the opposite. But the implicit changes in the position of the state are not clear. Upon what would the state rest once it had lost its power, though central planning, over the economy in general and over SOEs in particular? How could there be a 'Party without the plan'?

217-HDBT: political support

The decree had political support from central government. This can be seen from the detail and clarity of legislation passed to guide its implementation (BLD, 1988; BNgT, 1988; BNT, 1988; BTC, 1987; BVT, 1988; NHNN, 1987; TTKT, 1988), which can be contrasted with the tone of similar contributions to 76-HDBT (p. 186), and the rather clear explanations about how this new system was to work (e.g. Nguyen van Dam, 1988). It also received clear support from the conservative Premier, Pham Hung (1988).

It is useful to note that while 217-HDBT increased SOE autonomy it failed to clarify the status of the SOE as a form of property. This is hardly surprising. The draft statute on SOEs (50-HDBT, 22 March 1988) was followed by revisions to 217-HDBT (NXBST, 1990) that sought to govern just what the organs of the state were meant to do in a situation of extensive SOE autonomy. The situation remained unclear.

Towards the second trap: loss of Soviet aid, elimination of the 'two-price system' and the anti-inflationary measures of 1989

The history of 1989–1992 is in large part relatively straightforward, far more so than the 1980s. As the Soviet bloc collapsed and Soviet aid fell

From the 1986 Sixth Congress to the emergence of the SOE-focused model

away, the Vietnamese economy continued to experience hyperinflation. With policy focused upon inflation, top leaders were eventually convinced to adopt strong measures. Deposit interest rates at the state banks were raised sharply, to levels that were sufficiently positive in real terms to attract deposits, and the Chinese border was opened to trade, so the supply of consumer goods on Vietnam's markets increased sharply.[2]

After much debate, nominal interest rates charged to SOEs were also increased, though not to positive real levels. Inflationary expectations changed abruptly. People sold their hoards of goods, kept as a store of value against rapid price rises, and either put their money on deposit or bought valuable consumer goods, or both. At the same time the collapse of Soviet-bloc aid meant that central planners no longer had the resources that had previously allowed them to negotiate with SOEs for Plan A deliveries, and SOEs stopped being 'balanced' by their superiors. Supplies that continued to be allocated to them (such as coal and fuel) were now simply an allocation of inputs at state-determined prices. The economy was for the moment almost completely unprotected, as is shown by the negligible value of import taxes.

By 1991 the dust was starting to settle and output to recover. What emerged was a situation fraught with long-term difficulties, though a near-miracle had happened. Central to the emerging market economy was a radically changed trajectory for SOEs. This was because, while they had escaped from central planning, during the crisis the state's need for financial resources to replace the deliveries of planned SOE output had changed the relationship between SOEs and the state. And property rights, which had during the 1980s shifted downwards as SOE autonomy increased, now moved upwards.

To secure a tax base, and also to put money in the pockets of those outside SOEs who could exert power over them, rights to allocate surpluses and profits, to decide upon where investments should be made, to determine a unit's business strategy (in other words those things that form coherent answers to basic questions about property) all started to shift back *above* the SOE. As we shall see, channels for resources flows such as taxes, but more interestingly categories linked to capital such as depreciation and profits derived from own capital, were energised to shift resources outside the SOE. These changes were often strongly resisted. But in general these relationships between SOEs and outsiders, both formal and informal, occurred and meant that the trajectory of the nature of state capital shifted: while through the 1980s it had become increasingly private in character (though still in many ways influenced by its origins in central planning), now it became increasingly state in character (implying – for statist analysts (p. 6) – that the state was itself changing as commercial interests penetrated calculations and behaviour).

This meant, though, that as workers saw their wages increasingly set by supply and demand, so that their own access to surpluses generated by their SOEs' market operations were eroded, what faced them across the table were still officials. But now officials increasingly had direct interests in the profits generated by SOEs. It was almost as though, with the failure of traditional Marxism-Leninism, orthodox Marxist analysis of capitalism became increasingly valuable as classes emerged 'of and for themselves'; yet, with the nature of SOE ownership now tending to become increasingly statist, this meant that the relative autonomy of the state was being cut back at a time when globalisation and the market economy were both pushing for it. By the end of the 1990s, though, a relatively independent private sector was to emerge. But that is to run ahead of the story.

Grassroots comments

According to the panel, at the level of the SOE the anti-inflationary measures and loss of Soviet-bloc aid in 1989–1990 were important. With inflation at three-digit levels, SOEs and the population were extremely worried. Many conservatives argued that inflation was caused by *doi moi*. Soviet aid reduced very quickly and was then lost entirely. The danger that the Soviet system was about to collapse had direct implications for the very existence of the VCP.

The leadership could not reverse course any longer, but had to continue renovation to preserve the system and attract foreign capital. The main effect at this time was the slow eradication, and then termination, of the two-price system. This contributed to the end of inflation.

However, at the level of the SOE there was continued confusion, especially for those SOEs that received heavy price subsidies. At this time:

> We were looking for a way to setting up joint ventures with overseas, stimulating exports and imports (either directly or via trading companies) so as to compensate for the resources no longer supplied by the state.

The second trap and the recovery of 1990–1992

Political issues revisited: democracy, Yeltsin and the private sector

The background in terms of economic policy to the crucial period of 1989–1991 was stark. It had three main elements.

First, and dating back to perhaps 1983 or 1984, it had been learnt that attempts to preserve central planning (epitomised by 146-HDBT and 156-HDBT) lacked in the end both political support and economic rationality: it was better, in the national as well as particular interests, to go with the flow and accept and encourage SOE autonomy. 306-BBT, in 1986 but well before the Sixth Congress, showed this. 217-HDBT of 1987 as well as other policies followed this trajectory of shifting power and economic rights (and so in effect property rights) *downwards*. In political terms this suggested to analysts that political change must evolve in directions that reflected this, a clear example of which was the notion of contracting between autonomous entities early articulated by economists such as Dao Xuan Sam (1985, 1986), which seemed logically to lead to a view of the state as non-totalitarian and distinct from its subjects: economic and social agents.

This posed the question as to what these subjects would then grant to the state so as to give it authority over them, rather than simply power: how would it shift from rule to government? Viewing democratisation as but one way of securing popular support and so authority, and influenced by trends in Central Europe and the USSR itself, this linked economic and political reform and was underpinned by pragmatic thinking that sought political authority as a buttress to state power that could then be used developmentally. From this point of view elections, such as that of Yeltsin in the USSR, were one possibility, with the hope that this would support the construction of a non-totalitarian state, yet there was no obvious political process that could lead to selection of somebody to fill that role. Yet an important group of actors on the Vietnamese political stage was clearly the state business interest, which was in effect a nearly reborn commercial force capable of existing quite independently of central planning; indeed, its relationship with the plan was increasingly dependent not upon the political position of planners, but their position as controllers of the Soviet-bloc aid programme. Class tensions between workers and SOE owners were not important.

The second main lesson dated from the hyperinflation and chaos that had followed the price-wages-money programme of 1985. This had removed To Huu, and perhaps more importantly Tran Phuong, from the political arena, and had, by being blameable for the ensuing years, given great influence to advocates of the importance of macro-economic stability. Concretely, it gave considerable authority to the state bank and those around it, some of whom had come up from the State Prices Commission. This meant that the national polity was far more likely to remain intact under economic pressures, with claimants for subsidies and tax breaks likely to be put through processes that forced them to justify their claims in economic terms, and where political clout would not necessarily give a green light, since the state bank's veto would, far more often than not, be effective.

The third main lesson was that, in its starkest terms, the private sector did not itself appear to be of great importance. The *con rung* that had grown up were usually linked to SOE interests, and dependent upon them. Thus Vietnam's emerging market-oriented economic structures, and policy-makers' views of them, lacked a normal private sector. This meant, for example, that it was still very feasible to view industry-agriculture economic relations (such as marketing, processing and inputs supply) in terms of relations between SOEs and rural producers (either mediated by cooperatives or directly with family farms). The main contrasts between the 2000s and the 1990s were in the rise in the second decade of the private sector and foreign-invested companies, which highlighted the anachronism of the dominant element of the political economy, the close relationship between the state and SOEs that had underpinned the 1990s.

The collapse of the small-scale non-state sector: slaughter?

Non-state industry suffered very badly in the period 1989–1991 (Ngu Phong, 1990). This was in large part because of the nature of its relationship with the SOE sector and central planning. As we have seen, one method used to realise locally the value of resources obtained from the plan, usually originating in the Soviet aid programme but also created by the plan itself through the procurement of primary inputs (such as agricultural and forestry products), was to put them through satellite non-state units such as artisanal cooperatives, groups and so on. With better rights to sell on to markets, and with property rights over them such as to allow surpluses to be appropriated more securely, this meant they could not only generate such resources but also support primary accumulation – in others words, that these could become subject to clearer local or 'private' control and thus be put on the path to becoming capital, owned and used to generate profits.

One outcome of the loss of Soviet-bloc aid, as well as the processes that reduced SOE autonomy and shifted commercial property rights back up and outside SOEs, was thus naturally that these mechanisms became both less valuable and less feasible. Much capital was lost. And if, as is likely, it was through such channels that primary accumulation had started, and so a commercial class that was more private in character would emerge, then it was here that one must look for some of the reasons why a private sector took so long to develop through the 1990s.[3] Surveys carried out in the 1990s tended to show that private entrepreneurs had often had to reform and reconstitute capital after earlier failures (Ronnas, 1992, 1998).

Grassroots opinions

The panel had no clear sense of this period's overall trajectory, nor why the state sector recovered. One thought that it was simply because of the programme having a 'socialist direction'. Since the country was still socialist the state 'had to' restore the state sector. The state continued to subsidise the state sector but in new forms (priority allocations of capital, writing off unpaid debts, supplying land, permitting direct exports etc.). Because of this the small SOEs went under.

Because the state concentrated on the large companies it gave almost no support to the artisanal cooperatives, pushing them into crisis: 'throwing them in the deep end so they could sink or swim'. This meant that some cooperatives became dynamic and learnt to exploit opportunities in the new system, but some went under.

The recovery of 1990–1992

Changes to 217-HDBT – another U-turn

The beginnings of recentralisation within the heady air of success can be found in the ways in which 217-HDBT was modified as the 1989–1991 crisis developed. At this time (late 1989) the ministries had defined for themselves the following responsibilities:

- the preparation of plans;
- drafting of legal projects;
- construction of plans for international cooperation;
- preparation of relevant regulations;
- inspection and monitoring of other organs;
- regarding SOEs and other base units belonging to them, preparing policies to 'guide, stimulate and govern' them; issuing decisions to establish them; and inspecting them and allocating capital and other resources to them while approving their development directions and so on (NXBST, 1990: 284–9).

This, then, continued the direction of 217-HDBT – a freeing up of SOEs from state planning control without a clear sense of what would replace planning as the basis for the state: the trap was opening. Note also that 195-HDBT had in 1989 formally abolished the two-price system (HDBT, 1989).

Yet the circumstances of the time were pushing against the old 'reformist' trend to increase SOE autonomy. A central issue was that of restoring the tax base. For the authorities, SOEs were the most obvious source of funds. As early as 1989, therefore, we find changes to 217-HDBT that restored two parts of the range of silken threads that could be used to bind SOEs to higher levels: depreciation, and more importantly own capital. The former is easier to track, since it was an integral part of the traditional system (p. 187).

In mid-1989 93-HDBT was passed, revising the system of depreciation contributions of SOEs (HDBT, 1989). This stated clearly that 217-HDBT and 50-HDBT had stipulated that 100 per cent of basic depreciation was to be left to the SOE and only for a small number of large projects was some to be given to the state budget. 93-HDBT, however, bearing in mind the state's need for revenue, stipulated that new projects must pay 70 per cent of basic depreciation to the state for the first three years, with the remainder going to 'own capital' for use in the SOE's own investments. Further, for existing SOEs depreciation on assets paid for out of state budgetary funds will only be left to the units at an average rate of 50 per cent for all branches and the rest will be paid to the state budget.

Leeway for higher-level discretion was clear, as the Ministry of Finance was tasked to fix concretely the retention for each SOE in accordance with demand and requirements for replacement of the SOE's assets. This meant that any SOE which wanted to pay less could pay off the relevant cadres as part of the negotiation.

This retreat from 217-HDBT was then tightened up in 1992 and 1995.[4]

'Own capital' had been central to SOE commercial renaissance. 217-HDBT had maintained that it was subject to the direction of the SOE (p. 199). However, it was increasingly argued on various grounds that such assets should be subject to higher-level levies and guidance. Two arguments used in particular were that it had been created using state assets (these were of course SOEs), and that some form of levy was justified as a return on state investments or as a tax. If we compare Do Nguyen Khoat (1990) with Nguyen Quoc Khanh (1985) the change is very clear.

For Do Nguyen Khoat the issue is that the state had seen its power to implement central planning gravely weakened. The main reason for the low mobilisation of capital in SOEs is that capital comes from many sources, so their superior levels are ignorant. Far from being set by planners, prices differ greatly between branches and SOEs ignore the costs of fixed capital. There had been (partly due to inflation) a steep increase in demand for circulating capital, in part because of SOEs' increased demand for materials but also because of the large changes in prices of raw materials from agriculture due to rising free market prices. SOEs were finding 'own' inputs in many ways, such as exchange or barter for their output, exports or direct cash purchases.

This is a familiar picture. By 1990 the position has changed greatly and the issue is not that of an inability to implement central planning, but that of the tax base, and indirectly who can get at SOE profits. Do Nguyen Khoat's (1990) discussion focuses upon the rights to tax capital and the issue of the meaning and ownership of SOEs' own capital – referred to by him as capital 'supplemented by the unit'. While somewhat confused, we can see here how opinion is starting to try to sort out the relationship between the right to tax and the right to ownership. Should SOEs pay the state for capital because the capital is the state's or because they should pay taxes? For they were arguing that that capital tax could not be applied to their 'own capital'. It is noteworthy that the term 'own capital' seems to vanish from the legal record in 1986.[5]

In September 1989 decree 101-HDBT (1 August 1989) announced a capital survey of SOEs that was designed to find out what was there.[6]

The start of recentralisation – SOE management councils

In 1990 there was an interesting 'blip' in the process. Like 306-BBT it points to important steps in the political process prior to major events and so informing them.

If 306-BBT sought to secure support from the state business interest through promising largely unregulated autonomy, 143-HDBT (10 May 1990) attacked managers' autonomy by placing them under SOE management councils (Che Tuong Nhu, 1994: 20). In practice, given the Leninist practice of controlling such bodies through the MOs and/or the VCP directly, and that it would have involved people who had to have been 'sweet' for commercialisation to have happened, it is not surprising that this was a dead letter in terms of shifting towards some 'worker-managed' solution.

But if the focus is instead placed upon a drive to secure better control over SOEs, then the logic of 143-HDBT is far clearer, as can be seen from the intended composition and powers of the management councils. One half of the members, including the chairman, were to be appointed by the immediately superior state management organ. Of these, one was also to be a representative of the Ministry of Finance (*Cong Bao*, 1990: 178). The rest of the council were to be from the SOE and elected by its employee assembly. It was to meet quarterly, and its rights included approving the SOE business plan prepared by the manager; analysing and monitoring performance; and deciding upon and monitoring a number of key indicators, including depreciation, wages, materials use and profits. It was also to approve all expansion plans and long-term borrowing. Most importantly, it was to appoint and dismiss managers, monitor them and approve their wages and bonuses (*Cong Bao*, 1990: 178–9).

These powers, taken in their context, show the strong desire to regain influence over SOEs, realised tactically by the insertion of the externally appointed half of the council. Given that superior levels could also hope to exert influence – through MOs and the Party – upon elections of the internal members, this was a potentially powerful ploy.

Equitisation

Also in 1990 there started the policy circus referred to as 'equitisation' (*Cong Bao*, 1990: 180 et seq.). This involved in principle no more than re-establishing SOEs as share-issuing companies – an exercise similar to experiences in the West with the corporatisation of facilities previously kept wholly within ministries, such as dockyards and so on. This was an issue that was to last through the 1990s and on into the 2000s. It is reminiscent of the provisions in 25-CP for the bankrupting of SOEs, which also long remained inoperative (p. 136).

My view is that most SOEs by this time were highly commercialised and so *de facto* share companies anyway. Who controlled what, and how the proceeds were shared out, was understood by the relevant insiders and outsiders. This meant that a useful model to understand their behaviour was that of the 'virtual share company' (see p. 216). The language reflected this, with terms such as *lien doanh* used to refer to ventures that involved pooling of capital as the domestic capital market developed through the 1980s. Under these circumstances, any externally imposed change can be viewed as an attempted recapitalisation, which may or may not suit the interests of existing owners. They may see the outcome as useful, for example because their shares become more easily tradable or because it permits injections of capital they see as profitable; or they may see it as unwanted, for example because their own shares lose value or they lose too much control. In any case, the calculation would be expected to be primarily commercial in its logic rather than bureaucratic.

Renaissance? The SOE-focused model of the 1990s

With the end of central planning, SOEs' relationships with each other, with suppliers and with customers were now mediated through markets of various sorts. Two crucial inputs, however, were not yet mediated through markets: labour and capital. And while most SOEs occupied enough land for present purposes, and so access to it was not yet crucial, its sale (to whom?) and purchase also remained far from marketised.

To understand fully the extent to which the experiences of the 1980s and before had amounted to the renaissance of commerce in Vietnam it is important to step back from the fray and consider wider elements of what had happened.

The crisis that had faced the economy in 1989–1990 was considerable. While real GDP did not fall, this was largely because of a combination of good agricultural performance and the explosion of services that took place as neo-Stalinisation culminated in the return to the city streets of the vast range of services typical of the region – food, trade, petty production and so on. This soaked up labour, not least that shed from SOEs as state GDP fell by 5 per cent cumulatively in these two years (TCTK, 2004: tables 27 and 109). The SOEs were at this time producing around 40 per cent of total GDP. They were traditionally the main source of tax revenue for the state. As already mentioned, the MOs had, in the late 1980s, been told to prepare to go 'off budget'. And, as discussed above, SOEs offered various mechanisms for securing revenues.

So, as SOEs recovered activity levels in 1991 and 1992, so did the tax base. TCTK (1994: table 53) shows that between 1989 and 1992 state revenue rose by some 280 per cent – of this increase, 75 per cent came from SOEs. Almost none came from foreign trade taxes, which in 1992 amounted to less than 10 per cent of total state revenue. This was partly because the anti-inflation measures of 1989–1990 had included opening the borders so as to boost consumer goods supply on domestic markets, and they were still open. SOEs' share of state revenues rose from 48 per cent in 1989 to 68 per cent in 1992 (TCTK, 1994: table 54).

What is remarkable, and testimony to the dynamism of commercialised SOEs, is that these increased payments to the state, combined with having to operate in a largely open economy where the national market had already been largely unified (see p. 78), were consistent with a return to significant positive growth from 1991, and then to an average close to 10 per cent until the 1997 Asian crisis. The commercialised SOEs of the late 1980s, therefore, appeared quite capable of functioning without major subsidies in a relatively open economy while paying significant taxes.

Given this, and the fact that the VCP remained in many ways deeply unreformed, most importantly in its Leninist politics, it is hard to see, once the opportunity of avoiding the second 'trap' had been lost, how the 1990s could not have been dominated by a process of development focused upon SOEs (Fforde, 1997). What underpinned this entire process was the economic outcome: rapid growth without macro-economic instability.

Notes

1. The writings of reformists were very common at this time. For an example among many, reviewing the history of the 1980s in the Party journal on theoretical information, see Nguyen Van Ky (1989).
2. There are various enjoyable accounts of this period, for example Nguyen Manh Hung and Cao Ngoc Thang (1990); more academically see Wood (1989), Diehl (1993) and Lipworth and Spittaller (1993).
3. Formal policy towards the sector liberalised in the late 1980s (*Nhan Dan*, 1988).

4. The decrees were 135-CT (25 April 1992), 179-TTg (22 December 1992) and 51-TTg (21 January 1995).
5. A search through my own databases, which include all of the official gazettes for this period, shows that the last reference is in July 1986 (BTC, 1986).
6. One option was to discuss a 'capital tax' – Do Nguyen Khoat (1990), specifically referring to 'own capital'. But first-half 1990 revenues were below target and strong measures were needed (BTC, 1990).

9

State industry: from the early 1990s and the 'big surprise' to the gathering problems of the late 1990s and 2000s

Introduction

This chapter looks at the 1990s. The main reason its conclusions are provisional is that the trajectory after the emergence of the market economy in 1989-1991 is one of the birth of a Vietnamese capitalism, with the associated major issues to do with methods of rule and government, the emergence of modern consumers and classes – with their associated factor markets – and the pervasive impact of these changes upon attitudes and understanding.[1] For me, these have not yet been fully thought through (Fforde 2004a, 2005a) and so the points made here and in the next chapter are limited, provisional and exploratory. Central to these puzzles is the meaning to be attached to Vietnam's SOEs, whose reported share of GDP, as already mentioned (note 2 on p. xxiii), *rose* through the decade without, as would usually be expected, wrecking macro-economic stability through their demands for support: cheap credits, foreign exchange, tax breaks and so on.

How should this 'Vietnam paradox' (p. 1) be explained?

The past and its legacies

The 'shock and awe' to be expected after the collapse of the USSR had not extinguished the Vietnamese state sector. Far from it: after two or three years of creative chaos, by 1993 or so it was thriving and had transformed itself into an important tax base for the regime, generating resources for national development and legitimisation, and was an apparent foundation for Vietnam's integration into the world capitalist economy through foreign trade and as a counterpart for foreign investors. Had this turned a 'curate's egg' into 'dragon's teeth'? It had become part of the foundations of a regime that, to its own great astonishment as well as that of the by now well-tried population, was entering a period of 'economic miracle', with trend GDP growth rates at around 8 per cent and an economy sufficiently robust to endure not only the 1997 financial crisis but a series of substantial policy mistakes as the government, like others, persisted in learning through its own rather than others' errors. It was all a 'big surprise', granted the chaos of the late 1980s.

The 1990s were dominated by the need to come to terms with the major qualitative changes of 1989–1990, above all the absence of central planning. By the end of the decade, despite considerable pressure from reformers and foreign policy advisers, the state sector had maintained its share of the Vietnamese economy. The trajectory of a declining share seen in the second half of the 1980s was reversed from around 1992 (note 2 on p. xxiii). This was the 'Vietnam paradox', for developing countries normally find that high and rising state shares of GDP are accompanied by macro-economic instability as the sector pulls in cheap credit, weakens the tax base and fails to generate adequate exports.

Why did this not happen in Vietnam? The basis thesis advanced here is that, in the main, Vietnam's SOEs were best seen as 'virtual share companies', largely treated by their effective owners as private in nature, and so capable of performing under competitive conditions *without* economically destabilising state support. When placed into historical context, this fits well with the picture drawn of commercial renaissance based upon SOEs and the quote from Dao Xuan Sam on p. 46. The notion of the 'virtual share company' opens the way to exploring the real rather than the formal nature of SOEs as businesses, and here as I have already mentioned a preliminary result is that the centre of gravity of virtual share ownership moved 'upwards' and away from interests close to and within SOEs. This was experienced as a *reduction* in SOE autonomy.

There were I think two main aspects to this process: re-establishment of state influence over SOEs as a consequence of the need to re-establish a tax base, and the removal from workers of their effective rights to share in the proceeds from 'outside' activity that had grown up in the 1980s. A powerful trend from the early 1990s was towards a situation where SOE workers saw their wages set by the forces of supply and demand as the labour market developed.

The drive to prevent a macro-economic meltdown initially drove restoration of state authority over state commerce: state ownership was reimposed to an important degree. This meant that SOEs' freedoms were no longer rising; rather the reverse. SOE commercialisation during the 1980s (and earlier) meant that this could occur without excessively damaging the economy. The overall project, which could be called 'making SOEs pay for the regime', was successful. And, through the mid-1990s and on into the rural political crises of the late 1990s, this restoration of state revenues on the back of state commerce provided the resources to finance rural development spending, which, since most provincial party secretaries in the Central Committee were from tax-deficient rural provinces, underpinned a certain macro-politics. To put it more succinctly, not only were Ho Chi Minh City's commercial activities available to pay for around half of the state budget, but this could happen without creating political and economic instability – rather the reverse (Gainsborough, 2002). The origins of this are to be found in the commercial renaissance of Vietnam's SOEs through the 1980s. This process laid the ground for the shift towards a rather rapidly growing economy with a government that could and did spend significant resources on social policy.

Thus the trajectory of real ownership and control over SOEs changed direction after 1987's 217-HDBT. This brought the state feet-first back into the swampy mess of state capitalism, which was likely to lead to trouble as the consequences of such ways of socialising business risk were felt by politicians (Zysman, 1983; Wade 1988, 1990). But this, as I have already argued, requires an analysis of the overall political economy of Vietnam that is so far lacking.

Dragon's teeth? But blue ones...

Evidence for recentralisation of state property rights

There is thus a good but incomplete argument that around 1990 there appears a trajectory of *reducing* SOE autonomy. Elements above the SOEs – those who had been receiving the gifts and envelopes when they were expanding their market activities and looking for protection – extended their control, with intriguing effects upon the formation of Vietnam's commercial classes, not least as they tended to sit in state administrative offices. Any new dragon's teeth were thus no longer red, but increasingly blue...

Here I summarise my two pieces of research that point in this direction. These are based upon an in-depth but limited study of SOE property rights (Fforde, 2004b), and an examination of changes in policy and commentary between 1992 and 2002 (Fforde, 2005d). The panel also confirmed this shift in trend (p. 223).

Researching the 1990s: some preliminary results

Without a wider analysis it is not very useful to try to place piecemeal work into some critical context. There has been a large volume of research work into SOEs since the early 1990s. My personal problem with most of this is that it does not, on the whole, ask what I see as the basic question as to exactly what SOEs are, and so fails to select a persuasive analytical framework. Very few, for example, refer to Greenfield (1993, 1994), whose work, for all its polemic, is timely, based upon well-cited fieldwork and poses the right questions.

There is, for example, widespread evidence that it was quite normal for SOEs to act as the shells for various *de facto* joint ventures, via 'under-the-table' (*chui*) investments, and investors pay to lie in the shade (*nup bong*) offered by such shells. If this was normal, there is good reason to doubt whether SOEs should, as a matter of course, be viewed at this time as being economic agents with objectives such as profit maximisation. To use commercial metaphors, there is no point thinking of a business as an entity if it is really made up of a number of separate ventures that operate independently and just use it as a convenient source of inputs and legal cover. This is the old story of the distinction between form and content; in Vietnamese, the 'shell' (*vo*) and the 'gut' (*ruot*).

Property rights over SOEs

It seems clear to me that their history argues strongly that after 1990 SOEs as a form of property should be looked at in ways that can get behind their formal position as state-owned units to ask simple questions: who controls them, and who benefits from surpluses created by them? There is abundant evidence to confirm that, whatever answers research may give, they are *not* reasonably viewed as state-controlled.

Fforde (2004b) posed fundamental questions about SOEs as a form of property: who decides what, and who gets what? Data were then collected through 1998–1999 in various ways, often using 'anthropological' methods. The study concluded:

> The data is weak, and, were circumstances more favourable to the collection of data, likely unacceptable. However, the importance of the issues, and the problems in accessing this central problem – SOE 'ownership' – mean that it is extremely valuable. The sample has an investigative rather than a structured basis.
>
> It suggests that classic commercial issues – controlling profits, and preventing loss of equity control – are indeed central to understanding Vietnamese SOEs. Ownership and control are separate issues, and their implications are worked out in various ways. This suggests that any 'Weberian' view is off the mark.
>
> The interviews show managers and others capable of, to varying degrees, acting as informants both on the wider issues of state business management and their recent history. They reflect with considerable insight on the institutions around them.
>
> This tends to support the argument that the SOEs of the period are best viewed as VSCs [virtual share companies]. VSHs [virtual shareholders], in this sense, had varying rights, some of which were contingent. Apparent lack of ownership could then be understood as reflecting lack of agreement amongst VSHs, either permitting Managers to do what they liked, but only in very limited areas, or leading to paralysis. And such things are not peculiar to Vietnamese businesses.
>
> One important implication of this is that *it is not SOE managers who effectively control SOEs*. They certainly participate in such activities, but the story is far more complicated. Success or failure cannot be laid at their door, but must be shared with others.
>
> The VSC and VSH framework offers a promising approach to the analysis of Vietnamese SOEs, and therefore to refining and concretising what is meant by their de facto privatisation. This suggests in turn that research should focus upon the determinants of the VSC structure, and how it varies, for example between industrial sectors. In that a significant part of the literature has argued that the marketisation of the Vietnamese economy was a liberalisation, rather than a reform, it places to the fore the central issue of whether or not better economic performance will be attained through changes exogenous to SOEs (such as a hardening of budget constraints by changes in bank lending practice) rather

than through formal privatisation. And also just how such processes might, through an acceleration of unregulated de facto privatisation, lead to socially unacceptable concentrations of economic power, such as in Russia. This is perhaps more plausible at a local than at a national level, but in areas such as agricultural processing and exports it is not hard to make the argument that costs could easily be very high. One can ask, for example, who the VSHs of an SOE heavily involved in cash crop exports are, and then what their wider economic powers entail. More fundamentally, the real political economy is, or should be, central to the analysis. (Fforde, 2004b: 31–2)

The study then went on to look at details of the structures above SOEs that mediated patterns of control and profit-sharing. It concluded that these were dichotomous, divided between relationships with 'unions'[2] and more statist structures such as various departments under the Ministry of Finance, the state-owned commercial banks and so on. It hypothesised that this could be related to two quite different political strategies. Again to quote the study:

'Above the SOE' there were, as we have seen from both the sample and formal policy, usually but not always, essentially two sets of structures.

First, were the state bodies linking the SOE into the state apparatus. Following on various 'technocratic' reforms, strongly supported by donors such as the World Bank, the Ministry of Finance was the state body with formal control over various conduits for state resources, newly established. These were, most importantly, the State Treasury and the State Capital Management Department (SCMD). In addition, there was a range of development funds for various purposes.

Here can be envisaged an embryonic 'state-focused developmentalism' *where the Party rules and implements development through the classic bodies of a 'developmental state'*. Through the 1990s, party doctrine as taught to its members remained that the fundamental basis for party rule was the state apparatus, seen in terms of the local and central state 'authorities' (*chinh quyen*).

Second, there were other state business organisations, the descendants of the GDR 'Enterprise Unions', the various 'Groups' and 'General Companies' set up (either anew or based upon earlier forms) in the mid 1990s. These groups, with as we have seen typically hazy formal powers (apart from key and important rights, such as to move capital between their constituent SOEs), followed a quite different logic, where economic power is sited, not within state bodies, as such, but within large commercial units.

In the world economy of the late 1990s and early 2000s, it was perhaps clear that such bodies could hope to free themselves from local state control, to an important degree, through direct access to foreign capital, technology and markets through various mechanisms such as a stock market. They therefore offered a potential basis for political power *independent* from the state apparatus. This is, of course, the stuff of high politics.

It is possible that one amongst many causes of the lack of coherent state developmentalism in Vietnam during the 1990s was due to the contradictions between these two tendencies. Whilst internal Party relations would have integrated both sets of structures, their different logics are striking. Perhaps, effective subordination of one or other of these power structures to the other would have opened the way to a major exercise of state power in the cause of national development. For example, if the Ministry of Finance, the State Bank, the Ministry of Planning and Investment (MPI) and other state bodies had been brought under one authority, and then acted in coordination to select and then support priority sectors, for example as recommended by Japanese advisors (Ohno and Ohno, 1998), then we might have been able to observe such things as:

Clear subordination, in terms of authority and social deference, by General Companies and others to these peak state bodies.

Rapid and effective closure of areas of state business activity not in accord with the overall development strategy.

Development of various measures to cope with the socialisation of risk inherent in targeted allocation of resources, especially bank credits [Zysman, 1983; Wade, 1988] – for example, clear performance criteria for exporters.

We had in fact, prior to the Asian Crisis of 1997, seen none of these things.

Had the polarity been reversed, and large state capitals attained dominance (GCs), then perhaps we would have expected to see a different pattern. Available resources would have tended to go to them, they would have tended to seek self-publicity as important national 'developers', and budget constraints would have remained soft for them, but hard for their components. So far, however, they have been unable to escape important restrictions on their relations with foreign businesses and the global economy.[3]

It is thus striking, however, if we recall what SOE managers said, how the trajectory of the 1980s had been reversed, and how the confrontation and tensions between these two structures are what clarifies the character of their ownership structure. Thus, for what it is worth, the micro level data to a certain extent might be understood as expressing the consequences of fundamental political conflicts over development strategy and control over national assets occurring at a national level. In caricature, the dominant political issue of the 1980s was to obtain the support of the state business interest, which involved both creating it and then gaining its support. But then in the 1990s, the issue shifted, to re-establishing control over state business. If these conjectures are correct, the outcome of this politics was on the one hand to significantly curb trends to emergence of a relatively independent business sector out of SOEs, but on the other to fail to re-establish a coherent and relatively united set of control structures.

It is possible, but although interesting impossible to discuss at length here, that important changes were afoot in the late 1990s. The 1997 Asian Crisis came on top of the gathering balance of payment crisis that had been visible since late 1995, and added to widespread evidence that nature of state-SOE relations was threatening macroeconomic stability. In 1998–2000, focusing upon the State Bank, measures were taken to restore stability, boost exports and enhance growth. In these processes, it is likely that state rather than state business organisations gained power. Interestingly, the private sector also started to emerge rather fast, in part because harder budget constraints, and the passage of time, increasingly encouraged capital to move out of SOEs into more normal forms. VSHs, having seen their assets under attack, and with less attractive opportunities offered by the state, to move their capital out of SOEs and into more formally private forms. And, perhaps incidentally, since in these forms private assets could be matched by private liabilities, and techniques used were more labor-intensive, long-term prospects for less unhealthy economic expansion were thus probably enhanced. (Fforde, 2004b: 45–7)

I conclude from this that there is good provisional support for the view that the trajectory of SOE property changed around 1990, and that the state sector – producing around 40 per cent of GDP – was thereafter becoming less rather than more independent.

Contrast the following quote from an SOE manager with the rights to autonomy granted by 217-HDBT:

> We are subject to a number of influences... mainly these are from state policies and 'superior levels'... Let me give you an example. The finance department of the province decided to issue a directive that any SOE that wanted to buy, sell, invest or whatever over 100 million dong had to have the opinion of the department who would send somebody to check. It made no difference where the money came from, and so what that the SOE had been allocated state funds and granted autonomy. And if we want to sell cigarettes or act as an agent for a Vietnamese company we have to ask permission of the trade department of the province... [and] the trade department is our superior level, and it approves our plan and sets out guidelines for us... It has a very important role. (Fforde, 2004b: 27)

This has very important implications for how one characterises policy, politics and the nature of government in Vietnam.

Changes in policy and commentary between 1992 and 2002

Fforde (2005d) looked at articles about SOEs in the quality Vietnamese daily press in 1992 and 2002. This drew upon proprietary databases of newspaper articles about economic matters and simply involved searching through them for relevant references. The study was looking for various things, most importantly whether there was evidence for change, specifically the creation of any normal (in approximate Western terms) *legal* basis for governing relations between the state and SOEs implication. Its basic conclusions were that there was evidence neither for much change nor for legalisation:

> Examination of the legislation and the articles from the quality Vietnamese press seems to lead to the conclusion that there is no significant difference between the position taken by Stalin and that of the VCP at this time. Whilst the Law of Value is to be allowed to operate, and in Vietnam in the early 1990s this is clearly to a far greater extent than in early 1950s Soviet Russia, law and other

elements of state activities are part of a conscious attempt to subject it to the priorities of the socialist regime. Further, the apparent willingness to permit extra-legal activities that clearly could have a strong effect upon state control suggests that law was not perhaps the most important part of how the VCP governed SOEs, through various channels.

The argument here goes beyond the one, common in Vietnam studies, that it was the local market and players that were central to the dynamic of SOE change. Rather, viewed in terms of the overall political dynamic, and bearing in mind Beresford 1997's stress on the importance of the state as a *mediator* between interests, for the overall political goals of regime survival and order in relationships between higher and local levels, SOEs appear to have maintained an important political function. Their existence, and the possibility of mediating interest group conflicts through such levers as the Mass Organisations and Party organisations within them, the allocation of state credits, deliberations over access to FDI, to participation in development plans, export marketing exercises, and so on, all offered precisely what Beresford seems to be referring to. And, since this political project seems to have been successful, it follows, granted the widespread illegality, that law was not an important element of the 'techniques of rule'. Another way of putting this could be that if one focuses upon the 'rule' in 'rule by law', then law was not very important to this, at least as far as SOEs were concerned. Little real effort was put into dealing with the widespread illegality, and this reflected political realities and priorities. (Fforde, 2005d: 15)

In looking for change to relations between SOEs and the state, the results were similar:

The sources reveal a different but essentially similar treatment of relations between SOEs and the state as a decade previously. In 1992 SOEs were commercialised entities participating in a range of joint ventures and seeking to meet a variety of goals suited to the position in which they were placed by the party and state: a priority role in securing the general goals of national development and the specific political goals of securing the regime. At the time, conceptions were very much focussed upon the need for individual SOEs to survive the greatly increased pressures caused by the loss of Soviet aid and the need to tighten state support so as to maintain macroeconomic stability that had only recently been re-established. Law played a role in regulating and ordering SOEs, but was ignored by both SOEs and the party-state when viewed appropriate, and circumstances suited.

By 2002, Law was still essentially part of the treatment by a ruling Communist Party of the progressive opportunities offered to them (as to Stalin) by an expanded role of the Law of Value; it was not something that governed and determined the activities of either SOEs or the party-state, for, as we have seen, confusion in important areas remained, and the Law was ignored by both sides when viewed appropriate. What is quite different about the early 2000s, however, is the presence of a dynamic private domestic sector and the foreign invested sector. We can note the relative absence from the literature of reference to this, but we also need to note the considerable resources devoted to maintaining the state sector. In fact, the intense focus of legislation upon regulating the state sector can be interpreted as reflecting a pressing need to secure its position against these trends for the later years of the decade. The equitisation process itself, legally expressed, preserved considerable opportunity for hemming the operation of the Law of Value in many ways, consistent with the continuing socialist direction as discussed above. We can point to the residual powers to control SOEs when the state's share was below 50 percent, the commitment to use of the General Companies as a channel of influence, not at all clearly defined, and the ongoing negotiated relationship between the managers and workers in SOEs and the wider world of the state and party, still mediated by the party's local organisations and the mass organisations, whose attention could be increased and diminished as required. Law was not politically important to this; other forces existed to support and order the emergence of markets. (Fforde, 2005d: 27)

The study stressed, however, that the emergence of a private sector as well as important foreign commercial interests had clearly changed the environment within which SOEs and state operated.

Grassroots comments

Asked whether there had been a process of recentralisation in the 1990s, the panel commented that it is clear this was the case because the state continued with the statement that the state sector had a guiding role (*vai tro chu dao). Under many forms the state continued to assist the state sector, and following this forced many small SOEs to operate within the system of general companies. For example, the manager of one SOE did not want to be pushed into a general company but wanted to continue to operate independently. But this could not be done, as only if it belonged to the general company would it gain access to loans and be able to sell its products overseas.

Despite being retired, all members of the panel remarked that as of now (2005) the state still had a direction of 'recentralisation' regarding base units (SOEs). The old thinking about the system of centralised administration continued, and still remained in the minds of the leaders of ministries and branches. As ex-managers, the panel members thought that if you want to understand the Vietnamese economy it was not enough to rely solely upon the documents of the state. You have to visit SOEs themselves, to read the management documents of the ministries and provinces, and then you can appreciate the complexity of the situation. Often the documents of the Party committees of general companies, their leaders and the leaders of ministries or provinces are quite different from the decrees of the government, but the SOE has to follow the general company, the ministry or the province because they are its immediate superiors. If you disagree with them you suffer at once because 'the mandarin is far but the office is close'.

Thus, to reform, above all you must reform the leadership and policy-makers.

Notes

1. Greenfield (1993, 1994) argued that SOE managers, actively supported by the state, were already in 1990–1991 stealing and controlling state assets and so defining the particular nature of Vietnamese capitalism. I think this argument is overdone and requires more thought about the process of events through the 1990s.
2. These included the 'general companies' (GCs) and 'groups'; I refer to them all as 'unions' here for convenience.
3. For example, there has been no joint venture in television, bringing in outside programming and offering the possibility of relief from strong Party control over access to the mass media.

10

Conclusions – state industry and the Vietnamese experience

Capitalism and the state

Viewed in comparative context, Vietnam's state sector has to be seen as, despite all the shouting and screaming, successful. Transition to rapid growth in the 1990s relied upon energies and lessons from far earlier. Yet viewed in terms of what was possible, it has to be judged a failure. Crucial developmental problems of the mid-2000s can be blamed centrally upon the limits of SOE change: in particular, the failure to break out of the basic model of SOE-state relations, and the associated weaknesses of governance and delayed emergence of a private sector. Policy failure in 1989–1991, above all failure to secure political change, risked that Vietnam would, after a period during which the SOE-focused model ran its course, encounter a situation where it lacked effective means to compete internationally: good government and a healthy commercial sector. Rather, the basic structures of the early 2000s were, I argue, hardly different from the early 1990s: failure to distance business interests politically meant that corruption would eat deeply into the effectiveness of government.

But for many countries such problems would be welcomed, with GDP rising fast and poverty falling.

Lessons from Vietnam?

The emergence of capitalism

My work on Vietnam's emergent capitalism is unfinished and conclusions here are therefore limited.

It is clear that even the VCP, victor against the USA, ended up powerless to thwart the renaissance of commerce from within its SOEs. What does this suggest about the power of the VCP? Conclusions here are that the VCP's political effectiveness, in terms of its responsiveness to the rise of the 'state business interest' as well as its constitutional and somewhat pacific practices, had a lot to do with this outcome. Had it been North Korea or Romania neo-Stalinism would have been far less vulnerable.

Economic logics, especially 'Kim Ngoc's law', were crucial also. As the industrial sector became increasingly commercialised the 'slack' available from the inefficiencies of central planning was taken up. But this only had effective voice because of political conditions (and the ability economic success gave to SOEs' capacity to 'stroke' higher levels with envelopes and their equivalents).

But it did not stop there, and that is the meaning of the second 'trap'. Alternative sources of output gains were then needed. The economic question in the 1990s thus shifted to growth issues. Industrial output increases could no longer be found in efficiency gains within industry. This presented heavy policy questions about the relationship between agriculture and industry, the internal market and distribution of production, access to foreign markets and capital and above all the capital investment process, replacing the simple issue of resource allocation mechanisms within state industry. And such policy questions could only be answered politically, pointing towards the problems caused for the regime by its dependence upon SOEs and traditional socialist politics.

Lessons for developers?

In a wider context, I think that Vietnamese experience suggests the following conclusions.

- The starting point, a CPE, is not simply a strange variety of market economy.
- Change requires time to take hold at micro level.
- Against this, however, features peculiar to the central-planning model positively assist durable change at SOE level by creating rapidly mobilisable slack.
- Change takes even longer to implement at macro level.

- Commercialisation develops faster in product and labour markets than it does in capital and financial markets.
- There is therefore a need to expect a longer rather than a shorter transition period. A time scale of five to ten years may be appropriate.
- Inflation may be, temporarily, healthy.
- Difficulties in macro-stabilisation may simply show that the economy has not yet become adequately commercialised.

Lessons for those being developed?

The central lessons for those in developing countries, seeking development, are as follows.

- Change may be full of surprises, but within the flow of change there can be found order and meaning.
- It is worthwhile to develop local explanations of what is happening; these may be as valid as any other.
- Just because something is called an SOE means neither that you know what it actually is, nor whether you should like or dislike what it contributes to development.
- The relationships between business and politics are important, and they are path-dependent.
- Vietnamese experience is worth studying, but emulation of it is probably meaningless.
- Permit wide debate and listen to what different people say. Do not rely upon prestigious authorities as they are often silly. But persuasion is better than most of the alternatives – as long as people are prepared to listen (Fforde, 2005c).

Glossary

I mark in the text with an asterisk (*) words that I consider to have technical or specific meanings and uses, and this glossary attempts to explain in part how they were used. The English translation in the text may vary according to context and use. In the text I usually refer to the territory of the Democratic Republic of Vietnam as 'North Vietnam' – this refers in traditional terms to the north and the north-centre.

Ban can su – the Party Committee present in a state organisation and responsible for it.

Ban thuong – bonus sales; sold to add value to some other transaction.

Bo Chu quan – the 'head' or 'owning' ministry of an SOE, with important powers over it.

Bung ra – literally to 'explode'; used in the late 1970s to advocate a major increase in economic activity 'by any means'.

Cai tao – reform (in the sense of the reform of anti-socialist or problematic elements); the term used for the imprisonment of southern officers and others after 1975.

Can doi – to balance; used to refer to the way in which central planning calculated and delivered inputs to an SOE to balance its planned outputs.

Cap tren – the superior level within the state apparatus; 'The Man'.

Chan ngoai dai hon chan trong – the 'outside' foot is longer than the 'inside' foot; refers to the general tendency to prefer autonomous and/or market-oriented activity.

Chan trong chan ngoai – the 'inside' and the 'outside' feet; refers to situations where the relative attractiveness of the two are being compared.

Chi bo – Party cell; the basic Party organisational unit.

Chien si thi dua – emulation fighter; those who were struggling and succeeding in showing that they could meet the targets of Leninist emulation campaigns.

Chu dong – active, self-initiating; very hard to translate accurately due to its broad semantic range.

Chui – under the table, hidden.
Con rung – 'bastards'; but literally, children of the forest.
Cung cap – supply, in the sense of materials, inputs and so on.
Cuoc song – life; that which happens largely beyond human intentionality.
Dem ban ngoai – to take and sell 'outside'.
Dia phuong – local, as opposed to central (*trung uong*).
Dieu chinh – to regulate, or move things around so there is a better arrangement, with wide semantic range.
Doc – vertical, different from horizontal (*ngang*), relations between parts of the state.
Don vi co so – base unit; an SOE, a commune or a cooperative that receives orders from the state.
Gia ban buon cong nghiep – the industrial wholesale price.
Gia ban buon Nha nuoc – the state wholesale price.
Gia ban buon xi nghiep – the enterprise wholesale price.
Gia thanh – cost price; what it costs to produce something in accounting terms.
Hang ngoai – 'outside' commodities; goods and services outside the scope of central planning.
Ket nghia – to come together, of interests between parties; very demotic.
Khau – a link, a Soviet planning term referring to Taylorist methods of organising and regulating work.
Khoan san pham – output contracts, used in the reform of cooperatives and their relations with farming families.
Kinh doanh – latterly business aimed at making profits, earlier very unclear.
Lam ngoai – to work 'outside' the plan.
Lam ngoai, an ngoai – those who work 'outside' eat 'outside'.
Lam tu do – to work freely, autonomously.
Lien doanh – joint ventures involving pooling of resources with the intent of making a profit.
Lien ket – joint ventures involving pooling of resources so as to produce more.
Lon xon – confused, chaotic.
Mac ke – 'stuff it', as in attitudes to unwanted plan instructions that get in the way of local interests.
Moc ngoac – to 'hook', in the sense of get in cahoots with somebody.
Ngang – 'horizontal', opposed to *doc*, vertical, relationships within the state.
Nganh – 'branch'; the area of activity associated with a ministry.

Ngoai – 'outside', opposed to *noi*, 'inside'.

Nhom san pham – production groups; a group of entities brought together to *lien ket*, qv.

Noi – 'inside', opposed to *ngoai*, 'outside'.

Phan phoi noi bo – internal distribution, the practice of distributing SOE or another unit's output to its members or workers; the irony here is that *phan phoi* is what the rationing system was meant to do.

San pham giao nop – output for which the SOE has been given a target for contributions or deliveries to the state.

San xuat phu – minor production; production by an SOE of items that were not on its 'list' of planned goods.

Sap xep lai – to reorganise, but more realistically to rationalise, the organisation of an SOE and branch, qv.

Tap the – collective, as a in a group of people; not necessarily a cooperative.

Thanh phan – component; in Leninist terms the class category to which something or somebody was said to belong (in ID cards this usually referred to the family's classification during the 1950s' land reform).

Thi dua – emulation; see *chien si thi dua*.

Tieu thu – to sell or deliver products.

Trung uong – centre, opposed to *dia phuong*, local.

Tu can doi – self-balanced; see *can doi*.

Tu cung ung – self-supply; where an SOE arranged inputs by itself rather than getting them through the plan.

Tu lam – to do something oneself, for example self-balancing.

Tu lo – literally 'to worry about ('sort out') oneself'; for an SOE, to use an 'outside' solution to its problems; very demotic, often found referring to workers' incomes.

Tu phat – spontaneous.

Tu tieu thu – to 'self-dispose' (see *tieu thu*); to dispose of goods or services 'outside' the plan.

Tu tim kiem – to 'find for oneself'; to secure inputs 'outside'.

Uu tien phat trien cong nghiep nang mot cach hop ly – 'rational development of heavy industry'.

Vai tro chu dao – the 'leading role' of the state sector laid down in various SRV constitutions.

Von tu co – own capital; here *tu* has a stress rather than a logical function.

Acronyms

ANU	Australian National University
AVRP	Australian Vietnam Research Project, active at the ANU/Wollongong 1994–1997
BBT	Ban bi thu – Secretariat (of the Party)
BCH	Ban Chap hanh – Executive Committee (the Central Committee of the Party)
BCT	Bo Chinh tri – Politburo
BLD	Bo Lao dong – Ministry of Labour
BNgT	Bo Ngoai thuong – Ministry of Foreign Trade
BNN	Bo Nong nghiep – Ministry of Agriculture
BNT	Bo Noi thuong – Ministry of Domestic Trade
BVT	Bo Vat tu – Ministry of Materials Supply
CB	*Cong Bao* – the official government gazette, Hanoi
CIEM	Central Institute for Economic Management Research
CMEA	Council for Mutual Economic Assistance
CP	Chinh phu – the government, under the 1992 constitution
CPE	centrally planned economy
DMZ	demilitarised zone
DRV	Democratic Republic of Vietnam
EPU	Economics and Planning University
FBIS	Foreign Broadcast Information Service – US monitoring service
FDI	foreign direct investment
FYP	Five Year Plan
GoV	Government of Vietnam
GSO	General Statistical Office (Tong cuc Thong ke)
HDBT	Hoi dong Bo truong – Council of Ministers
IMF	International Monetary Fund
JPRS	Joint Publications Research Service – US monitoring service
JSP	joint state private
KHH	*Ke hoach hoa* (*Planning*) – journal of SPC

MO	mass organisation
NCDS	National Centre for Development Studies
NCKT	*Nghien cuu kinh te* (*Economic Research*) – journal of the Economics Institute, Hanoi
NEU	National Economics University
NhD	*Nhan Dan* (*The People*) – official Party daily, equivalent to the old Soviet *Pravda*
NHNN	Ngan hang Nha nuoc – the state bank (the central bank)
NIA	national income accounting
NXB	Nha Xuat ban – publishing house
NXBST	NXB Su That – Truth Publishing House
SEA	South-East Asia
SIDA	Swedish International Development Agency
SOE	state-owned enterprise
SPC	State Planning Commission
SRV	Socialist Republic of Vietnam
SWB	Summary of World Broadcasts – BBC monitoring service
TCCS	*Tap chi Cong san* (*Communist Studies*) – theoretical journal (monthly) of the Vietnamese Communist Party
TCTK	Tong cuc Thong ke – General Statistical Office
TTg	Thu tuong (Premier)
TTKT	Trong tai Kinh te – the economic 'referee'
TWD	Truong uong Dang – the Party 'centre': BCT, BBT, BCH etc.
UBKHNN	Uy ban Ke hoach Nha nuoc – see SPC
VCP	Vietnamese Communist Party

Bibliography

Abrami, Regina (2002) 'Self-making, class struggle and labor autarky: the political origins of private entrepreneurship in Vietnam and China', PhD thesis, Department of Political Science, University of California, Berkeley.

Abrami, Regina and Henaff, Nolwen (2004) 'The city and the countryside: economy, state and socialist legacies in the Vietnamese labor market', in Melanie Beresford and Angie Tran Ngoc (eds *Reaching for the Dream: Challenges of Sustainable Development in Vietnam*. Copenhagen: Nordic Institute of Asian Studies.

Almond, Gabriel A. (1988 'The return to the state', *American Political Science Review*, 82(3): 853–74.

Arndt, H.W. (1981) 'Economic development: a semantic history', *Economic Development and Cultural Change*, 29(3): 457–66

BBT (1981) 'Cai tien cong tac khoan, mo rong khoan san pham den nhom nguoi lao dong va nguoi lao dong trong hop tac xa nong nghiep', *Nhan Dan (The People)*, 20 January.

BCH (1963) 'Nghi Quyet Cua Hoi Nghi Trung Uong Lan Thu Tam Ve Ke Hoach Phat Trien Kinh Te Quoc Dan 5 Nam Lan Thu Nhat (1961–1965) (Resolution of the Eighth Plenum on the First National Socio-economic Development Plan)', mimeo. Hanoi: BCH.

BCT (1988) 'Nghi Quyet Bo Chinh tri ve Doi moi quan ly kinh te nong nghiep (10) (Resolution of the Politburo on the reform of agricultural economic management (10))', *Nhan Dan (The People)*, 12 April.

Beresford, Melanie (1989) *National Unification and Economic Development in Vietnam*. London: Macmillan.

Beresford, Melanie (1993) 'The political economy of dismantling the "bureaucratic centralism and subsidy system" in Vietnam', in Kevin Hewison, Richard Robison and Garry Rodan (eds) *Southeast Asia in the 1990s: Authoritarianism, Democracy and Capitalism*. Sydney: Allen and Unwin.

Beresford, Melanie (1997) 'Vietnam: the transition from central planning', in Garry Rodan, Kevin Hewison and Richard Robison (eds)

The Political Economy of South-East Asia. Oxford: Oxford University Press.

Beresford, Melanie and Fforde, Adam (1997) 'The origins of the market economy in Vietnam: a comment and some questions on the reform of domestic trade', *Journal of Communist Studies and Transition Politics*, 13(4): 99–128.

BLD (1981) *Tim hieu chinh sach moi ve kinh te* (*Understanding the New Economic Policies*). Hanoi: Bo Lao Dong.

BLD (1988) 'TT 9/1/88 huong dan thuc hien QD 217 HDBT cua Hoi Dong Bo Truong ve lao dong tien luong va xa hoi- So 01 LDTBXH TT (Circular letter, 9 January 1988, of the Ministry of Labour on the implementation of decree 217-HDBT on labour, wages and social issues)', in NXBST *Quyet dinh 217 va huong dan thuc hien* (*Decree 217 and Guidance on its Implementation*). Hanoi: NXB Su That.

BNgT (1988) 'T/T 2-BNgT/CS cua Bo Ngoai thuong 18/1/88 giai thich va huong dan viec nhap xuat khau va hop tac kinh te voi nuoc ngoai theo Q/D 217 HDBT (Circular letter 2-BNgT/CS of the Ministry of Foreign Trade, 18 January 1988, explaining and guiding exports and foreign economic cooperation in accordance with decree 217-HDBT)', in NXBST *Quyet dinh 217 va huong dan thuc hien* (*Decree 217 and Guidance on its Implementation*). Hanoi: NXB Su That.

BNN (1991) 'Du thao: Danh gia 3 nam thuc hien nghi quyet 10 cua Bo chinh tri ve doi moi quan ly kinh te nong nghiep (Draft: evaluating three years of implementing decree 10 of the Politburo on the reform of the economic management of agriculture)', mimeo, 23 April. Hanoi: Bo Nong Nghiep (Ministry of Agriculture).

BNN (n/d) 'Diem qua qua trinh hop tac hoa nong nghiep va cac che do quan ly hop tac xa (Points to the process of cooperativisation and the cooperative management system)', mimeo. Hanoi: Bo Nong Nghiep (Ministry of Agriculture).

BNT (1988) 'T/T 1 NT cua Bo Noi thuong 8/1/88 huong dan thi hanh viec tieu thu san pham theo Q/D 217 HDBT (Guiding letter of the Ministry of Domestic Trade, 8 January 1988, guiding implementation of the procurement of products in accordance with decree 217-HDBT)', in NXBST *Quyet dinh 217 va huong dan thuc hien* (*Decree 217 and Guidance on its Implementation*). Hanoi: NXB Su That.

Boudarel, G. (ed.) (1983) *La bureaucratie au Vietnam*. Paris: L'Harmattan.

Bramall, Chris (1993) 'The role of decollectivisation in China's agricultural miracle, 1978–90', *Journal of Peasant Studies*, 20(2): 271–95.

Bramall, Chris (1995) 'Origins of the agricultural "miracle": some evidence from Sichuan', *China Quarterly*, 143(3): 731–55.

Bray, Francesca (1983) 'Patterns of evolution in rice-growing societies', *Journal of Peasant Studies*, 11(October): 3–33.

BTC (1986) 'Thong tu so 10-TC/DTXD huong dan viec trich lap, quan ly va su dung von tu co ve dau tu xay dung co ban cua cac to chuc san xuat, kinh doanh thuoc thanh phan kinh te quoc doanh (Circular letter 10-TC/DTXD, 22 July 1986, guiding the appropriation, management and use of own capital and basic construction investment of state producers and businesses)', *Cong Bao*, 31 August.

BTC (1987) 'T/T 78 TC/CN cua Bo Tai Chinh 31/12/87 huong dan thuc hien quyen tu chu tai chinh cua cac don vi kinh te co so theo QD 217 HDBT 14/11/87 (Circular letter 78-TC/CN of the Ministry of Finance, 31 December 1987, guiding implementation of the rights to financial autonomy of base economic units in accordance with decree 217-HDBT, 14 November 1987)', in NXBST *Quyet dinh 217 va huong dan thuc hien (Decree 217 and Guidance on its Implementation)*. Hanoi: NXB Su That.

BTC (1990) 'Finance ministry reviews budget results for first half of 1990', Hanoi Radio, SWB, 18 August.

Bui Cong Trung (ed.) (1959) *Ban ve cai tao cong thuong nghiep tu ban chu nghia o mien Bac (A Discussion of the 'Cai Tao' of Capitalist Industry and Trade in the North)*. Hanoi: NXB Su That.

BVT (1988) 'TT 5 VT VP cua Bo vat tu 6/1/88 huong dan viec mua ban vat tu doi voi cac xi nghiep quoc doanh de thuc hien QD 217-HDBT (Circular letter 5-VT/VP of the Ministry of Materials, 6 January 1988, on the purchase and sale of materials regarding SOEs in order to implement decree 217-HDBT)', in NXBST *Quyet dinh 217 va huong dan thuc hien (Decree 217 and Guidance on its Implementation)*. Hanoi: NXB Su That.

Chaliand, Gerard (1969) *The Peasants of North Vietnam*. Harmondsworth: Penguin.

Chanda, Nayan (1986) *Brother Enemy: The War After the War*. New York: Macmillan.

Che Tuong Nhu (1994) 'The sequence of economic reforms to the industrial state-owned enterprises of Vietnam', mimeo. Canberra: Australia National University/NCDS.

Cong Bao (1975) *Cong Bao*, 31 July.

Cong Bao (1976) *Cong Bao*, 31 August.

Cong Bao (1982a) *Cong Bao*, 31 July.

Cong Bao (1982b) *Cong Bao*, 15 October.

Cong Bao (1982c) *Cong Bao*, 31 October.

Cong Bao (1982d) *Cong Bao*, 15 December.
Cong Bao (1985) *Cong Bao*, 15 July.
Cong Bao (1986) *Cong Bao*, 31 October.
Cong Bao (1990) *Cong Bao*, 31 May.
Conyngham, W.J. (1982) *The Modernisation of Soviet Industrial Management*. Cambridge: Cambridge University Press.
Cowen, Michael and Shenton, Robert (1996) *Doctrines of Development*. London: Routledge.
Dahm, Bernard and Houben, Vincent J.H. (eds) (1999) *Vietnamese Village in Transition*, Passau Contributions to Southeast Asian Studies. Passau: Passau University.
Dam Van Nhue and Le Si Thiep (1981) 'Ket hop loi ich cua tap the nguoi lao dong trong cong nghiep dia phuong (Integrating the interests of the collective of workers in regional industry)', *Nghien cuu kinh te (Economic Research)*, 10.
Dang Phong and Beresford, Melanie (1998) *Authority Relations and Economic Decision-making in Vietnam: An Historical Perspective*. Copenhagen: Nordic Institute of Asian Studies.
Dang Quoc Tuyen (ed.) (1990) *Thong tin chuyen de: bao toan va phat trien von o xi nghiep cua cac nuoc (Topical Information: Protecting and Developing Capital in Enterprises in Various Countries)*. Hanoi: BTC Vien Khoa hoc tai chinh (Financial Science Institute).
Dang Tho Xuong (ed.) (1992) 'Chuong trinh KX-08-01-03 – Bao cao tong thuat quan diem cua dang tu 1945–1980 (Programme KX-08-01-01 – overview of the Party's "point of view", 1945–1980)', mimeo, 16 November, Hanoi.
Dao Xuan Sam (1985) 'May khau co ban cua viec xay dung co che quan ly co ke hoach gan voi hach toan, kinh doanh (The basic links to the construction of a management system close to accounting and business)', in Le Thi (ed.) *Mot so van de ly luan va phuong phap luan nghien cuu thoi ky qua do o nuoc ta (Some Theoretical and Methodological Research Problems of the Transitional Period in Our Country)*. Hanoi: NXB Khoa hoc Xa hoi.
Dao Xuan Sam (1986) 'Kinh doanh xa hoi chu nghia va quyen tu chu cua nguoi kinh doanh (Socialist business and the rights to autonomy of the businessman)', *Nhan Dan (The People)*, 18 March.
Darre, M. (1985) 'Le Vietnam dans le 3e guerre de l'Indochine', *Defence Nationale*, November.
DCSV (1977) *Phuong huong, nhiem vu va muc tieu chu yeu cua ke hoach 5 nam 1976–1980 (The Direction, Tasks and Main Targets of the 1976–1980 Five Year Plan)*. Hanoi: NXB Su That.

DCSV (1987) *Dai hoi VI Nhung phuong huong co ban cua chinh sach kinh te (The Sixth Congress – Basic Directions of Economic Policy)*. Hanoi: NXB Su That.

DCSV (1988) *Nghi quyet Bo chinh tri ve doi moi quan ly kinh te nong nghiep (10) (Politburo Decree 10 on the Reform of Agricultural Economic Management)*. Hanoi: NXB Su That.

de Lestrange, Alexandre and Richet, Xavier (1998) 'Economic reform and behaviour of state-owned enterprises in Vietnam', *MOCT-MOST*, 8(4): 77–95.

de Vylder, Stefan and Fforde, Adam (1988) *Vietnam – An Economy in Transition*. Stockholm: SIDA.

de Vylder, Stefan and Fforde, Adam (1996) *From Plan to Market: The Economic Transition in Vietnam*. Boulder, CO: Westview Press.

Dic Lo (1999) 'Reappraising the performance of China's state-owned enterprises, 1980–96', *Cambridge Journal of Economics*, 23(6): 693–718.

Diehl, Markus (1993) 'Stabilization without crisis: the case of Vietnam', Working Paper No. 578, Kiel Institute of World Economics, May.

Diehl, Markus (1995) 'Structural change in the economic transformation process: the case of Vietnam 1986–1992', *Economic Systems*, 19(2): 147–82.

Digregorio, Michael (1994) 'Urban harvest: recycling as a peasant industry in northern Vietnam', East-West Center Occasional Papers, Environment Series No. 17, East-West Center, Honolulu.

Dinh Thu Cuc (1977) 'Qua trinh tung buoc cung co va hoan thien quan he san xuat xa hoi chu nghia trong cac hop tac xa san xuat nong nghiep o mien bac nuoc ta (The process of step-by-step reinforcement and improvement of socialist production relations in agricultural producer cooperatives in the north of our country)', *NCLS*, 175(7/8).

Do Nguyen Khoat (1990) 'Van de bao toan von o cac xi nghiep quoc doanh (The problem of capital protection in SOEs)', *Nhan Dan (The People)*, 28 February.

Doan Hai, Nghiem Phu Ninh and Do Khac Dan (eds) (1979) *To chuc va quan ly hop tac xa tieu cong nghiep, thu cong nghiep (The Organisation and Management of Small and Artisanal Industrial Cooperatives)*. Hanoi: NXB Uy ban Ke Hoach Nha nuoc (SPC).

Doan Trong Truyen (1965) *Van de thuong nghiep va gia ca trong cuoc cach mang xa hoi chu nghia o mien Bac nuoc ta (The Problem of Trade and Prices in the Socialist Revolution in the North of Our Country)*. Hanoi: NXB Su That.

Doan Trong Truyen (1977) *Dua quan ly kinh te vao nen nep va cai tien mot buoc, phu hop voi phuong huong xay dung he thong quan ly kinh te xa hoi chu nghia* (*Bring Order to Economic Management and Reform at a Step, in Ways Suited to the Direction of Constructing a Socialist Economic Management System*). Hanoi: NXB Su That.

Dodsworth, John R., Spitaller, Erich, Braulke, Michael, Lee, Keon Hyok, Miranda, Kenneth, Mulder, Christan, Shishido, Hisanobu and Srinivasan, Krishna (1996) *Vietnam: Transition to a Market Economy*. Washington, DC: IMF.

Dollar, David, Glewwe, Paul and Litvack, Jennie (1998) *Household Welfare and Vietnam's Transition*. Washington, DC: World Bank.

Drabek, Zdenek (1990) 'A case study of a gradual approach to economic reform: the Vietnam experience of 1985–88', World Bank Asia Regional Series IDP 74, September.

Duiker, William F. (2000) *Ho Chi Minh*. New York: Hyperion.

Duong Bach Lien and Le Trang (1983) *Tim hieu quyet dinh 25-CP va quyet dinh 146-HDBT sua doi, bo sung quyet dinh 25-CP* (*Understand Decree 25-CP and Decree 146-HDBT Correcting and Supplementing 25-CP*). Hanoi: NXB Su That.

Ellman, Michael (1979) *Socialist Planning*. Cambridge: Cambridge University Press.

Ellman, Michael and Kontonrovich, Vladimir (1998) *The Destruction of the Soviet Economic System – An Insiders' History*. Armonk, NY: M.E. Sharpe.

EPU (1970) *25 nam xay dung va phat trien kinh te mien bac* (*Twenty-five Years of the Construction and Economic Development of the North*). Hanoi: NXB Truong dai hoc kinh te ke hoach (EPU).

EPU (1975) *Kinh te Cong nghiep – Giao trinh Tap I, Tap II* (*Course in Industrial Economics, Vols I and II*). Hanoi: NXB Truong dai hoc kinh te ke hoach (EPU).

EPU (1979) *Giao trinh Kinh te Cong nghiep tap I* (*Course in Industrial Economics, Vol. I*), ed. Nguyen Lang. Hanoi: NXB Dai hoc va Trung Hoc Chuyen Nghiep.

Ericson, R.E. (1984) 'The "second economy" and resource allocation under central planning', *Journal of Comparative Economics*, 8(17): 1–24.

Far Eastern Economic Review (1984) 13 December.

Feldbrugge, F.J.M. (1984) 'Government and shadow economy in the Soviet Union', *Soviet Studies*, 36(4): 528–43

Fforde, Adam (1982) 'Problems of agricultural development in North Vietnam', PhD dissertation, University of Cambridge.

Fforde, Adam (1983) 'The historical background to agricultural collectivisation in North Vietnam – the changing role of "corporate" economic power', Discussion Paper No. 148, Department of Economics, Birkbeck College, University of London.

Fforde, Adam (1985) 'Economic aspects of the Soviet-Vietnamese relationship', in Robert Cassen (ed.) *Soviet Interests in the Third World*. London: Sage Publications.

Fforde, Adam (1986) 'The unimplementability of policy and the notion of law in Vietnamese communist thought', *South East Asian Journal of Social Science*, 62(1): 62–75.

Fforde, Adam (1987) 'Vietnam – historical background and macro-analysis', in Rita Liljestrom, Adam Fforde and Bo Ohlsson (eds) *The Living Conditions of the Workers Associated with the Bai Bang Project*. Stockholm: SIDA.

Fforde, Adam (1989) *The Agrarian Question in North Vietnam, 1974–79: A Study of Co-operator Resistance to State Policy*. New York: M.E. Sharpe.

Fforde, Adam (1993) 'The political economy of "reform" in Vietnam – some reflections', in Borje Ljunggren (ed.) *The Challenge of Reform in Indochina*. Cambridge, MA: Harvard University Press.

Fforde, Adam (1997) 'The Vietnamese economy in 1996: events and trends – the limits of doi moi?', in Adam Fforde (ed.) *Doi Moi – Ten Years After the 1986 Party Congress*, Political and Social Change Monograph 24. Canberra: Australian National University.

Fforde, Adam (1999) 'From plan to market: The economic transitions in Vietnam and China compared', in Anita Chan, Benedict J. Tria Kerkvliet and Jonathan Unger (eds) *Transforming Asian Socialism: China and Vietnam Compared*. Canberra: Allen and Unwin.

Fforde, Adam (2000) 'The institutions of transition from central planning – the case of Vietnam', in Colin Barlow (ed.) *Institutions and Economic Change in Southeast Asia: The Context of Development from the 1960s to the 1990s*. Cheltenham: Edward Elgar.

Fforde, Adam (2001) 'Vietnamese farmers' organisations', with Nguyen Dinh Huan, CERUDEV/NISTPASS, Hanoi, AARES Conference, Adelaide, 2001. Also available from: *www.aduki.com.au/Farmers'%20Organisations%20-%20Final.pdf* in the form of the original consultancy report (Report for SIDA and the Policy Department, MARD).

Fforde, Adam (2002) 'Resourcing conservative transition in Vietnam: rent-switching and resource appropriation', *Post-Communist Economies*, 14(2): 203–26.

Fforde, Adam (2004a) 'Vietnam in 2003: the road to un-governability?' *Asian Survey*, 44(1): 121–9.

Fforde, Adam (2004b) 'Vietnamese state owned enterprises (SOEs) – "real property", commercial performance and political economy', Working Paper Series No. 69, August, SEARC City University of Hong Kong. Also available from: *www.cityu.edu.hk/searc/WP69_04_Fforde.pdf*.

Fforde, Adam (2005a) 'Vietnam in 2004: popular authority seeking power', *Asian Survey*, 45(1): 146–52.

Fforde, Adam (2005b) 'Civil society, the state and the business sector – protagonists of a democratisation process?', in Heinrich Boell Foundation (ed.) *Towards Good Society: Civil Society Actors, the State and the Business Class in Southeast Asia – Facilitators of or Impediments to a Strong, Democratic and Fair Society?*. Berlin: Heinrich Boell Stiftung, pp. 173–92.

Fforde, Adam (2005c) 'Persuasion: reflections on economics, data and the "homogeneity assumption"', *Journal of Economic Methodology*, 12(1): 63–91.

Fforde, Adam (2005d) 'SOEs, law and a decade of market-oriented socialist development in Vietnam', in P. Nicholson and J. Gillespie (eds) *Asian Socialism and Legal Change: The Dynamics of Vietnamese and Chinese Reform*. Canberra: Asia Pacific Press, pp. 241–70. See also: *www.cityu.edu.hk/searc/WP70_04_Fforde.pdf*.

Fforde, A.J. and Paine, S.H. (1987) *The Limits of National Liberation – Problems of Economic Management in the Democratic Republic of Vietnam, with a Statistical Appendix*. London: Croom-Helm.

Furuta, Motoo (1988) 'The Sixth Party Congress in the history of Vietnamese communism', in Tadashi Mio (ed.) *International Relations Around Indochina*. Tokyo: Japan IIA.

Gainsborough, Martin (2002) *Changing Political Economy of Vietnam: The Case of Ho Chi Minh City*. London: RoutledgeCurzon.

Gillespie, John and Nicholson, Pip (eds) (2005) *Asian Socialism and Legal Change: The Dynamics of Vietnamese and Chinese Reform*. Canberra: Asia Pacific Press.

Gordon, Alec (1981) 'North Vietnam's collectivisation campaigns: class struggle, production and the middle peasant problem', *Journal of Contemporary Asia*, 11(1): 19–43.

Greenfield, Gerard (1993) 'The emergence of capitalism in Vietnam', *Socialist Register*, 29: 203–35.

Greenfield, Gerard (1994) 'The development of capitalism in Vietnam', in Ralph Miliband and Leo Panitch (eds) *Between Globalism and*

Nationalism: Socialist Register 1994. London: Merlin Press, pp. 211–18.

HDBT (1989) 'QD 195 HDBT ban hanh nhung quyet dinh bo sung 217 HDBT (Decree 195-HDBT promulgating decrees supplementing 217-HDBT)', Hanoi, December.

Heng, Russell Hiang-Khng (1999) 'Of the state, for the state, yet against the state – the struggle paradigm in Vietnam's media politics', PhD dissertation, Australian National University,

Hindess, Barry (1996) *Discourses of Power: From Hobbes to Foucault.* Oxford: Blackwell.

Ho Phuong (1977) 'Lai ban ve viec thanh lap cac lien hiep san xuat trong cong nghiep nuoc ta (Another discussion of the establishment of industrial production associations in our country)', *Nghien cuu kinh te (Economic Research)*, 12.

Hoang Lien (1980) 'Khu pho Hoan Kiem (trung tam Ha Noi) dang ky kinh doanh cong, thuong nghiep (Hoan Kiem locality (central Hanoi) registering industry and trade)', *Nhan Dan*, 6 November.

Hoang Quoc Viet (1974) *Tang cuong phap che XHXN trong quan ly kinh te (Strengthening Socialist Law in Economic Management).* Hanoi: NXB Su That.

Humphry, C. (1983) *Karl Marx Collective: Economy, Society and Religion in a Siberian Collective Farm.* Cambridge: Cambridge University Press.

Huu Hanh (1980) 'Khoan Lua (Rice contracts)', *Tap chi Cong san (Communist Studies)*, 12.

Huynh Kim Khanh (1982) *Vietnamese Communism 1925–45.* Ithaca, NY: Cornell University Press.

Jerneck, Anne (1995) 'Adjusting state and market in Vietnam – the story of enterprise unions', PhD thesis, Department of Economic History, University of Lund.

Joint Publications Research Service (1985) 25–26 June.

Joint Publications Research Service (1986a) 23 April.

Joint Publications Research Service (1986b) 20 June.

Kerkvliet, Benedict (1995) 'Village-state relations in Vietnam: the effect of everyday politics on decollectivization', *Journal of Asian Studies*, 54(2): 396–418.

Kerkvliet, Benedict (2001) 'An approach for analysing state-society relations in Vietnam', *Sojourn*, 16(2): 179–86.

Kerkvliet, Benedict (2005) *The Power of Everyday Politics: How Vietnamese Peasants Transformed National Policy.* Ithaca, NY and London: Cornell University Press.

KHH (1986) *QD cua HDBT so 76 HDBT 26/6/86 ve Viec ban hanh cac ban quy dinh tam thoi ve bao dam quyen tu chu san xuat, kinh doanh cua cac don vi kinh te co so (Decree 76-HDBT, 26 June 1986, on the Promulgation of Temporary Regulations on Guaranteeing the Rights to Autonomy in Production and Business of Economic Base Units)*. Hanoi: Ke hoach hoa (Planning).

Kleinen, John (1999) *Facing the Future, Reviving the Past: A Study of Social Change in a Northern Vietnamese Village*. Singapore: ISEAS.

Kleinen, John (2001) 'La comédie de l'État-parti. Le Viêt Nam depuis la réunification', *Raisons Politiques*, 3: 37–54.

Kokko, Ari (1998) 'Vietnam – ready for Doi Moi II?', Working Paper in Economics and Finance No. 286, December. Stockholm: SSE/EFI.

Kornai, J. (1980) *The Economics of Shortage*. Amsterdam: North Holland.

Kornai, J. (1985) 'Comments on papers prepared in the World Bank about socialist countries', CPD Discussion Paper, March. Washington, DC: World Bank.

Krueger, Anne O. (1974) 'The political economy of the rent-seeking society', *American Economic Review*, 64(3): 291–303.

Le Duan (1968) *Nam vung duong loi cach mang xa hoi chu nghia, tien len xay dung kinh te dia phuong vung manh (Hold Strong to the Line of the Socialist Revolution, Advance Towards the Construction of a Stable Regional Industry)*. Hanoi: NXB Su That.

Le Duan (1979) *May van de ve kinh te dia phuong (Problems of the Local Economy)*. Hanoi: NXB Su That.

Le Duc Tho (1981) 'Thuc hien mot su chuyen bien sau sac ve to chuc… (Realising a profound change in organisation…)', in Le Duc Tho (1985) *Xay dung Dang trong cach mang xa hoi chu nghia o Viet nam (Party Construction in the Socialist Revolution in Vietnam)*. Hanoi: NXB Su That.

Le Duc Tho (1985) Xay dung Dang trong cach mang xa hoi chu nghia o Viet nam (*Party Construction in the Socialist Revolution in Vietnam*). Hanoi: NXB Su That.

Le Duc Tho (1986a) *Nhung nhiem vu cap bach cua cong tac xay dung Dang (Pressing Tasks in Party Construction Work)*. Hanoi: NXB Su That.

Le Duc Tho (1986b) 'Carry out ideological work satisfactorily in preparation for the CPV Congress', SWB, 6 August.

Le Huy Ngo (1990) *Vinh Phu*, 30 May.

Le Huy Phan and Ho Phuong (1972) 'May van de ve to chuc quan ly cap tren xi nghiep trong cong nghiep nuoc ta (Problems in the organisation of management by the superior level of industrial SOEs in our country)', in Nguyen Tri (ed.) *Ve to chuc san xuat trong cong nghiep mien bac nuoc ta (On the Organisation of Production in the Industry of the North of Our Country)*. Hanoi: NXB Dai hoc va Trung Hoc Chuyen Nghiep (Higher and Specialised Middle Education).

Le Mai Trinh (1984) 'Nha may det Thanh cong, mot mo hinh can doi ke hoach nang dong (*Thanh cong*, an active model of planned balancing)', *Ke hoach hoa (Planning)*, August.

Le Monde (1986) *Le Monde*, 24 June.

Le Thanh Binh (1972) 'To chuc nhom san xuat – mot phuong huong co hieu qua de tang cuong quan ly cong nghiep (The organisation of production groups – an effective way to strengthen industrial management)', in Nguyen Tri (ed.) *Ve to chuc san xuat trong cong nghiep mien bac nuoc ta (On the Organisation of Production in the Industry of the North of Our Country)*. Hanoi: NXB Dai hoc va Trung Hoc Chuyen Nghiep (Higher and Specialised Middle Education).

Le Thanh Nghi (1977a) *Quan triet va thi hanh Dieu le Xi nghiep Cong nghiep Quoc doanh (Master and Implement the Industrial Enterprise Statute)*. Hanoi: NXB Su That.

Le Thanh Nghi (1977b) *Tu tuong chi dao ke hoach 5 nam 1976–1980 (Ideas Guiding the 1976–1980 FYP)*. Hanoi: NXB Su That.

Le Trang (1990) 'Nhung van de cot loi cua viec chuyen cac xi nghiep cong nghiep quoc doanh sang kinh doanh co che thi truong (Core issues in the shift of SOEs to market business operations)', mimeo. Hanoi: CIEM.

Leipziger, D.M. (1992) *Awakening the Market – Viet Nam's Economic Transition*. Washington, DC: World Bank.

Liljestrom, Rita and Fforde, Adam (1987) 'Voluntariness and force in labour', in Rita Liljestrom, Adam Fforde and Bo Ohlsson (eds) *The Living Conditions of the Workers Associated with the Bai Bang Project*. Stockholm: SIDA.

Liljestrom, Rita, Fforde, Adam and Ohlsson, Bo (eds) (1987) *The Living Conditions of the Workers Associated with the Bai Bang Project*. Stockholm: SIDA.

Lindauer, David L. and Pritchett, Lant (2002) 'What's the big idea? The third generation of policies for economic growth', *Economia*, 3(1): 1–39.

Lipworth, Gabrielle and Spitaller, Erich (1993) *Vietnam – Reform and Stabilization 1986–1992*. Washington, DC: IMF.

Ljunggren, Borje (1993) *The Challenge of Reform in Indochina*. Cambridge: HIIB.

Luong, Hy van (1989) 'Vietnamese kinship: structural principles and the socialist transformation in northern Vietnam', *Journal of Asian Studies*, 48(4): 741–59.

Luong, Hy van (1992) *Revolution in the Village: Tradition and Transformation in North Vietnam*. Honolulu: University of Hawaii Press.

Luong, Hy van (1997) 'Capitalism and noncapitalist ideologies in the structure of northern Vietnamese ceramics enterprises', in Timothy Brook and Hy van Luong (eds) *Culture and Economy: The Shaping of Capitalism in East Asia*. Ann Arbor, MI: University of Michigan Press.

Malarney, Shaun (1993) 'Ritual and revolution in Viet Nam', PhD dissertation, Department of Anthropology, University of Michigan.

Mallon, Ray and Van Arkardie, Brian (2003) *Vietnam: A Transition Tiger?*. Canberra: Asia Pacific Press.

Marr, David (1995) *Vietnam 1945: The Quest for Power*. Berkeley, CA: University of California Press.

McMillan, John (1994) 'China's nonconformist reforms', Policy Paper No. 11, Institute on Global Conflict and Cooperation, San Diego, December.

McMillan, J. and Woodruff, C. (1999) 'Interfirm relationships and informal credit in Vietnam', *Quarterly Journal of Economics*, 114(4): 1285–320.

Ministry of Light Industry (1984) *Light Industry*, 1.

Ministry of Light Industry (1985) 'Nghi quyet cua Hoi Dong Bo Truong "Ve mot so van de cai tien quan ly cong nghiep quoc doanh" 156 HDBT (Decree of the Council of Ministers "On some problems in the reform of state industrial management" 156-HDBT)', *Light Industry*, 1.

Mitchell, Timothy (1991) 'The limits of the state: beyond statist approaches and their critics', *American Political Science Review*, 85(1): 77–96.

n/a (1989) 'Bao cao (du thao) so ket tinh hinh thuc hien nghi quyet 10 cua Bo chinh tri ve doi moi quan ly kinh te nong nghiep (Draft report on the results of the implementation of decree 10 of the Politburo in agricultural economic management reform)', mimeo, Hanoi (thought to be internal document of the Ministry of Agriculture and Rural Development).

Naughton, Barry (1994) *Growing Out of the Plan: Chinese Economic Reform, 1978–1993*. New York: Cambridge University Press.

NCKT (1985) *Nghien cuu kinh te (Economic Research)*, 3: 13.

Ngo Dinh Giao (1972) 'Mot so y kien ve phan cong va hiep tac lao dong trong xi nghiep co khi mien bac nuoc ta (Some opinions on labour division and cooperation in engineering enterprises in the north of our country)', in Nguyen Tri (ed.) *Ve to chuc san xuat trong cong nghiep mien bac nuoc ta* (*On the Organisation of Production in the Industry of the North of Our Country*). Hanoi: NXB Dai hoc va Trung Hoc Chuyen Nghiep (Higher and Specialised Middle Education).

Ngo Vinh Long (1985a) 'The national political economy of rural development in Vietnam, 1975–84. I – rural development in Vietnam, 1975–1984', mimeo, SSRC Conference, Chiangmai.

Ngo Vinh Long (1985b) 'The national political economy of rural development in Vietnam, 1975–84. II – the reform years, 1980–1984', mimeo, SSRC Conference, Chiangmai.

Ngoc Van (1980) 'Qua mot so xi nghiep tra luong khoan san pham tap the (A look at some SOEs paying wages according to collective output contracts)', *Nhan Dan* (*The People*), 19 November.

Ngu Phong (1990) 'Phai chang gan ba trieu lao dong tieu, thu cong nghiep khong la doi tuong van dong quan chung cua Dang? (So are nearly 3 million workers in small and artisanal industry not something that the Party wants to mobilise?)', *Nhan Dan* (*The People*), 14 March.

Nguyen Cao Thuong (1980) *Khai thac kha nang tiem tang trong san xuat cua xi nghiep cong nghiep* (*Exploiting the Production Potential of Industrial Enterprises*). Hanoi: NXB Lao dong.

Nguyen Duy Trinh (1976) *Mien bac xa hoi chu nghia trong qua trinh thuc hien hai nhiem vu chien luoc* (*The Socialist North in the Process of Implementing Two Strategic Tasks*). Hanoi: NXB Su That.

Nguyen Duy Trinh and Nguyen Van Tran (1966) *Nhung thang loi ve vang cua Nhan Dan ta trong cong cuoc xay dung nen kinh te xa hoi chu nghia o mien Bac (1955–1965)* (*The Golden Victories of Our People in the Construction of a Socialist Economy in the North, 1955–1965*). Hanoi: NXB Su That.

Nguyen Khac Truong (1991) *Manh dat lam nguoi nhieu ma* (*Land with Many Ghosts*). Hanoi: NXB Hoi Nha Van.

Nguyen Lam (1980a) *Phat trien cong nghiep hang tieu dung va cong nghiep dia phuong* (*Develop Consumer Goods Industry and Local Industry*). Hanoi: NXB Su That.

Nguyen Lam (1980b) 'May van de ve tu tuong chinh sach kinh te hien nay (Some problems of current economic policy thinking)', *Tap chi Cong san* (*Communist Studies*), 3.

Nguyen Lang (1969) 'Mot vai y kien ve co cau cong nghiep dia phuong (Some opinions on local industrial structure)', *Nghien cuu kinh te* (*Economic Research*), 6.

Nguyen Lang and Nghiem Phu Ninh (1972a) 'Ve viec ket hop hinh thuc thu cong nghiep gia dinh voi xi nghiep cong nghiep xa hoi chu nghia (On the combination of family-based forms of artisanal industry with socialist industrial enterprises)', in Nguyen Tri (ed.) *Ve to chuc san xuat trong cong nghiep mien bac nuoc ta* (*On the Organisation of Production in the Industry of the North of Our Country*). Hanoi: NXB Dai hoc va Trung Hoc Chuyen Nghiep (Higher and Specialised Middle Education).

Nguyen Lang and Nghiem Phu Ninh (1972b) 'To chuc san xuat cong nghiep trong cac hop tac xa nong nghiep (The organisation of industrial production in agricultural cooperatives)', in Nguyen Tri (ed.) *Ve to chuc san xuat trong cong nghiep mien bac nuoc ta* (*On the Organisation of Production in the Industry of the North of Our Country*). Hanoi: NXB Dai hoc va Trung Hoc Chuyen Nghiep (Higher and Specialised Middle Education).

Nguyen Manh Huan (1980) 'Hop tac xa nong nghiep Dinh Cong (Dinh Cong agricultural cooperative)', *Nghien cuu kinh te* (*Economic Research*), 8.

Nguyen Manh Hung and Cao Ngoc Thang (1990) *Viet nam co mot nam nhu the!* (*Vietnam Had a Year!*). Hanoi: NXB Su That.

Nguyen Nien (1973) 'Mot so van de phap ly trong quan ly tai chinh o xi nghiep cong nghiep quoc doanh hien nay (Some current legal issues in the financial management of SOEs)', *Luat Hoc* (*Legal Studies*), 2.

Nguyen Nien (1974a) 'Quyen quan ly nghiep vu cua xi nghiep doi voi tai san nha nuoc trong tinh hinh cai tien quan ly xi nghiep cua ta hien nay (Enterprise rights to task management regarding state assets in the current situation of enterprise management reform)', *Luat Hoc* (*Legal Studies*), 7.

Nguyen Nien (1974b) 'Quyen quan ly nghiep vu cua xi nghiep doi voi tai san luu dong va cac quy xi nghiep theo che do quan ly moi hien nay (Enterprise rights to task management regarding circulating capital and enterprise funds according to the current system)', *Luat Hoc* (*Legal Studies*), 8.

Nguyen Nien (1977) 'Dia vi phap ly cua xi nghiep cong nghiep quoc doanh (The legal position of industrial SOEs)', *Luat Hoc* (*Legal Studies*), 3.

Nguyen Nien (1985) 'Xoa bo tap trung quan lieu-bao cap, tu goc nhin phap ly (Getting rid of the centralised adminstrative-subsidy system, from the legal point of view)', *Luat Hoc* (*Legal Studies*), 4.

Nguyen Quoc Khanh (1985) 'Quan ly va su dung von san xuat – van de co ban dam bao quyen tu chu tai chinh cua xi nghiep

(The management and use of production capital – the basic issue in guaranteeing the financial autonomy of the enterprise)', *Nghien cuu kinh te* (*Economic Research*), 2.

Nguyen Sinh (c. 1988) 'Thuc trang quoc doanh nong nghiep sau nghi quyet 10 (The situation of agricultural SOEs after decree 10)', mimeo, Hanoi.

Nguyen Tri (ed.) (1972a) *Ve to chuc san xuat trong cong nghiep mien bac nuoc ta* (*On the Organisation of Production in the Industry of the North of Our Country*). Hanoi: NXB Dai hoc va Trung Hoc Chuyen Nghiep (Higher and Specialised Middle Education).

Nguyen Tri (1972b) 'Loi noi dau (Introduction)', in Nguyen Tri (ed.) *Ve to chuc san xuat trong cong nghiep mien bac nuoc ta* (*On the Organisation of Production in the Industry of the North of Our Country*). Hanoi: NXB Dai hoc va Trung Hoc Chuyen Nghiep (Higher and Specialised Middle Education).

Nguyen Tung (ed.) (1999) *Mong Phu – Un village du Delta du Fleuve rouge* (*Viet Nam*. Paris: Editions L'Harmattan.

Nguyen van Chinh (2000) 'Work without name – changing patterns of children's work in a north Vietnamese village', PhD thesis, University of Amsterdam.

Nguyen van Dam (1988) 'Doi moi cong tac tin dung von luu dong nham thuc hien QD 217 HDBT (Reform of credit and circulating capital in order to implement decree 217 HDBT)', *Tap chi Ngan Hang* (*Journal of Banking*), 1(2).

Nguyen Van Ky (1989) 'Chinh sach tich luy va tieu dung trong thoi ky qua do hien nay o nuoc ta (The accumulation and consumption policy during the current transitional period in our country)', *Thong tin ly luan* (*Theoretical Information*), 1.

Nguyen van Tran (1974) *Nhung van de co ban trong duong loi cong nghiep hoa xa hoi chu nghia cua Dang* (*Basic Problems in the Party Line on Socialist Industrialisation*). Hanoi: NXB Su That.

Nhan Dan (1979a) *Nhan Dan* (*The People*), 4 January.
Nhan Dan (1979b) *Nhan Dan* (*The People*), 5 January.
Nhan Dan (1979c) *Nhan Dan* (*The People*), 19 February.
Nhan Dan (1979d) *Nhan Dan* (*The People*), 21 February.
Nhan Dan (1979e) *Nhan Dan* (*The People*), 23 February.
Nhan Dan (1979f) *Nhan Dan* (*The People*), 10 May.
Nhan Dan (1979g) 'Editorial', *Nhan Dan* (*The People*), 2 June.
Nhan Dan (1979h) 'Editorial', *Nhan Dan* (*The People*), 5 June.
Nhan Dan (1979i) 'Editorial', *Nhan Dan* (*The People*), 14 June.
Nhan Dan (1979j) *Nhan Dan* (*The People*), 22 June.

Nhan Dan (1979k) *Nhan Dan (The People)*, 17 July.
Nhan Dan (1979l) *Nhan Dan (The People)*, 7 August.
Nhan Dan (1979m) *Nhan Dan (The People)*, 6 September.
Nhan Dan (1979n) *Nhan Dan (The People)*, 6 October.
Nhan Dan (1979o) *Nhan Dan (The People)*, 24 October.
Nhan Dan (1979p) *Nhan Dan (The People)*, 25 October.
Nhan Dan (1979q) *Nhan Dan (The People)*, 1 November.
Nhan Dan (1979r) *Nhan Dan (The People)*, 13 November.
Nhan Dan (1979s) *Nhan Dan (The People)*, 4 December.
Nhan Dan (1979t) *Nhan Dan (The People)*, 12 December.
Nhan Dan (1979u) *Nhan Dan (The People)*, 27 December.
Nhan Dan (1980a) *Nhan Dan (The People)*, 10 March.
Nhan Dan (1980b) *Nhan Dan (The People)*, 19 March.
Nhan Dan (1980c) *Nhan Dan (The People)*, 1 April.
Nhan Dan (1980d) *Nhan Dan (The People)*, 16 April.
Nhan Dan (1980e) *Nhan Dan (The People)*, 24 April.
Nhan Dan (1980f) *Nhan Dan (The People)*, 6 May.
Nhan Dan (1980g) *Nhan Dan (The People)*, 27 May.
Nhan Dan (1980h) *Nhan Dan (The People)*, 5 June.
Nhan Dan (1980i) *Nhan Dan (The People)*, 15 July.
Nhan Dan (1980j) *Nhan Dan (The People)*, 29 July.
Nhan Dan (1980k) *Nhan Dan (The People)*, 31 July.
Nhan Dan (1980l) *Nhan Dan (The People)*, 16 September.
Nhan Dan (1980m) *Nhan Dan (The People)*, 27 October.
Nhan Dan (1980n) *Nhan Dan (The People)*, 28 October.
Nhan Dan (1980o) *Nhan Dan (The People)*, 11 November
Nhan Dan (1980p) *Nhan Dan (The People)*, 19 November.
Nhan Dan (1980q) *Nhan Dan (The People)*, 9 December.
Nhan Dan (1981a) *Nhan Dan (The People)*, 7 April.
Nhan Dan (1981b) *Nhan Dan (The People)*, 28 April.
Nhan Dan (1981c) *Nhan Dan (The People)*, 23 June.
Nhan Dan (1981d) *Nhan Dan (The People)*, 24 September.
Nhan Dan (1982a) *Nhan Dan (The People)*, 7 January.
Nhan Dan (1982b) *Nhan Dan (The People)*, 9 February.
Nhan Dan (1982c) *Nhan Dan (The People)*, 17 February.
Nhan Dan (1982d) *Nhan Dan (The People)*, 10 March.
Nhan Dan (1982e) *Nhan Dan (The People)*, 13 March.
Nhan Dan (1982f) *Nhan Dan (The People)*, 23 March.
Nhan Dan (1982g) *Nhan Dan (The People)*, 24 March.
Nhan Dan (1985a) 'Editorial', *Nhan Dan (The People)*, 24 September.
Nhan Dan (1985b) *Nhan Dan (The People)*, 15 October.

Nhan Dan (1985c) *Nhan Dan (The People)*, 4 November.
Nhan Dan (1986) 'Editorial', *Nhan Dan (The People)*, 14 May.
Nhan Dan (1987) 'Editorial', *Nhan Dan (The People)*, 12 September.
Nhan Dan (1988) *Nhan Dan (The People)*, 29 November.
NHNN (1988) 'T/T 130 Nh/TT 30/12/87 huong dan trien khai cong tac tien te, tin dung, thanh toan de thuc hien ban Q/D ban hanh kem theo QD 217-HDBT 14/11/87 cua HDBT (Circular letter 130-Nh/TT, 30 December 1987, guiding dissemination of the work regarding money, credit and account settling so as to implement the resolution on the implementation of decree 217-HDBT, 14 November 1987)', in NXBST *Quyet dinh 217 va huong dan thuc hien (Decree 217 and Guidance on its Implementation)*. Hanoi: NXB Su That.
NXBST (1976) *Phap luat ve quan ly kinh te – nhung quy dinh co ban cua nha nuoc (Economic Management Law – Basic State Regulations)*. Hanoi: NXB Su That.
NXBST (1978) *Mot so van kien cua Dang va Chinh phu ve tieu cong nghiep va thu cong nghiep (Some Documents of the Party and Government on Small and Artisanal Industry)*. Hanoi: NXB Su That.
NXBST (1980) *Mot so van kien cua trung uong Dang ve phat trien cong nghiep (Some Documents of the Party Centre on Industrial Development)*. Hanoi: NXB Su That.
NXBST (1988) *Quyet dinh 217 va huong dan thuc hien (Decree 217 and Guidance on its Implementation)*. Hanoi: NXB Su That.
NXBST (1990) *Nhung quy dinh moi sua doi va bo sung quyet dinh 217 HDBT (New Regulations Revising and Supplementing Decree 217-HDBT)*. Hanoi: NXB Su That.
Pham Hung (1988) 'Doi moi hoat dong cua cac xi nghiep quoc doanh (Reform of SOE activities)', speech at cadre conference to research 217, 2 December 1987, in NXBST *Quyet dinh 217 va huong dan thuc hien (Decree 217 and Guidance on its Implementation)*. Hanoi: NXB Su That.
Phan van Tiem (1992) 'Nguyen nhan cua tinh trang lam phat keo dai o nuoc ta. Luan cu khoa hoc cua nhung bien phap kiem che va giam lam phat o Viet Nam (Tai lieu hoi thao de tai K.03.10) (The causes of long-term inflation in our country. The scientific basis and ways of controlling and reducing inflation in Vietnam)', mimeo, November. Hanoi: Vien NCKH Thi truong Gia ca (Institute for Prices and Markets).
Podolski, T.M. (1972) *Socialist Banking and Monetary Control: The Experience of Poland*, Cambridge Russian, Soviet and Post-Soviet Studies. Cambridge: Cambridge University Press.

Polanyi, Karl (1975) *The Great Transformation*. New York: Octagon Books.

Porter, Gareth (1990) 'The politics of "renovation" in Vietnam', *Problems of Communism*, 39(3): 72–88.

Porter, Gareth (1993) *Vietnam: The Politics of Bureaucratic Socialism*. Ithaca, NY: Cornell University Press.

Prostiakov, Igor (1998) 'Economic reform in the interregnum between Andropov and Gorbachev-Ryzhkov', in Michael Ellman and Vladimir Kontonrovich (eds) *The Destruction of the Soviet Economic System – An Insiders' History*. Armonk, NY: M.E. Sharpe.

Riedel, James and Turley, William S. (1998) 'The politics and economics of transition to an open market economy in Vietnam', mimeo. Paris: OECD.

Ronnas, Per (1992) *Employment Generation Through Private Entrepreneurship in Vietnam*. New Delhi and Stockholm: ILO/SIDA.

Ronnas, Per (1998) 'The transformation of the private manufacturing sector in Vietnam in the 1990s', Working Paper in Economics and Finance No. 241, May, Stockholm School of Economics.

Ronnas, Per and Sjoberg, Orjan (eds) (1991) *Socio-economic Development in Vietnam: The Agenda for the 1990s*. Stockholm: SIDA.

Shonfield, Andrew (1965) *Modern Capitalism: The Changing Balance of Public and Private Power*. Oxford: Oxford University Press.

Shore, C. and Wright, S. (1997) 'Policy: A new field of anthropology', in Chris Shore and Susan Wright (eds) *Anthropology of Policy: Critical Perspectives on Governance and Power*. London: Routledge.

Sikor, Thomas (1999) 'The political economy of decollectivisation: a study of differentiation in and among Black Thai villages of northern Vietnam', PhD dissertation, University of California, Berkeley.

Smith, Ralph B. (1983) *An International History of the Vietnam War*. London: Macmillan.

Spoor, Max (1985) 'The economy of North Vietnam – the first ten years: 1955–1964 (a study of economic policy and performance of socialism in the third world)', MPhil thesis, Institute of Social Studies, The Hague.

Spoor, Max (1988) 'Reforming state finance in post-1975 Vietnam', *Journal of Development Studies*, 24(4): 102–14.

Suiwah Leung (ed.) (1996) *Vietnam Assessment: Creating a Sound Investment Climate*. Singapore: ISEAS.

SWB (1980) BBC Summary of World Broadcasts, 23 April.

SWB (1981) BBC Summary of World Broadcasts, 25 March.

SWB (1982) BBC Summary of World Broadcasts, 26 April.
SWB (1986) BBC Summary of World Broadcasts, 18 December.
SWB (1987) BBC Summary of World Broadcasts, 2 September.
Ta Nhu Khue (1974) 'Ban ve tinh chat va noi dung quyen tai san cua XNQD (Discussion of the nature and content of SOE rights over assets)', *Luat Hoc (Legal Studies)*, 8
Tap chi Cong san (1985) 'Cai tien co che quan ly hop tac xa nong nghiep (Reform of the agriculture cooperative management system)', editorial, *Tap chi Cong san (Communist Studies)*, 5.
TCTK (1977) *Tu dien thong ke (Statistical Dictionary)*. Hanoi: Tong cuc thong ke.
TCTK (1978) *Tinh hinh phat trien Kinh te ca Van hoa mien bac xa hoi chu nghia Viet nam 1960–75 (The Economic and Cultural Development of Socialist North Vietnam 1960–1975)*. Hanoi: NXB Thong ke.
TCTK (1980) *So lieu thong ke 1979 (Statistical Materials 1979)*. Hanoi: Tong cuc thong ke.
TCTK (1981) *So lieu thong ke 1976–1980 (Statistical Materials 1976–1980)*. Hanoi: NXB Thong ke.
TCTK (1982) *So lieu thong ke cong nghiep 5 nam 1976–1980 (Statistical Materials on Industry for 1976–1980)*. Hanoi: NXB Thong ke.
TCTK (1983) *So lieu thong ke cong hoa xa hoi chu nghia Vietnam 1982 (Statistical Materials 1982)*. Hanoi: Tong cuc thong ke.
TCTK (1985) *So lieu thong ke 1930–1984 (Statistical Materials 1930–1984)*. Hanoi: NXB Thong ke.
TCTK (1990) *So lieu thong ke cong hoa xa hoi chu nghia Vietnam 1976–89 (Statistical Materials for the SRV 1976–1989)*. Hanoi: NXB Thong ke.
TCTK (1991) *So lieu thong ke 1976–1990 (Statistical Materials 1976–1990)*, Hanoi: NXB Thong ke.
TCTK (1994) *Economy and Finance of Vietnam 1986–1992*. Hanoi: NXB Thong ke.
TCTK (1995) *Nien giam Thong ke 1994 (Statistical Yearbook 1994)*. Hanoi: NXB Thong ke.
TCTK (2000) *So lieu thong ke kinh te – xa hoi Viet nam 1975–2000 (Statistical Data of Vietnam Socio-economy 1975–2000)*. Hanoi: NXB Thong ke.
TCTK (2001) *Nien giam Thong ke 2000 (Statistical Yearbook 2000)*. Hanoi: NXB Thong ke.
TCTK (2004) *Nien giam Thong ke 2003 (Statistical Yearbook 2003)*. Hanoi: NXB Thong ke.

Thayer, C.A. (1983) 'Vietnam's two strategic tasks: building socialism and defending the fatherland', in *Southeast Asian Affairs*. Singapore: Institute for South-East Asian Studies.

Thayer, C.A. (1992) 'Political reform in Vietnam: Doi moi and the emergence of civil society', in R.F. Miller (ed.) *The Development of Civil Society in Communist Systems*. Sydney: Allen and Unwin.

Thayer, C.A. (1995) 'Mono-organisational socialism and the Vietnamese state', in Benedict Kerkvliet, J. Tria and Dong J. Porter (eds) *Vietnam's Rural Transformation*. Boulder, CO: Westview Press.

The Dat (1981) *Nen Nong nghiep Viet Nam tu sau Cach mang thang tam nam 1945 (Vietnam's Agriculture After the 1945 August Revolution)*. Hanoi: NXB Nong Nghiep.

To Duy (1969) *Mot so van de ve luu thong phan phoi trong thoi ky xay dung chu nghia xa hoi va chong my cuu nuoc hien nay (Some Problems of Distribution and Circulation in the Current Period of Socialist Construction and the Fight Against the US to Save the Country)*. Hanoi: NXB Su That.

Tran Duc Hoat (1983) 'May van de ve tuyen truyen kinh te trong nhung thang cuoi nam 1983 (Problems in economic propaganda in the closing months of 1983)', *Tuyen truyen (Propaganda)*, 8–9.

Tran Duc Luong (1988) 'Nhung van de then chot trong quy dinh cua HDBT ban hanh theo QD 217 HDNT (Core issues in regulations of the Council of Ministers promulgated in accordance with decree 217-HDBT)', speech at cadre conference to research 217-HDBT, 1 December 1987, in NXBST *Quyet dinh 217 va huong dan thuc hien (Decree 217 and Guidance on its Implementation)*. Hanoi: NXB Su That.

Tran Duc Nguyen (1988) *Mot so quan diem kinh te cua Dai hoi VI (Some Economic Positions Taken by the Sixth Congress)*. Hanoi: NXB Su That.

Tran Phuong (1966/1967) 'Ban ve buoc di cua cong nghiep hoa (Discussion of the stages of industrialisation)', *Nghien cuu kinh te (Economic Research)*, 36, 37 and 39.

Tran The Duong (1994) *Thi truong lao dong va cong doan trong doanh nghiep (The Labour Market and the Trade Union in the Enterprise)*. Hanoi: NXB Lao Dong.

Tran Trong Huy (1967) 'Van de tieu cong nghiep va thu cong nghiep trong tinh hinh moi (The problem of small and artisanal industry in the new situation)', *Nghien cuu kinh te (Economic Research)*, 6.

Truong Chinh (1968/1969) 'Weaknesses, shortcomings and mistakes in agricultural cooperatives', Vietnamese documents and research notes. Saigon: US Embassy.

Truong Chinh (1981) 'Van de the che hoa duong loi xay dung nen kinh te moi (The problem of institutionalising the line on constructing the new economy)', *Nghien cuu kinh te (Economic Research)*, 2.

TTKT (1988) 'T/T 104 TT/PC cua Trong tai kinh te nha nuoc 31/12/87 huong dan mot so van de ve hop dong kinh te va trong tai kinh te nham thi hanh Q/D 217 HDBT (Circular letter 104-TTPC of the State Referee, 31 December 1987, guiding a number of issues to do with economic contracts and economic refereeing in order to implement 217-HDBT)', in NXBST *Quyet dinh 217 va huong dan thuc hien (Decree 217 and Guidance on its Implementation)*. Hanoi: NXB Su That.

TTXVN (1981) '6 cong ty, lien hiep xi nghiep, xi nghiep nhan ke hoach quy tien luong theo khoi luong san pham (Six companies, enterprise unions and enterprises have received planned-for wage funds based upon output)', *Nhan Dan (The People)*, 20 October.

Turley, William S. (1993) 'Political renovation in Vietnam: renewal and adaptation', in Ljunggren, (ed.) *The Challenge of Reform in Indochina*. Cambridge, MA: Harvard University Press.

Turley, William S. and Riedel, James (1998) *Viet Nam: Ordeals of Transition*. Paris: OECD.

Turley, William S. and Selden, Mark (1993) *Reinventing Vietnamese Socialism: Doi Moi in Comparative Perspective*. Boulder, CO: Westview.

TWD (1979) *Tang cuong xay dung Dang trong hop tac xa tieu cong nghiep va thu cong nghiep (Reinforcement of Party Construction in Small and Artisanal Industrial Cooperatives)*. Hanoi: NXB Su That.

UBKHNN (1989) *Quyet dinh 217 HDBT va huong dan thuc hien (tai ban co bo sung B: Tap chi ke hoach hoa (Decree 217-HDBT and Guidance for its Implementation (Republished with Supplements)*. Hanoi: UBKHNN.

UNDP (1990) *Report on the Economy of Vietnam*. Hanoi: UNDP.

UNIDO (1989) *Vietnam's Industrial Development: An Assessment*. Vienna: UNIDO.

Van Dac (1983) 'Nhung quan diem co ban cua mot so chinh sach kinh te lon hien nay – QD: 25 CP va 146 HDBT ve cai tien cong tac quan ly xi nghiep quoc doanh (The basic ideas of some important contemporary economic policies – 25-CP and 146-HDBT on the improvement of SOE management)', *Tuyen truyen (Propaganda)*, 8–9.

Van Dyke, Jon M. (1972) *North Vietnam's Strategy for Survival*. Palo Alto, CA: Pacific Books.

Vasavakul, Thaveeporn (1993) 'Vietnam: sectors, classes and the transformation of a Leninist state', in James W. Morley (ed.) *Driven by*

Growth: Political Change in the Asia-Pacific Region. New York: M.E. Sharpe.

Vasavakul, Thaveeporn (1995) 'Viet Nam – the changing models of legitimation', in M. Alagappa (ed.) *Political Legitimacy in Southeast Asia: The Quest for Moral Authority*. Stanford: Stanford University Press.

Vasavakul, Thaveeporn (1996) 'Politics of the reform of state institutions in post-socialist Viet Nam', in Suiwah Leung (ed.) *Vietnam Assessment: Creating a Sound Investment Climate*. Singapore: ISEAS.

Vasavakul, Thaveeporn (1997) 'Sectoral politics and strategies for state and party building from the VII to the VIII Congress of the VCP (1991–1996)', in Adam Fforde (ed.) *Doi Moi – Ten Years After the 1986 Party Congress*, Political and Social Change Monograph No. 24. Canberra: Australian National University.

VCP (1987) *Dai hoi VI Nhung phuong huong co ban cua chinh sach kinh te* (*The Sixth Congress: Basic Directions in Economic Policy*). Hanoi: NXB Su That.

Vickerman, Andrew (1986) 'The fate of the peasantry – premature "transition to socialism" in the Democratic Republic of Vietnam', Southeast Asian Studies Monograph Series No. 28, Centre for International and Area Studies, Yale University.

Vo Nhan Tri (1986) 'Soviet-Vietnamese cooperation since 1975', *Indochina Report*, October.

Vo Nhan Tri (1990) *Vietnamese Economic Policy Since 1975*. Singapore: Institute of South-East Asian Studies.

Vu Khien and Vu Quoc Tuan (1974) 'Buoc dau nghien cuu luat ke hoach hoa – Noi dung phap che cua luat ke hoach hoa (A first step in researching planning law)', *Luat Hoc* (*Legal Studies*), 6.

Vu Ngoc Hoanh (1972) 'Ve to chuc san xuat theo quy luat tap trung hoa trong cong nghiep nuoc ta (On the organisation of production according to the law of industrial centralisation in our country)', in Nguyen Tri (ed.) *Ve to chuc san xuat trong cong nghiep mien bac nuoc ta* (*On the Organisation of Production in the Industry of the North of Our Country*). Hanoi: NXB Dai hoc va Trung Hoc Chuyen Nghiep (Higher and Specialised Middle Education).

Vu Quoc Tuan (1983) 'Cong tac tuyen truyen ve ke hoach nha nuoc nam 1983 (Propaganda work and the 1983 state plan)', *Tuyen truyen* (*Propaganda*), 1.

Vu Quoc Tuan and Dinh Van Hoang (1960) *Ban ve nhip do phat trien kinh te quoc dan mien Bac* (*Discussion of the Speed of National Economic Development in the North*). Hanoi: NXB Su That.

Vu Tuan Anh (1985) 'Thu phan tich nen tai san xuat xa hoi ta duoi goc do co cau nganh kinh te (An attempt at analysing production assets from the point of economic structure)', *Nghien cuu kinh te (Economic Research)*, 2.

Vu Tuong (n/d) 'Dependent but not dependable: The making of a socialist working class in North Vietnam, 1945–1970', mimeo. Berkeley, CA: Department of Political Science, University of California.

Vu Tuong (2001) 'Policies and illusions of order: state-labor relations and the organizational roots of labor peace in socialist Vietnam', mimeo. Berkeley, CA: Department of Political Science, University of California.

Wade, Robert (1988) 'The role of government in overcoming market failure: Taiwan, Republic of Korea and Japan', in Helen Hughes (ed.) *Achieving Industrialization in East Asia*. Cambridge: Cambridge University Press.

Wade, Robert (1990) *Governing the Market: Economic Theory and the Role of Government in East Asian Industrialization*. Princeton, NJ: Princeton University Press.

Wadekin, K.-E. (1973) *The Private Sector in Soviet Agriculture*. London: University of California Press.

Wadekin, K.-E. (1982) *Agrarian Policies in Communist Europe*. London: Martinus Nijhoff.

Warren, Bill (1973) 'Imperialism and capitalist industrialization', *New Left Review*, I/81 (September/October): 3–44.

Waterbury, John (1999) 'The long gestation and brief triumph of import-substituting industrialization', *World Development*, 27(2): 323–41.

Wiles, Peter (1962) *The Political Economy of Communism*. Cambridge, MA: Harvard University Press.

Wiles, Peter (1977) *Economic Institutions Compared*. Oxford: Blackwell.

Williams, M. (1987) 'Vietnam's Sixth Party Congress', *Journal of Communist Studies*, 3(2): 185–90.

Wood, Adrian (1989) 'Deceleration of inflation with acceleration of price reform: Viet Nam's remarkable recent experience', *Cambridge Journal of Economics*, 13 December.

Woodside, A.B. (1970) 'Decolonization and agricultural reform in North Vietnam', *Asian Survey*, 10(8): 705–12.

Woodside, A.B. (1976) *Community and Revolution in Modern Vietnam*. Boston, MA: Houghton Mifflin.

Woodside, A.B. (1997) 'The struggle to rethink the Vietnamese state in the era of market economies', in Timothy Brook and Hy van Luong (eds) *Culture and Economy: The Shaping of Capitalism in East Asia*. Ann Arbor, MI: University of Michigan Press.

World Bank (1990a) 'Viet Nam – stabilization and structural reforms – an economic report', mimeo. Washington, DC: World Bank.

World Bank (1990b) 'Aide memoire: statistics in Vietnam, consultant's report', mimeo. Washington, DC: World Bank.

World Bank (1995a) 'Vietnam – economic report on industrialization and industrial policy', World Bank document. Washington, DC: World Bank.

World Bank (1995b) *Bureaucrats in Business: The Economics and Politics of Government Ownership*. Washington, DC: World Bank.

Zysman, John (1983) *Governments, Markets and Growth: Financial Systems and the Politics of Industrial Change*. Ithaca, NY: Cornell University Press.

Note: the varying Vietnamese terms for various legal and political instructions are translated as 'decree'.

Index

1978–1979 economic crisis, 144
1979–1980 crisis, 127–9
1980 Ninth Plenum, 28
1986 Sixth Congress, 31, 37–40
1997 Asian crisis, 17, 210, 214, 220
Abrami, Regina, 5–6
accounting, costs, prices and profitability, 167–9
accumulation:
  pattern of, 160
  processes of, 63
aggravated shortage, 11, 24, 30, 56, 58, 60–3, 84, 86, 112, 119, 125, 136, 190
agriculture:
  collectivisation, 152
  cooperatives, 59, 198
  tax system, 36
ai thang ai (who wins), 7
allocative mechanisms, 10, 19–21, 39, 58, 60, 89, 167
  nature of, 83
  relations, 139
Almond, Gabriel., 7
analytical frameworks, 11–13
anarchy in markets, 36
anti-inflationary measures of 1989, 200–2
Arndt, H.W., 57

artisanal industry, 77–9, 152
  reintegration of, 90–2
  workers' wages, 116
authority and power of SOEs, 199
AVRP transcripts, 64

ba quy (three funds), 68
balancing, 179
Ban can su (Ministry's Party Unit), 78
basic property forms, 47
Beresford, Melanie, 5, 55, 57, 64, 103
BLD (Bo Lao dong), 134, 136–9, 170, 200
BNgT (Bo Ngoai thuong), 200
BNN (Bo Nong nghiep), 198
BNT (Bo Noi thuong), 200
Bo chu quan (head ministries), 100, 102
Boudarel, G., 198
branch:
  issue of, 101
  ministry, 74, 109
Bray, Francesca, 10, 22, 56,
BTC, 200
Bui Cong Trung, 38
bung ra (burst out), 24, 26, 40
bureaucracy:
  conflicts within, 73–4
  subsidised administrative supply system, 40

business-based growth, 63
BVT (Bo Vat tu), 200

cai tao (reform), 78, 97
can doi (balanced), 68
cap tren (superior levels), 24
capital:
  and output, state industry, 128
  assets, 69
  stock, 70
  survey of SOEs, 207
  tax, 211
capitalism:
  and the state, 225
  emergence of, 225–7
Central Cooperative Association, 79
centrally planned economy (CPE), 10
  model, 11
  programme, 39
Chaliand, Gerard, 6
chan trong chan ngoai (outside), 124
changes in policy, 1990–1992 and 2002, 205–7, 221–3
che do quan lieu bao cap (bureaucratic subsidised administrative supply system), 40
Che Tuong Nhu, 208
chi tieu phap lenh (legally binding plan targets), 68
China:
  aid cuts, 161
  SOE reforms, 84
chu quan (owning), 74
chuc nang (functional), 73
chui (under the table), 61, 70, 216
CIEM (Central Institute for Economic Management Research), 51, 182
CMEA (Council for Mutual Economic Assistance), 129

collectivisation:
  comments, 169
  effects of, 4
commercial:
  commercialisation, 62, 105–11
  capital accumulation, 48
  political economy, 63
  renaissance, 3, 12, 190
communist:
  economy, Vietnam, 10–13
  statistical theory, 10
Communist Studies, 26
con rung (bastard offspring), 119, 122, 126–7
Cong Bao, 35–6, 46, 51, 102–3, 108, 165–6, 168, 191, 208
cong nghiep dia Phuong, (local industry), 77
conservatism degree, 187
consumer demand:
  content, 198–200
  exploitation, 147–8
continuity and change, 131
control mechanism, 69
  control organs, 79–80
  planning and balancing the SOE, 68
Conyngham, W.J., 84
cooperatives, 110
  associations, 109–10, 124
  rights, 185
Cowen, Michael, 57
cuc (departments), 75
cung cap (supply), 85
cuoc song (life), 87
currency reform, 183

Dam Van Nhue, 132–3
Dang Phong, 5, 103
Dao Xuan Sam, 1, 46, 137, 194–5, 203, 214
Darre, M., 49, 51

Index

data, 10–11
   analysis problems, 10–13
DCSV, 33, 198
decrees:
   306-BBT, 39–40, 177–8, 184–7, 190, 196, 203, 207
   19-CP, 86, 99
   24-CP, 98, 103–4
   25-CP, 25, 35, 38, 70, 84, 112–13, 138–40, 159, 163, 169, 171, 173, 176, 190, 208
   64-CP, 171
   93-CP, 171
   119-CP, 97
   134-CP, 108, 123
   135-CP, 102
   143-CP, 106
   172-CP, 98, 103
   182-CP, 182
   236-CP, 97
   279-CP, 70, 113, 146, 159, 171
   318-CP, 49
   135-CT, 211
   191-CT/CW:41, 79
   191-CT/TW:33, 79
   50-HDBT, 200, 206
   76-HDBT, 184, 186–8, 191, 200
   93-HDBT, 206
   101-HDBT, 207
   113-HDBT, 35
   146-HDBT, 23, 35, 38, 164–8, 173–6, 186, 203, 208
   156-HDBT, 23, 35, 37–8, 178–82, 186, 203
   160-HDBT, 35
   162-HDBT, 37
   177-HDBT, 38
   188-HDBT, 36
   217-HDBT, 185, 200, 203, 206, 215, 221
   26-NQ/TW, 28, 38, 133, 135, 159, 161, 172
   105-NQ/TW, 105
   3-TTg, 82, 106
   21-TTg/TN, 82
   51-TTg, 211
   179-TTg, 211
   274-TTg, 97
de facto:
   autonomy, 99
   commercialisation, 56
   decentralisation, 41
   freedom, 111–12
   liberalisation of 1979–1980, 38
de Lestrange, Alexandre, 7
de Vylder, Stefan, 4, 6, 11, 18, 49, 182, 193
debate, conflict and policy development, 169–77
decapitalisation, 160
decentralisation, 41, 86
dem ban ngoai (taken for sale outside), 150
democracy:
   centralism, 73
   Yeltsin and the private sector, 203–4
depreciation system, 206
de-Stalinisation, 116, 178
development:
   policy, 57–8, 120
   state industry reform, 78
dia phuong (local), 24, 74, 99
Dic Lo, 9
Diehl, Markus, 7
dieu chinh (adjustment), 179
different allocative mechanisms, 87
Digregorio, Michael, 5
Dinh Thu Cuc, 29
Dinh Van, 14
direct contracting, 27
direct horizontal relations, 27
distributionalism, 87
Do Muoi, 25, 187

Do Nguyen Khoat, 207, 211
Doan Trong Truyen, 113
doc (vertical production unit), 85
doi moi, 24, 37, 40–1, 189, 195
  congress, 44, 63, 178
Dollar, David, 1
don vi co so (base units), 24, 85, 86
dong thoi thua thieu (abundant and short supply), 11
double-entry book keeping, 112
Drabek, Zdenek, 5
DRV, 6, 11, 17, 54, 144
  defending the DRV, SOE policy, 164–9
  development goals of communism, 53–66
  economy, 4, 12, 26, 34, 129
  legacy, 21–2
  model, 44–5
  nation-state, 55
  neo-Stalinist models, 55
  neo-Stalinist system failure, 34
  population, 16
  programme, 45, 57, 67, 112
  socio-economic programme, 121
dual-pricing system, 181
Duiker, William F., 30, 158
Duong Bach Lien, 170, 172–6

early policy debates, 85–6
East Germany, 30
economy/economic:
  and business, 195
  crisis, 12, 25, 29, 143
  data, 10
  development, 8–9, 16–17, 54–8
  growth, 18
  indicator, 26
  liberalisation 1990–1991, 45
  logic, 54–6, 111
  management system, 29, 76, 132, 198
Economic Management Law – Basic State Regulations (NXBST), 99
Eighth Plenum, 37–40, 105
Ellman, Michael, 84
EPU (Economics and Planning University), 56, 88, 97
  study, 88–9
EPU/NEU, 94
equitisation, 208–9
Ericson, P.E., 11
exogenous shocks, 1978–1979, 143–5

Farmers Union, 46
FDI (foreign direct investment), 43
Feldbrugge, F.J.M., 11
fence-breaking:
  beneficiaries of, 159
  harbingers of, 76–83
Fforde, Adam, 1, 4, 6, 11, 13–14, 16, 18, 23, 29, 32–4, 39, 43, 49–50, 55–7, 61, 65–7, 77, 80–1, 85, 114, 117, 121, 130, 132, 143, 163, 182, 186, 193–4, 198, 213, 216, 221–2
Fifth Congress, 32–41, 64
Fifth Plenum, 36
finance, 187
first trap, 22, 119–20
Five Year Plan (FYP), 11, 13, 16, 18, 29, 40, 48, 54, 56, 67, 84, 95, 98, 152
  commercialisation, 81
  role of non-state sector, 105–8
foreign trade, 187
Fourteenth Plenum, 78
Fourth Central Committee of the VCP, 22

Fourth Plenum, 17, 36
free market, 71, 153, 155
  activity, 156
  behaviour, 13
Furuta, Motoo, 195

Gainsborough, Martin, 6, 215
general companies (GCs), 224
gia ban buon cong nghiep (industry wholesale price), 68, 167
gia ban buon xi nghiep (SOE wholesale price), 68, 167
gia cong (putting-out), 81–2, 90
gia thanh (cost price), 68, 91, 166
glasnost, 195
global capitalist system, 9
globalisation, 23
Gordon, Alec, 31
Greenfield, Gerard, 8, 198, 216, 224
growth 1954–1975, 13

Ha Tinh, 89
Haiphong, 156–8
hang ngoai (outside commodities), 124
Ho Chi Minh City, 24–5, 27–8, 30, 33, 35, 38, 145–6, 158, 173, 180, 215
Ho Phuong, 95–7
Hoa Binh, 89
Hoang Quoc Viet, 97
Hoang, 14
hyperinflation, 184, 201

ideological logic, 56–8
IMF (International Monetary Fund), 11
impact and meanings of 25-CP, 160–1
import dependency, differential impact of, 144–5

incentives:
  changing balance of, 143–4
  structure, 175
industry/industrial:
  complexes, 144
  cooperatives, 107, 109, 123,
  gross output, 108
  growth, 20
  management ministries, 110
  management system of, 72
  policy, 194
  production, 78
  reform pattern of, 178
inflation, 194
  finance, 5
inputs supply problem, 148–9
inside/outside dichotomy, 4
institution:
  intentions, 164–5
  types of, 102
interpretations of new legislation, 169–77

ke hoach bo sung (supplementary plans), 109
Kerkvliet, Benedict, 5–7, 130
ket nghia (alliances), 125
khau hao coban (depreciation), 69
khau (links), 37
KHH, 187
khoan san pham (output contract), 23
Kim Ngoc, 31
  law, 21, 47, 226
kinh doanh (occupying themselves), 107
Kleinen, John, 58
Kokko, Ari, 7
Kontorovich, 84
Kornai, J., 11–12, 70
Krueger, Anne O., 9
kto kogo, 7
  labour and wages, 187

263

labour:
　problems 151
　relations, 149–50
lam ngoai (work outside), 150
lam tu do (work freely), 153
Lao Cai, 89
law:
　centralisation of production, 94
　value, 114, 223
Le Duan, 15, 24, 28, 30–1, 39–40, 49, 57, 85, 94, 152, 158, 163, 178
Le Duc Tho, 24, 30–1, 57
　programme, 31, 71
Le Huy Ngo, 66
Le Huy Phan, 95, 97
Le Mai Trinh, 50
Le Monde, 38
Le Si Thiep, 132–3
Le Thanh Nghi, 26, 86, 122
Le Trang, 170, 172–6
legally binding plan targets, 68
Leipziger, D.M., 5
Leninist institutions, MOs, 22
Leung, Suiwah, 7
Level II organisations, 134
Lindauer, David L., 8–9
liquidation of kulaks, 29
Ljunggren, Borje, 23
local industry:
　development of, 79
　in economic policy, 89–90
loi nhuan don thuan (pure profits), 174
lon xon (confusion), 87
Luong, Hy van, 4

macro-dynamics, 19–21
macro-economics, 199
　analysis, 19
　performance, 127–9

situation, 39
stability, 9, 220
macro-stabilisation, 41–2
Mallon, Ray, 7
management, 74, 198
market economy, 23, 62
　growth, 6
　regulation, 6
　shift, 45
　transition, 3
market scepticism, 8
market-based commerce, 63
marketisation, 48
　processes, 76, 189
market-oriented:
　economy, 5, 43
　liberalisation, 185
　system, 2
Marr, David, 31
Marx, Karl, 115
Marxist-Leninist analysis, 22
mass consumption, 90
mass organisations (MOs), 1
material incentive system, 151
material supply system, 62, 199
McMillan, J., 7
Mekong delta, 17, 34, 152
military-technocratic alliance, 49
ministries or departments, 102
ministries, 73
Ministry of Engineering and Metallurgy, 75, 95
Ministry of Planning and Investment (MPI), 219
Mitchell, Timothy, 6
moc ngoac (hooking), 130
money, role of, 59
multi-plan system, 25, 136

Nam Ha, 89
national income accounting (NIA) methods, 10

Index

national markets, 78
Naughton, Barry, 16
neo-Stalinism, 6, 33, 47, 119–31
  assumptions, 10
  correctness, 6
  development model, 40, 56
  doctrine, 26
  dominance, 94
  machine, 61
  model, 12
  programme, 2, 12, 25–6, 67, 82
  project, 84
  system, 167
  theory, 87
  tradition, 12
new course, 169–77
new policy, 153
ngang (horizontal production unit), 12, 85
nganh (branch), 73, 100–1
Nghiem Phu Ninh, 90–2
Nghien cuu kinh te, 66
Ngo Dinh Giao, 95–6
Ngo Vinh Long, 143
ngoai (outside), 24
Ngoc Van, 50
Ngu Phong, 204
Nguyen Ai Quoc Party Academy, 31
Nguyen Cao Thuong, 115
Nguyen Duy Trinh, 15–16, 110
Nguyen Khac Truong, 58
Nguyen Lam, 26–7, 32–3, 49, 90–2, 126, 185
Nguyen Lang, 89
Nguyen Manh Huan, 29
Nguyen Nien, 97
Nguyen Quoc Khanh, 207
Nguyen Sinh, 198
Nguyen Tri, 29, 86, 88–90, 115
Nguyen van Dam, 200
Nguyen van Linh, 24, 178, 186

Nguyen Van Tran, 15, 97
Nhan Dan, 38, 50, 113, 127, 131, 144, 147–55, 157–8, 186
NHNN (Ngan hang Nha nuoc), 200
nhom san pham (product groups), 107
Nineteenth Plenum, 96
noi (inside), 24
noi/ngoai (inside/outside), 85
non-state sector policy, 105–11
North Vietnam:
  economy 1954–1975, 13–16, 21
  industrial management system, 85
NQ/TW, 28
NXBST (NXB Su that), 78, 80, 100–1, 103, 105–7, 109, 199

Ohno, 219
output contract system (BBT), 25, 156
output growth rates (BCH), 15
outside, 124
  economy, 56, 66, 78, 123
  plan, 172
  work, 158
own capital, 200, 207, 211
owning and branch ministries 73–4

Paine, S.H., 4, 6, 11, 13–14, 16, 55–6, 61, 66–7, 80, 117
Paris Agreements, 106
partial reforms, 22–5
Party-state:
  control mechanisms, 70
  relations, 72–3
People's Committees of provinces or cities, 102–3, 110
perestroika, 195
peripheral autonomy, 75, 87

pha rao (fence-breaking), 25, 28, 61, 132, 139
Pham Hung, 66, 200
Pham van Dong, 24
phan phoi noi bo (internal distribution), 148, 150, 167
Phan van Tiem, 193
phe lieu (waste products), 76
phe pham (by-products), 77
planned economy, 22
planning system, 187
  decentralisation, 98
  reform, 109
Poland, 32
Polanyi, Karl, 78
policy:
  events, 1954–2005, 21–42
  explosion, 98
  U-turn, 184–6
Politburo:
  attitude through 1980, 28
  resolution, 80
political analysis, 55
political economy:
  analyses, 9
  characteristic of, 62
  Vietnamese, 120–1
political support, 200
political tensions, 156-HDBT, 177–83
position of local authorities *vis-à-vis* central government, 103
post-Second World War reconstruction, 8
pragmatism, 57
predates 25-CP, 70
pre-modern rural socio-economy, 4
Prices Commission, 187
price-wages-money, 22, 183–4
  débâcle, 178

measures, 178
programme, 1985, 204
priority to heavy industry, 18
Pritchett, Lant, 8–9
privileged access resources, 42
problems of:
  land reform, 24
  local economy, 29
process of commercial renaissance, 44
production, 10
productionism and distributionism, 84, 86–8
pro-market, 20
  policy analysis, 83–8
pro-plan incentives, 20
Prostiakov, 84
proto civil society, 82–3
provinces, 151–6
  cooperatives, 155
  People's Committees, 100

Quang Tri, 29
quy luat (natural law), 84

rational structure, 90
recentralisation, 1980–1985, 33–5, 163–91, 205
  decree, 163
  legislation, 35–7
  programme, 37
  structures, 28
  tendency, 36
Red River delta, 17, 31, 152, 154
reforms, 98–101
  debate, 85
  rationales, 72
reformists, 171–7
regional economies, development of, 151–9
reinforcement of control, 114

relative stability of production, 139
rents, 48
rent-seeking, 9
retail price inflation, 19
reunification, 58–60
　reform, 102–3
Riedel, James, 7
Romania, 30

san pham giao nop (planned system), 181
sap xep lai (rationalisation), 179
second FYP (Five Year Plan), 17–19, 121–2, 132
Second Plenum 1977, 28
second trap, 203–5, 226
　de-Stalinisation, 41
　loss of Soviet aid, 200–2
separation:
　notion of, 84
　problem, 84–5
Seventh Plenum, 37, 105
Shenton, Robert, 57
Shonfield, Andrew, 8
Sino-Soviet split, 23
Sino-Vietnamese border war, 22
Sixth Congress, 178, 189–90, 195–8, 203
Sixth Plenum, 23–4, 26–7, 29, 37, 87, 131–5
　origins, 119–20
small-scale industry, 81, 94, 106–7, 109
　cooperatives, 123
　eve of economic crisis, 125–6
　large-scale socialist production, 85
　non-state sector collapse, 204–5
　Party organisations, 123–7
　production importance, 78

socialism:
　conservative policy, 93–8
　construction, 120
　division of labour, 88
　industry, 77
　transformation, 11, 78, 80
socio-economic change, laws of, 88
state-owned enterprises in Vietnam (SOEs), 1, 5–8
　autonomy, 12, 38, 200
　balance, 198–200
　balloons, 43
　categories of, 136
　commercial renaissance, 163, 207
　commercialisation, 69–70, 135–9
　employment, 16
　focused model, 1990s, 43, 193–211
　investments, 33
　life, mid-1970s, 53–4
　outside activities, 25
　participation, 22
　plan indicators, 181
　position of, 6
　property rights, 216–21
　recovery, 23
　shared rights, 182
　transition of political economy, 63–5
south and *tiep quan*, 122
Soviet-bloc aid,
　effects, 1965–1975, 81–3
　elimination of two-price system, 200–2
　loss of, 17
　programme, 169, 204
specialised labourers 20–1
spontaneous decentralisation, 1979–1980, 143–61
　cause of, 132
　grassroots experiences, 145–9

Spoor, Max, 6, 55
SRV (Socialist Republic of Vietnam), 10, 54
  economy, 23, 40
  planning system, 19
stabilisation measures, 199
start of recentralisation, SOE management councils, 207–8
state authority, assertion of, 98–100
state business:
  interest, 24, 39, 63
  organisations, 218
State Capital Management Department (SCMD), 218
state economic management reform, 198
state industry, 213–24
  management, early legislation, 96–8
  national self-expression, 61–2
  planning reform, 104
  policy debates, 1979, 67–118
  politics and political economy, 68–70
  reform, meaning, 100–1
state management, aim of, 100
state material supply system, 121
state plan 1976, 86
State Planning Commission (SPC), 26
state planning system, internal reform, 98–100
State Prices Commission, 112
state property rights, 71
  recentralisation, 215–24
state sector, 110
State Treasury, 218
state-society:
  approach, 6
  relations, 7
statist developmentalism limits, 54–8
subsidiary economy, 21

subsidisation, 5
superiors, 24, 85
SWB (Summary of World Broadcasts), 28, 32

Ta Nhu Khue, 97
Tap chi Cong san, 37, 126
tax and credit systems, 106
TCTK (Tong cuc Thong ke), 14–15, 17–19, 43, 48, 153, 209–10
technical materials, 166
technico-economic norms, 181
technocratic reforms, 218
Tenth Plenum, 1964, 61
Thai Nguyen, 144
Thanh Cong, 28
Thanh Hoa, 89
thanh phan (economic components), 10, 27
Thayer, C.A., 30, 33, 64
three-contracts controversy, 31, 86
three interests, 27
three-plan system, 131, 136, 140, 167, 171, 178
Three Year Plan (1958–1960), 15, 67, 78
thu quoc doan (state income), 68
tiet kiem (economising), 68
tieu thu cong nghiep (small and artisanal industry), 77
tieu thu san pham (output disposal), 138
tieu thu (disposal), 85
To Huu, 25, 35, 38, 204
tracking reaction, 35–7
trade, 135
  regulations, 38
traditional:
  central planning, 67
  economic programme, 70–1
  socialism, 119
Tran Duc Hoat, 36

Tran Duc Luong, 187, 198–9
Tran Duc Nguyen, 197
Tran Phuong, 22, 27, 38, 64, 184
Tran The Duong, 160
Tran Trong Huy, 81
transition:
    economy, 163
    essence of, 40
    fiscal crisis, 19, 33
    model, 4–5, 12–13, 23, 41, 44, 64, 131–41, 159
    period, 27
    political economy, 64
transitive development programme, 57
traps and their significance, 42–4
Treaty of Friendship and Cooperation, 127
trung uong and dia phuong (centre and locality), 24, 85
trung uong (central), 74
Truong Chinh, 24, 31–2, 40, 49, 57, 158, 163, 178, 186
TTKT (Trong tai Kinh te), 200
TTXVN, 50
tu can doi (self-balancing), 10
tu duy (issue of cognition), 57
tu phat (spontaneity), 87
tu tieu thu (self-disposal), 108
TWD (Truong uong Dang), 123–4
Twelfth Plenum, March 1982, 32
Twentieth Plenum, 97
Twenty-fourth Plenum, 122
Twenty-second Plenum, 97
two-price system, 12

UBKHNN (Uy ban Ke hoach Nha nuoc), 198
UNDP, 5
UNIDO, 5
USSR, 32, 40
    collectivisation, 66

U-turn, 40–1, 66
Uu tien phat trien cong nghiep nang mot cach hop ly (rational priority to development of heavy industry), 15

vai tro chu dao (leading role), 193
Vasavakul, Thaveeporn, 22, 30, 64
VCP (Vietnamese Communist Party), 41, 65
Vickerman, Andrew, 6, 13, 130
Viet Minh, 56
Viet Tri, 144
Vietnam/Vietnamese:
    analysis, 23
    central planning, 42
    communism, 56
    economy, 2
    paradox, 1, 17, 213–14
    Vietnam War, 23
Vinh Phu, 31
Vo Chi Cong, 24
Vo Nguyen Giap, 24
Vo Nhan Tri, 32–3
Vo Thuc Day, 24
Vo van Kiet, 27, 32
von tu co (own capital), 13, 113, 140
VSCs (virtual share companies), 217
VSHs (virtual shareholders), 217
Vu Khien, 97
Vu Ngoc Hoanh, 94
Vu Quoc Tuan, 14, 36, 97
Vu Tuan Anh, 18, 34
Vu Tuong, 5
vu (sections), 75

Wade, Robert, 219
wage/price system, 172
wage-price reform, 183
Warren, Bill, 9
Waterbury, John, 8

welfare and bonus funds, 174
Williams, M., 196
Women's Union, 46
Woodruff, C., 7
Woodside, A.B., 6–7
working class, creation of, 94

World Bank, 8

y lai (dependency), 95
Yen Bai, 89

Zysman, John, 219

Printed in the United Kingdom
by Lightning Source UK Ltd.
128399UK00001B/100-105/A